Forsyth's Guide to Trusts and Estate Practice

Edition 9

Disclaimer

Forsyth's Guide to Trusts and Estate Practice

Wolters Kluwer

Edition 9

CCH New Zealand Limited
PO BOX 33-270, Takapuna
Auckland 0740
Telephone: 0800 500 224
https://books.wolterskluwer.co.nz

About Wolters Kluwer

Wolters Kluwer enables legal, tax, finance, and healthcare professionals to be more effective and efficient. We provide information, software, and services that deliver vital insights, intelligent tools, and the guidance of subject-matter experts.

We create value by combining information, deep expertise, and technology to provide customers with solutions that improve their quality and effectiveness. Professionals turn to us when they need actionable information to better serve their clients.

Wolters Kluwer. When you have to be right.

Enquiries are welcome on 0800 500 224.

A catalogue record for this book is available from the National Library of New Zealand.

ISBN 978-1-77547-438-8 (print)

ISBN 978-1-77547-439-5 (ebook)

Published by CCH New Zealand Limited

First published: 1973

This edition published June 2022

Contents

Expanded Table of Contents

Page

CHAPTER 1

Wills

Page

Page

CHAPTER 7

Administrators

CHAPTER 8

Functions of a Personal Representative

Page

CHAPTER 9

Succession on Intestacy

CHAPTER 10

Application of Assets in Payment of Debts

CHAPTER 11

Introduction to Trusts

CHAPTER 12

Creation of an Express Trust and the Parties to a Trust

CHAPTER 13

Illegal Trusts

Page

Preface to the Ninth Edition

The aim of this book is to provide, in a readable form, a basic outline of this area of law for tertiary students, legal executives and the lay reader.

The Trusts Act 2019 (Act) came into force on Saturday, 30 January 2021. The Act constitutes a major reform for trust law in New Zealand. While the Act largely restates existing common law principles, the Act introduces new duties on trustees. The Act applies to all express trusts governed by New Zealand law. This includes trusts made from 30 January 2021, as well as existing trusts. The Act is geared towards discretionary family trusts; however, its application is modified for certain kinds of trusts. The reforms are largely based on recommendations for modernising and clarifying trust law made by the Law Commission in 2013. They also reflect advice from a reference group of experts who considered the Law Commission's recommendations. The Act is included in this edition.

The present edition updates the law until 2022.

In this edition, additional references to recent cases have been included to illustrate the legal concepts. However, the emphasis has remained on producing a straightforward guide rather than a legalistic text.

I would like to thank and acknowledge Tom Forsyth for his efforts in producing the early editions of this book.

Cordelia Thomas
Wellington
March 2022

Preface to the First Edition

This little book was written for Technical Institute students and for the lay reader.

Those wanting a fuller coverage of this area of the law are referred to *Nevill's Concise Law of Trusts, Wills and Administration in New Zealand*. The present text stands on its own feet, but I also mention that I have not hesitated in making a few specific references to Nevill where I have thought that these would be useful to the industrious student.

The writing of this text has been a pleasure. I will consider myself amply rewarded if Technical Institute students find it readable and informative.

TA Forsyth
Wellington
July 1973

About the Author

Dr Cordelia Thomas LLB (Otago), LLM (VUW) (Hons first class), PhD (VUW) was a senior lecturer in law at Wellington Polytechnic, then at Massey University, where she taught a variety of subjects, including estates law and practice. She completed a PhD thesis in medical law, developing a legal framework for the collection, retention and use of human body parts. In 2005 she became the senior legal adviser for Toi te Taiao: the Bioethics Council, where she was involved in a number of projects, mostly relating to the cultural, ethical and spiritual issues arising from biotechnologies related to human reproduction. Subsequently, she became the specialist senior legal advisor at the office of the Health and Disability Commissioner and she is currently an Associate Commissioner.

Dr Thomas continues to teach public health law at Massey University. She is a member of the Central Health and Disability Ethics Committee.

Chapter 1
Wills

1.0 Introduction

During their lifetime, most people usually acquire certain assets, some of which they will still own at the time of their death. In addition, they may incur debts and liabilities, which may be outstanding at the time of their death. The sum of these assets and liabilities at the time of death is known as the deceased's estate.

So that the debts and liabilities of the deceased should be satisfied, and the assets disposed of, the law provides for the appointment of a person to administer or manage the estate — the deceased's personal representative; and it is the representative's responsibility:

- to take over the rights of the deceased
- to bring in the assets
- to satisfy the debts and liabilities, and
- to realise or transfer the assets, that is, to dispose of what remains according to the deceased's directions if they had made a will (that is, if the deceased died testate) and, if the deceased had not made a will (died intestate), according to certain statutory rules.

If the deceased had made a will, they would usually have appointed as their personal representative someone in whom they had confidence to carry out the instructions in the will. This person is known as the executor. Though, if the deceased person had died intestate, or if no executor had been appointed in the will or if the executor is unable or unwilling to act, the court will appoint a person or an institution to act as personal representative. Such a personal representative is known as the administrator.

In this chapter and those that follow, the procedure from the making of a will to the completion of the administration of the estate by the personal representative will be considered.

1.1 What essentially is a will?

A will is a written statement made by a person setting out their wishes as to how their estate shall be disposed of after their death. The Wills Act 2007 sets out the law with regard to the wills of persons who die on or after 1 November 2007. Section 40 of the Wills Act sets out the provisions that apply to wills made before 1 November 2007, and s 39 sets out the provisions that apply to the wills of persons who died before 1 November 2007.

It is now taken for granted that people have the right to direct how all their assets should be disposed of after their death, but very early English law did not recognise such a right. In those times, people could dispose by will of their movable goods, subject to certain restrictions, but they could not thus dispose of land. Over the years, the restrictions were gradually removed, and, by the 16th century, English law recognised a person's right to direct during their lifetime how the assets they owned at the time of their death, including land, should be disposed of. As we have said, a person's express declaration in this respect is appropriately called their will (sometimes, testament), which is the declaration of the person's will or intention about the disposal of their assets after their death.

Obviously a person's assets change from day to day and year to year, and the assets owned at the time of death may differ greatly from those owned when the will was made, perhaps years earlier. However, the making of a will does not restrict the will-maker's (previously referred to as the testator or testatrix) right to freely dispose of their assets during the will-maker's lifetime, even though they may be specifically mentioned in the will. A will does not constitute a gift of the will-maker's assets, nor is it a contract whose terms are binding on the will-maker. It is simply an expression of how the will-maker intends to dispose of any assets owned at the time of death, whether they were acquired before or after the will had been made.

The persons named in the will as intended recipients of the assets (the beneficiaries) acquire no rights over the assets until the will-maker's death. If the will-maker sells or otherwise disposes of the assets in the meantime, the beneficiaries have no claim. A will is thus said to "speak" from the moment of the will-maker's death, unless a contrary intention is expressed in the will. It is sometimes described as "ambulatory", meaning that its operation is suspended until death and that it is freely revocable in the meantime. This basic principle has an important bearing both on the making of a will and on how the estate will be distributed after the will-maker's death. This will presently become clear.

Law: Wills Act 2007, s 8

1.2 The form of a will

Not every person makes a will, but, if they do, they must conform to certain formalities. Apart from the informal wills made by military or seagoing persons, which topic is summarised in Subsection 1.3.5 — *Informal wills* of this text, to be valid, a will must be *in writing* and must be signed by the will-maker or by some person signing on the will-maker's behalf and in their presence (an amanuensis).

Section 8(1) of the Wills Act defines a will as "a document. . .". This suggests that the previous law, which states that a will may be typed, printed or written, or may be a composite of these, still applies. It may also contain photocopied material whereby standard clauses relating to trusts and the like can be used, without the costly and repetitious task of retyping on each occasion. (A will that is written entirely by the will-maker is called a holograph will.)[1]

The formalities for the execution of a will are set down in the s 11 of the Wills Act. The Wills Act 1837 prescribed that the will-maker must sign the will "at the foot or end thereof"; however, s 11 of the Wills Act 2007 does not include this requirement, and so the signature may appear anywhere on the document.

The will-maker's signature (or mark, if they cannot write) must be witnessed by 2 witnesses, who must sign after the will-maker has either signed or acknowledged the will-maker's signature[2] in their presence. The Wills Act was amended in 2012 to provide that both the witnesses must see the will-maker sign or acknowledge the signature. However, they do not have to see each other sign as witness.

Although the requirements for signing wills were previously rigidly applied, the Wills Act has provided greater flexibility — although the statutory formalities must still generally be met. However, s 14 of the Wills Act allows the High Court to make an order declaring the document valid if the Court is satisfied that the document expresses the testamentary intentions of the deceased.

Apart from the formalities of writing, signing, and witnessing, a will may be in any form whatsoever — no legal language is necessary, but, as with most legal documents, a set pattern and standard phraseology have over the years been adopted by will draftspersons.

The possible variations in the form of a will are infinite, and the will of a wealthy will-maker will often run into many pages containing very complicated provisions. However, it will usually follow the same basic form. Nevertheless, the average citizen usually makes a simple will, such as that set out below.

A fairly simple will, in typical form, might read as follows:

This is the Last Will and Testament of me, *John Henderson* of Wellington, Builder.

1. I revoke all wills and testamentary dispositions at any time heretofore made by me and I declare this to be my last will and testament.
2. I Appoint my wife, Helen Henderson, and my brother, James Henderson, to be the executors and trustees of this my will.

1 *Re Jaray* [1978] 2 NZLR 26.

2 To accomplish an acknowledgment of their signature, will-makers must show their signature to both witnesses simultaneously — no *formal* acknowledgment is required.

3. I Give and Devise unto my brother, James Henderson, the property situate at 99 Main Street, Auckland.
4. I Give and Bequeath unto my sister, Jean Henderson, all photographic equipment owned by me at the time of my death.
5. I Give and Bequeath unto my daughter, Joan Henderson, the sum of six thousand dollars ($6,000).
6. Subject to payment of all my just debts, funeral and testamentary expenses, I Give Devise and Bequeath the remainder of my estate, both real and personal, of whatsoever kind and wheresoever situate (hereinafter called "my residuary estate") unto my said wife, Helen Henderson, provided that she shall survive me by fourteen (14) days, and, if she shall fail to do so, I Direct my trustee to hold my residuary estate upon trust for such of my children who shall survive me and attain the age of twenty (20) years, and if more than one, equally.

In Witness Whereof I have to this my last will and testament set my hand this 5 th day of March Two Thousand and Twenty Two (2022).

Signed by the will-maker, John Henderson, as and for his last will and testament in the presence of us both present at the same time who at his request in his sight and presence have hereunto subscribed our names as witnesses:

J Henderson

A B Smith,	C D Jones,
Builder,	Grocer,
Wellington.	Wellington.

Now let us look at this will clause by clause.

Clause 1 effectively cancels any prior wills made by the will-maker. It is the usual practice to include such a clause, whether or not the will-maker is known to have made an earlier will. (The revocation of a will shall be dealt with in more detail presently.)

Clause 2 appoints the executors, the personal representatives of the deceased, who will be responsible for seeing that the estate is administered according to the will. It is customary, as here, to use the term "executor(s) and trustee(s)", even though the will may not set up any trusts, and so, strictly speaking, no trustee is needed. The position and duties of trustees are considered later in Chapter 16 — *Trustees.*

Clause 3 concerns a gift of land. The term "devise" can be used both as a verb and a noun about gifts of land. The beneficiary is called a "devisee".

Clause 4 concerns a gift of movable goods and is called a "bequest" (verb: "bequeath").

1.2

Property is divided into "real property" (or "realty") and "personal property" (or "personalty"). Real property comprises land and things permanently fixed to the land, such as buildings and fences. Strictly speaking, real property refers only to freehold interests in land. This is the usual way in which land is owned in New Zealand. "Freehold" does not mean "free of mortgage", as some people think, but is contrasted with "leasehold", where the land is held only for a term of years. A leasehold interest is called a "chattel real" or a "chattel interest in land", and with all movable property comes within the definition of "personal property". Hence, you may "devise" a freehold interest, but "bequeath" a leasehold interest in land. It is not logical that leasehold interests in land should be classified as personal property, but this is the result of an anomaly in the Common Law.

However, in some of the relevant legislation, for example, the Administration Act 1969, the term "real property" now includes leasehold as well as freehold interests in land.

Clause 5 concerning a gift of money, is also a bequest; but the term "legacy" is often, but not exclusively, reserved for gifts of money. If amounts are included in a will, it is better practice to specify them in words as well as in figures.

Clause 6 is called the "*Residuary Clause*" and disposes of all the will-maker's property not already specifically devised or bequeathed. If no residuary clause were included, if the will-maker had not specifically disposed of every item in their estate, they would be deemed to have died intestate in relation to the balance of their estate. Note that it is sometimes stated, but not obligatory to state, that specific gifts shall be free of expenses. This means that all expenses will be paid out of the residuary estate, and the residuary beneficiary will receive what remains. Clause 6 has expressly stated this to make it clear what remains.

It is always wise to have a substitutional gift (as in this clause) to provide against an intestacy or a partial intestacy.

The next clause in the will, beginning "In Witness Whereof. . .", is called the "Testimonium". This carries the date of the will, which is obviously very important as it establishes which is the last will if several are found.[3]

The last clause is the "Attestation Clause", the wording of which makes clear the correct procedure to be followed for signing and witnessing the will. As

3 If the will-maker executes a document changing a will (often referred to as a codicil) containing reference to the will (or the will is re-executed with intent to carry the date forward), the will is *republished*. This means that the will-maker is deemed to have made a new will that includes the contents of the codicil as at the date of the codicil, and this can be significant, for example, if there is a change in the law affecting wills between the date of the will and the date of the codicil — *Skinner v Ogle* (1845) 163 ER 1067. The concept of *republication* is similar to, but theoretically different from, the concept of *revival* discussed in Section 1.9 — *Revival of a revoked will*, and is achieved by similar means. The difference between the two is that mere *republication* will not revive a will that has been revoked.

we have already noted, this procedure must be strictly followed because, if it can be proved that the will was not correctly signed and witnessed, it will be invalid, unless the High Court declares it is valid under s 14.

A person who has made a will may later wish to alter, add to, or delete a part of that will. A new will can, of course, be executed, revoking the earlier one. But, if the alteration or addition is a minor one, it may be affected by executing a "Codicil". A codicil to the above will might read as follows:

> "*This is the first Codicil* to the will of *John Henderson* of Wellington, Builder, which will is dated the 5th day of March, 2022.
>
> I *Give and Bequeath* unto my daughter, *Mary Henderson,* the sum of Two Thousand Dollars ($2,000), and, in all other respects, I confirm my said will.
>
> In *Witness Whereof,* and so on.
>
> *Signed* by the said *John Henderson* as the first Codicil to his last will in the presence of us, and so on."

J Henderson

(Witnesses)

The codicil becomes part of the will and must be executed with the same formalities (Wills Act 2007, s 8(3)(e)).

Some solicitors prefer to use a more elaborate form of will appointing trustees — even in cases where this is not strictly necessary, and an example of such a will is set out in the Appendix 1.

Law: Wills Act 2007, s 8

1.3 Other points relating to wills

1.3.1 Conditional wills

An essential feature of every will is that it is conditional on its being unrevoked at the time of the death of the will-maker but, over and above this, it is quite possible to make a conditional will. A will may be conditional on an event and, in such a case, does not become operative on the will-maker's death, unless the condition has been fulfilled. For example, a will-maker may declare in their will that the will is conditional upon the will-maker dying before the age of fifty. If the will-maker survives this age, the will will be inoperative, even though it has not been specifically revoked at the time of death.

However, it is sometimes difficult for the courts to interpret whether it was the intention of the will-maker that the will be conditional, or whether, in referring to the event or events in question, the will-maker was merely recording reasons for making the will (or, indeed, whether the reference was mere surplusage).[4]

If will-makers wish to make a *conditional* will, they must make this *clear*.

1.3.2 Who may make a will?

The general rule is that anyone who has attained the age of 18 may make, change, revoke and revive wills (Wills Act 2007, s 9). A person under the age of 18 may do so if they are or have been married, in a civil union or in a de facto relationship. If not, they must satisfy the Family Court that they understand the effect of the proposed testamentary action and have obtained the approval of the Court. A person who is, or is about to become, a military or seagoing person may also make a will in spite of being under the age of 18 (Wills Act 2007, s 9).

However, the general statement is subject to certain qualifications. To make a valid will, a person must have *testamentary capacity*. The general rule is that every person of sound mind, and who is 18 years of age and over, has testamentary capacity, whether man or woman, married or single. A person under the age of 18 who is or has been married, in a civil union or in a de facto relationship may make a will, but, if unmarried, in a civil union, or in a de facto relationship, their will is invalid, and does not become valid on their attaining the age of 18. (If the will-maker is 16 or 17 years of age and their will was made with the approval of a District Court or the Public Trust, the will would be valid.)

The requirement of "*sound mind*" does not mean a perfectly balanced mind, nor does it exclude eccentricity or even some forms of mental incapability. A person suffering from fits of mental incapability may make a valid will during a lucid period. A sound mind in this instance means that a person must have a "disposing mind". That is, they must understand the nature of their act in disposing of their property, and they must also be able to understand the amount and nature of the property available for disposal, and to recall the persons whom they should consider to have "claims on their bounty". That a will-maker excludes persons for whom they have a moral obligation to provide, does not mean that they were not of sound mind, but they must be mentally able to appreciate their obligations, whether or not they give effect to them.

A number of further points need to be mentioned.

1. The basic position is that will-makers must have testamentary capacity at the *time* of executing their will. In *Bishop v O'Dea* (1999) 18 FRNZ 492 (CA), Tipping J held that those seeking probate must demonstrate that the will-maker had sufficient understanding of:

4 See *Re Panapa* [1993] 1 NZLR 694, where a question arose as to whether or not the will was conditional upon marriage (and where the will was held not to be conditional).

- the fact that they were making a will and the effect of doing so
- the extent of the property being disposed of, and
- the moral claims to which they ought to give effect when making testamentary dispositions.

He added that a person who lacked capacity before making the will can still make a will after recovery or during a lucid period. However, in such a case, the will is regarded with particular distrust and there is, at first instance, a strong presumption against it, particularly if it displays lack of moral responsibility in the nature of the dispositions.

However, the courts have allowed some latitude regarding capacity. In *Parker v Felgate* (1883) 8 PD 173,[5] the testatrix, who was suffering from an illness and had to be roused from a coma, executed her will by means of an amanuensis at a time when she realised that her will was being executed but was not capable of recalling its contents. Her illness had recently become serious, and she had previously given instructions to her solicitor to prepare the will at a time when it was not disputed that she had testamentary capacity. The Court upheld the will because she recalled that she had given instructions and believed that the will was in accordance with them. There is thus authority for the view that, if the will-maker clearly had testamentary capacity at a time when she gave instructions to her solicitor, and those instructions were carried out, a court should uphold the will, even though the will-maker was not of "disposing mind" at the time when she executed it. The matter is obviously one of practical importance in the case of a failing will-maker. This case was recently approved of in *Hoogeveen v Public Trust* [2008] BCL 799 (HC). In that case, 6 months passed between the giving of the instructions and the date on which the will was executed. During that time, the will-maker had attempted suicide twice and suffered depression and various events such as a family bereavement. The Court concluded that, when she was unwell, she was unable to assess the moral claims on her estate. The previous probate of that will was revoked and her earlier will treated as unrevoked.

2. It is not essential that a will-maker have testamentary capacity in relation to the *whole* of the will. If it is proved that they were suffering from an insane delusion in relation to a particular matter, the court can disregard the provision relating to that particular matter, and uphold the rest of the will.
3. The will-maker must know and approve of the will at the time of execution (related to 1. above). This requirement satisfies itself in the case of a holograph will, but, in the case of a will prepared by a solicitor for a client, it does not; and a legal executive should take steps to ensure that the client does know of and approve the will that has been prepared. If

5 Approved of in *Perera v Perera* [1901] AC 354.

the client glances over the will, executes it, and the will then turns out to contain a mistake, s 31 of the Wills Act allows the High Court to make an order correcting the will if it does not carry out the will-maker's intentions, because it contains a clerical error or does not give effect to the will-maker's instructions. The High Court may use external evidence to interpret the words in the will if the words used in the will make the will meaningless, ambiguous, uncertain, ambiguous in light of the surrounding circumstances or uncertain in light of the surrounding circumstances. External evidence includes evidence of the will-maker's testamentary intentions, but the will-maker's intentions may not be used as surrounding circumstances (Wills Act 2007, s 32).

If the evidence is that the deceased lacked capacity before the will was signed, those people who support the will have a particularly heavy burden of then trying to establish that the testator recovered or made the will during a lucid interval. Generally speaking, this is how the Courts approach cases of mental capacity or incapacity. At the end of the day, much will depend upon the opinions of the doctors as to the extent the will-maker had capacity at the date when the will was signed. In addition, all the surrounding circumstances will be taken into account including the opinion of the lawyer who prepared the will (presumably on instructions) and who witnessed the signing of the will.

A good practice for a legal executive to follow, if at all possible, is to post out a copy of the will to the proposed will-maker before the appointment for execution, so that the latter has ample opportunity to get familiar with its contents. However, many will-makers will, in addition, need a careful explanation of the provisions of the will to ensure that it does, in fact, comply with the will-maker's intentions. Failing this, at least give a copy of the will to the client after it is executed.

If the will is apparently rational and the will-maker's sanity has not been disputed, their soundness of mind will be presumed. However, if the will is disputed and evidence is advanced casting doubt on the will-maker's mental capacity, this will displace the presumption that they were of sound mind. That the will-maker had a sound disposing mind at the time of making the will must then be proved.

1.3.3 Who may take under a will?

The general rule is that anyone may take under a will — anybody can be a beneficiary. Moreover, it is not necessary that a beneficiary be in existence when the will is made, or even at the death of the will-maker when the will comes into operation. Nevertheless, there are definite limitations on how far into the future a person may be born and still qualify as a beneficiary. The law permits will-makers to tie up their property for only a limited period of time after their death, and the "Rule against Perpetuities", dealt with later in Chapter 13 — *Illegal Trusts*, is concerned with this topic. The most common length of this period is the remaining life of some nominated person living at the will-maker's death plus 21 years, and that beneficiaries will have to be born within this period to legally qualify as such. Of course, the fact that a person legally qualifies as a beneficiary does not necessarily mean that they are instantaneously entitled to receive their share of the estate. For example, will-makers frequently direct that their children are not to receive property until they are a specified age.

There are 2 main exceptions to the general rule that anyone may take under a will, and the reasons for these are fairly obvious.

The first is based on the principle that a person may not profit from their own criminal act. A beneficiary, who has killed the will-maker, whether the killing amounts to murder or manslaughter, will not be allowed to take a gift under the will. The Succession (Homicide) Act 2007 codifies the law that prevents a person (the "killer"), who kills another person (the "victim") by committing homicide, from benefiting as a result of the victim's death from the victim's estate; or any other property arrangement. Homicide means the killing of a person or a child who has not become a person, by another person, intentionally or recklessly by any means that would be an offence under New Zealand law, whether done in New Zealand or elsewhere, but does not include—

- a killing caused by a negligent act or an omission
- infanticide under s 178 of the Crimes Act 1961
- the killing of a person by another in pursuance of a suicide pact, or
- an assisted suicide.

The killer cannot take under the intestacy of the victim, nor can any person claiming through them, for instance, the wife of a beneficiary who has been convicted of the murder of the will-maker and has subsequently died.

The second exception concerns persons who have witnessed the signing of the will, or the husband or wife or civil union partner or de facto partner of a witness (Wills Act 2007, s 13). They may not take a gift under the will either, unless there are sufficient independent witnesses apart from them. A will witnessed by a beneficiary will be valid and effectual in every respect except for the gift to the witness. The will will be read as if the clause making the gift had not been included, and the subject-matter of the gift will become part of the residuary estate. A gift that is invalidated because the beneficiary was an attesting witness will be made effective if will-makers subsequently make a codicil, witnessed by other persons, confirming their will. Moreover, a beneficiary under a will who has not witnessed the will does not lose the gift if the beneficiary later witnesses a codicil made by the will-maker, so long as the codicil does not vary the gift in the beneficiary's favour. The rule is clearly included to avoid the possibility of fraud on the part of witnesses.

If the will contains a gift to a solicitor draftsman, special considerations again are raised. As was said in the House of Lords in *Wintle v Nye* [1959] 1 WLR 284, the law is not that a solicitor draftsman cannot take under the will, but the court must be satisfied that the gift was specifically approved of by the will-maker. A good solicitor-draftsman-beneficiary usually refers the will-maker to another preferably independent solicitor, so that the necessary evidence can be gathered in writing.

One further point should be noted here. Usually a gift will lapse if the beneficiary predeceases the will-maker. The gift will fail as discussed in Subsection 3.3.2 — *Lapse*. However, where a will-maker leaves a gift to their child or other issue (for example, grandchild), and the beneficiary dies before the will-maker leaving a child or children living at the will-maker's death, such a child or children will take the gift in place of the deceased parent. This is an important statutory exception to the general rule that the court will not re-write a will-maker's will by substituting a beneficiary for one who is unable to take the gift. The provision applies to children or other issue born out of wedlock as well as within it, by virtue of the Status of Children Act 1969. However, the provision will not apply if it is clearly contrary to the will-maker's intention as it appears from the will.

1.3.4 Joint and mutual wills

The terms "joint wills" and "mutual wills" have entirely different meanings and should not be confused.

Joint wills are simply documents incorporating the wills of 2 people, each of whom executes their will in the usual way. Except that the 2 wills are combined in the same document, no special significance is attached to a joint will. The joint will-makers may or may not leave their property to each other. The dispositions are treated as 2 separate wills.

Mutual wills, on the other hand, have a greater significance. For instance, a husband and wife are said to make mutual wills when they make corresponding wills leaving their property to each other. But strictly speaking, the term applies only where such wills are made pursuant to an agreement between the parties. The making of mutual wills does not prevent either party from revoking their will. However, if the agreement to make mutual wills were a binding contract, the revoking of one will would be a breach of that contract, and the revoking party would be liable to an action for damages. Section 30 of the Wills Act provides that, if one of the persons does not keep the promise, the other person may claim any of the benefit that the estate does not provide which was agreed to be made. The promise may be made orally, in writing or electronically.

1.3.5 Informal wills

Those members of the armed forces and sailors at sea, who are described as "military or seagoing persons" by subpart 3 of the Wills Act, are exempt from the general rule that a will must be in writing, signed, and witnessed. Such persons, who must be members of the armed forces, or seafarers at sea, respectively, are permitted by the Act to make informal wills, which do not necessarily even have to be in writing. In some of the cases, statements made in postcards sent home by servicemen have been held to be valid informal wills under those provisions. This includes prisoners of war.

The reason for this exception is obvious. Neither the facilities nor the expert advice on the correct formalities for executing a formal will may be available, and such persons should not be denied the right of making a will in a critical situation.

As we have said, such persons must come within the definition of "military or seagoing persons". The most practical consideration in modern times is the position of servicemen who comprise New Zealand's contributions to the various peace-keeping forces around the globe. The Ministry of Defence rarely exercises the power it possess under s 37 of the Act to bring such servicemen within the Act's provisions, but instead ensures, as a matter of policy, that they have made a valid formal will before they depart from New Zealand.

A will made wholly by word of mouth before witnesses is called a **nuncupative** will, and witnesses to such a will may, unlike witnesses to a formal will, take a gift under the will. Unless a "military or seagoing person" is being held prisoner of war, a nuncupative, or a partly oral will, will remain valid for only one year.

An informal will may also be revoked informally.

Law: Wills Act 2007, ss 13, 23, 24, 33–38

1.4 The free expression of the will-maker's intentions

It is not enough merely to have a will signed and witnessed in the prescribed manner. In addition to the formalities of signing and witnessing necessary for a valid will, certain other conditions must be fulfilled.

1. *Animo testandi* — The document must be executed "animo testandi". This means that it must be made with the intention of disposing of the will-maker's property after their death, and with the intention that it shall not operate during their lifetime but shall take effect at their death, and that, in the meantime, it shall be freely revocable by the will-maker. If it can be proved that the will-maker did not intend the document to operate in this way, it will not be admitted to probate as a valid will, even though it may conform to all the formalities of a will.

If a document, though executed in the form of a will, clearly intends to make an irrevocable gift of the maker's property, or if it is intended to become effective on the happening of some event before the will-maker's death, it is not a will, although it may be effective as a gift or settlement of the property "inter vivos" (between living persons).

Again, if a person executes a document in the form of a will, which they intend to use only as a draft or perhaps for the sole purpose of showing to a "beneficiary" to induce that person to comply with their wishes, there is clearly no animo testandi, and the document is a nullity.

2. *Free and voluntary act* — The second requirement is that the execution of the will must be the free and voluntary act of the will-maker and not the result of *coercion, undue influence or fraud.*

In the general law,[6] if a special relationship exists between the parties, such as between a parent and a child or a doctor and a patient, there is presumed to be undue influence, which must be rebutted if the dominant person seeks to enforce the contract or other transaction. Such is not the case with wills though, for obviously such a special relationship is all the more reason for one person's wishing to leave a gift to another. There is also nothing against a person inducing or persuading another to name them as a beneficiary in their will, so long as the will-maker can still exercise their own judgment. If the persuasion or inducement completely deprives the will-maker of their free judgment or willpower, however, it is undue influence or coercion, and the gift will be set aside. The will-maker may be led but must not be driven. In *Harrison v Harrison* (2007) 26 FRNZ 532 (HC), the will-maker was 92 years old and ailing. The new principal beneficiary was a grandson and the primary family care giver who was also exercising the power of attorney. The will-maker's son was excluded from face-to-face contact with the will-maker, the grandson had drafted the will and, when one lawyer assessed the will-maker as lacking capacity, the grandson arranged for another lawyer and a medical examination of the will-maker. The Judge stated that the onus was on the grandson to satisfy the Court that the will was the exercise of the will-maker's free will. He noted that direct evidence of undue influence will seldom be available, and the Court must infer matters from all the surrounding circumstances. Consequently, probate was declined.

Similarly, if the will-maker has been induced by fraud to make the will, the will can be set aside.

If the will is apparently rational and properly executed, the burden of proving coercion, undue influence, or fraud, is usually on the person alleging it.

6 Dealt with in Chapter 15 — *Revocation and Avoidance of Trusts.*

1.5 The implementation of the will-maker's intentions

The purpose of a will, as we have said, is to enable the will-maker's intention and wishes to be carried out after their death, and this is normally done. However, today, the factor of the will-maker's intention is not the paramount factor that it was in Victorian times. Today, there exist some grounds, created by the legislature, upon which the will-maker's intention may be varied by the courts if this is considered desirable, and these possibilities are worthy of specific mention.

We are going to see in this section that, while will-makers may, in basic theory, make whatever will they choose, the position is, in practice, that many will-makers do not now possess complete testamentary power.

1.5.1 The Law Reform (Testamentary Promises) Act 1949

While a person who makes a will contrary to agreement by contract will be liable for damages for breach of contract, this did not always help people who had been led to believe by the will-maker, either expressly or implicitly, that, if they did certain work required by the will-maker during the latter's lifetime, they would be reimbursed or provided for by the will-maker in their will. Formerly, if the will-maker failed to honour this promise, such people had no right of action, unless they could prove a binding contract. A housekeeper, for example, may have continued working for a will-maker for many years for very little reward on the understanding that they would be provided for in that will-maker's will, only to find that no provision had been made for them. They were usually unable to prove a binding contract, and so were left without a remedy.

To eliminate this injustice, New Zealand passed legislation that is now contained in the Law Reform (Testamentary Promises) Act 1949. Briefly, this Act says that:

1. When a person has served another on the express or implied understanding that the latter will recompense the former in their will, but no specific contract can be proved, or
2. Even though a contract can be proved, it cannot be enforced because the amount of the promised reward is uncertain, or because the promise to leave land is unenforceable through no evidence in writing, the court has power to make an order enforcing the promise against the estate. The court will consider all the circumstances, and award what it thinks reasonable for the services given.[7]

7 See *Wright v Holland* [1996] 1 NZLR 213.

A warning that claimants under the Act should not expect too much of a bonanza came from Casey J in *Brown v Jobbins* HC Auckland, A519/82, 15 August 1983. The Act enables relief only to the extent of the work and services rendered.

Previously, such actions had to be brought to the High Court, but now, if none of the parties to the proceedings object, the action can be determined in the Family Court, which is a division of the District Court (with right of appeal).

Atkinson v Samuels HC Auckland, CIV 2006-404-7878, 30 May 2008, Priestly J, related to a successful application by members of the Atkinson family for an order vesting shares in them under the Law Reform (Testamentary Promises) Act. Sydney Samuels left his entire net estate jointly to his nephew and niece. The estate was substantial and included shares in a private company, Glenholme Farms Limited. The Atkinsons were close family friends of Samuels for around 70 years. They submitted that:

- The services, particularly family support, given for more than fifty years by their family to Samuels and his wife went far beyond what one would expect from mere friends.
- There had been the promise of Glenholme Farms Limited shares at a relatively early stage of their family's involvement with Samuels.
- There was a clear nexus between the promise made and the services rendered.
- The value of the services, although non-monetary, far exceeded the valuation of shares.

The application was granted because:

- Samuels had promised that he would leave his Glenholme Farms Limited shareholding to the Atkinsons.
- The relationship with them was of great significance to both Samuels and his wife because of their inability to have children.
- The promise of shares was linked to the services rendered by the Atkinsons.
- The services rendered to a very close family friend went well beyond what one might normally expect of mere friends.
- The just and appropriate award under s 3(1) was to order that Samuels' shares in Glenholme Farms Limited were to vest in each of plaintiffs as tenants in common in equal shares.

1.5.2 The Family Protection Act 1955

It is now convenient to consider a further inroad into a will-maker's freedom of disposition — the Family Protection Act 1955, which consolidates the old

In this case, the plaintiff had lived with the now deceased intestate since 1975. They had bought two cottages, one in 1976 registered in the intestate's name, and the other in 1978 registered in the names of the intestate and the plaintiff as tenants in common in equal shares. The Court found that the intestate's statement that the plaintiff "would get everything" amounted to a promise, within the meaning of the Act, to make provision for her from his estate. The Court ordered the 1976 cottage to be vested in the plaintiff and in the intestate's estate as tenants in common in equal shares, but declined to make further provision for the plaintiff.

Will-maker's Family Maintenance Act 1900. This is a part of the social legislation in which New Zealand has led the world. It was not until 1938 that a similar statute was passed in England.

In short, the Act enables a claim to be made to the court to provide from the deceased's estate for certain members of their family, when the claimant would not receive adequate provision for their proper maintenance or support under the will or under the rules of intestate succession. The Act, as applied and developed by the court over many years, has been a piece of living legislation and, in the concept of moral duty that has been developed, both the financial and the sentimental well-being of the family has assumed a central place in the judges' priorities.[8]

When a claim is made under the Act, the court must decide, after considering all the circumstances, whether the claimant, who under the terms of the will or the rules of intestate succession receives no share or what they claim is an inadequate share, should be granted a share or an increased share of the deceased's estate.

For some years, the legislation was considered to impose a legal duty on a person to provide adequately for their family, and as limiting their free disposing power. However, that this is not the correct theoretical base was established by the Court of Appeal in *In Re Allardice, Allardice v Allardice* (1910) 29 NZLR 959 (CA).[9]

Fundamentally, the court has "no power to recast the will-maker's will" into something that the court considers just. Notwithstanding the legislation, the will-maker's disposing power remains fundamentally unrestricted, but the court may nevertheless vary a will-maker's will by forcing their estate to meet the claims of those entitled to a share. The concept is one of breach of moral duty, not limitation of testamentary power. A person may still make whatever will they choose, but, if they ignore their moral duty to provide for their dependants, their gifts to others may be cut down to meet the claims of their family.

The end result is, admittedly, not very different to that disclaimed in *In Re Allardice, Allardice v Allardice*. Will-makers have disposing power over their estates, but must meet their moral duty to their dependants. As Cooke J said in the Court of Appeal in *Little v Angus* [1981] 1 NZLR 126, where an award was increased:

> "The inquiry is as to whether there has been a breach of moral duty judged by the standards of a wise and just testator; and, if so, what is appropriate to remedy that breach. Only to that extent is the will to be

8 See Nicola S Peart "*The Direction of the Family Protection Act 1955*" [1994] NZ Recent Law Review 1 at 193.

9 Approved of by the Privy Council in *Bosch v Perpetual Trustee Co (Ltd)* [1938] AC 463; [1938] 2 All ER 14 (PC).

disturbed. The size of the estate and any other moral claims on the deceased's bounty are highly relevant".

In *Re Shirley* CA155/85, 6 July 1987, the estate was worth $97,000 as at the date of death and $120,000 at the date of the hearing in the High Court. Under the will, one son received assets worth, at the date of the will-maker's death, $45,000; and he and the other 3 sons were entitled to a 25% share each in the residue, distributable on the death of the widow. The High Court held that the testator had breached his moral duty to the other 3 sons and awarded further provision equivalent in the case of one son to $15,400 and to $13,800 each to the other 2. On appeal, the Court of Appeal held, first that the emphasis laid by the Judge on the disparity between the benefits conferred by the will on Graham as compared with those conferred on his brothers was not appropriate; and that what each had to establish was that the provision made for him by the will was not in the context of his own means and obligations and all other relevant circumstances adequate to provide for his proper maintenance and support.

The Court of Appeal went on to review the individual claims. It concluded that there had been a breach of duty to one son and made an award in his favour. As to the other 2 sons, it said:

> "We are of opinion that neither Kenneth nor Ian established a breach of moral duty by the testator. Neither established any relevant 'needs' which he cannot adequately meet from his own resources which by the date of the hearing were substantial. Their position as sons of the testator was recognised by the bequest of a share of residue. The award made, equivalent in each case to about $13,500, was rightly described by Mr Barton as 'just a little more than a token'".

The bequest to each son of a share in the residue on the widow's death was in present value terms of less than 10% of the estate. The Court, while accepting that family recognition as distinct from economic need could be the basis of a duty to provide proper support for an adult child, saw a relatively modest provision as adequate provision in that regard.

In *Williams v Aucutt* [2000] 2 NZLR 479 at [52], the Court of Appeal stated:

> ". . . we reject the argument that the Court must expressly find a need for proper maintenance and support. The test is whether adequate provision has been made for the proper maintenance and support of the claimant. 'Support' is an additional and wider term than 'maintenance'. In using the composite expression, and requiring 'proper' maintenance and support, the legislation recognises that a broader approach is required and the authorities referred to establish that moral and ethical considerations are to be taken into account in determining the scope of the duty. 'Support' is used in its wider dictionary sense of 'sustaining, providing comfort'. A child's path through life is supported not simply

by financial provision to meet economic needs and contingencies but also by recognition of belonging to the family and of having been an important part of the overall life of the deceased. Just what provision will constitute proper support in this latter respect is a matter of judgment in all the circumstances of the particular case. It may take the form of lifetime gifts or a bequest of family possessions precious to its members and often part of the family history. And where there is no economic need it may also be met by a legacy of a moderate amount. On the other hand, where the estate comprises the accumulation of the family assets and is more than sufficient to meet other needs, provision so small as to leave a justifiable sense of exclusion from participation in the family estate might not amount to proper support for a family member".

In *Henry v Henry* [2007] NZFLR 640, the Court of Appeal stated that the award, once a failure to make adequate provision was established, should be no more than is necessary to remedy the failure. A conservative approach should be adopted. Unfairness is not enough to disturb a will. The court must conclude that the claimant has established that they have not received adequate provision for proper maintenance and support.

The application of the Family Protection Act was extended to apply to de facto relationships from 1 February 2002 and to civil union partners from 26 April 2005, by s 7 of the Relationships (Statutory References) Act 2005 (No 3).

The de facto partner must have been living in a de facto relationship at the deceased's date of death.

1.5.3 Meaning of de facto relationships

A de facto partner has the same meaning as in s 2 of the Property (Relationships) Act 1976. That Act contains a "check list" of factors to be looked at in order to guide the court in making a determination of what a de facto relationship is.

Section 2D provides that a de facto relationship is one between 2 persons, whether a man and a woman, or a man and a man, or a woman and a woman—

- who are both aged 18 years or older
- who live together as a couple, and
- who are not married to one another.

In determining whether 2 persons live together as a couple, all the circumstances of the relationship are to be taken into account, including any of the following matters where relevant:

- the duration of the relationship
- the nature and extent of common residence

- whether or not a sexual relationship exists
- the degree of financial dependence or interdependence, and any arrangements for financial support between the parties
- the ownership, use and acquisition of property
- the degree of mutual commitment to a shared life
- the care and support of children
- the performance of household duties
- the reputation and public aspects of the relationship.

In determining whether 2 people live together as a couple, the court is not required to make any finding in respect of any of the matters stated above or in respect of any combination of them. A court may have regard to such matters and attach such weight to any matter as may seem appropriate to the court in the circumstances of the case.

Brown v Ferrow FAMC Auckland, FAM 2006-070-564, 25 June 2008 was an unsuccessful application by Brown for an order that she and Ferrow had a qualifying relationship under the Property (Relationships) Act. The issue was whether they lived together as couple under s 2D(1) of the Property (Relationships) Act by considering factors under s 2D(2) of the Property (Relationships) Act.

It was held that they had formed a relationship in 1994, which had ended in 2004. While they had used homes occupied by Brown for many joint activities and had spent a significant amount of time together there, they never used these homes as common residences. While they had enjoyed an active sexual relationship, this became less frequent as the years went by and was likely to have ceased by early 2004. Although they did not have joint bank accounts and their financial affairs were not intertwined, Ferrow provided very significant financial support to Brown and her children, which enabled her to maintain a much higher standard of living than she would otherwise have been able to enjoy. They did not purchase any property in their joint names, and Ferrow retained the household furniture and the whiteware that he had purchased. It was accepted that though each of them, independently at some point in the ten-year relationship, had a commitment to fully share a relationship, their commitment did not coincide and could not be described as mutual. Ferrow put a lot of time, effort, and money into caring for and supporting Brown's children, performed a large part of the household duties and effectively managed the household. To most of their friends and acquaintances, they appeared to be a couple. Taking an overall view, the Court concluded that they did not live together as couple, and they did not have a qualifying relationship for the purposes of the Property (Relationships) Act, so the application was declined.

In *C v A* (2007) 26 FRNZ 389, Mr A died in May 2005. Two women laid claim to his estate — his separated wife and the applicant, with whom he had a relationship in the 4 years prior to his death. It was held that the applicant and the deceased were not in a de facto relationship. They did not live together and, apart from their sexual and emotional connection, they had not intermingled the practical aspects of their lives relating to their households, finances and children.

The Family Protection (Amendment) Act 2001 also provides that a claim may be made for maintenance or support by a child of a marriage, or a child of a de facto relationship of the deceased. A child of a de facto relationship includes a child whose parents have a de facto relationship with each other after the child's birth. A child of a marriage includes a child whose parents marry each other after the child's birth. A step-child of the deceased may claim, if the step-child was being maintained, or is legally entitled to be maintained, by the deceased immediately before their death.

1.5.4 Relationship of short duration

There is a restriction on the entitlement of a de facto partner to claim against the estate of a deceased under the Family Protection Act, where the relationship is of a short duration. Pursuant to s 2E of the Property (Relationships) Amendment Act 2001 in relation to a de facto relationship, if the partners have lived together as de facto partners for a period of less than 3 years, or for 3 years or longer if the court considers it just, the relationship will be treated as one of short duration. With respect to a relationship of short duration, the court cannot make an order under the Family Protection Act in favour of a de facto partner, unless either there is a child of the de facto partnership or the de facto partner has made a substantial contribution to the de facto relationship, and failure to make an order would result in serious injustice to the de facto partner.

1.5.5 Classes of persons entitled to claim under the Family Protection Act

The following classes of persons are entitled to claim under the Family Protection Act:

- The spouse, either as a consequence of marriage, civil union or de facto relationship, is entitled to claim under the Family Protection Act.
- The children, including adopted children, children of a de facto relationship, step children and ex-nuptial children, are entitled to claim.
- Grandchildren, including adopted grandchildren, grandchildren of a de facto relationship, step grandchildren and ex-nuptial grandchildren.
- Parents, if that parent was being maintained at least in part by the deceased immediately before their death and there is no spouse, de facto partner or child of the relationship who can claim.

1.5.6 Basis for decision

In deciding a claim (or a later variation of an award), the court must take into account all circumstances, of which it is impossible to make an exhaustive list, because they will obviously differ in every case. However, they may include such matters as:

- the provision (if any) made for the claimant in the will, or the share taken under an intestacy
- the wishes of the deceased, and their reasons for making the dispositions made by the will (if any)
- the age, health, earning powers, and financial position of the claimant
- the style of living to which the deceased has accustomed the claimant
- other sources of maintenance available to the claimant
- the size of the estate
- the character and conduct of the claimant
- the assistance given by the claimant in the accumulation of the estate
- whether strangers are the only ones who will be affected by an award
- whether the parties who will be affected by an award consent to it.

On the same terms as we have seen in the case of actions under the Law Reform (Testamentary Promises) Act, claims under the Family Protection Act can now be determined in the Family Court.

There are restrictions on the courts' powers to make orders under both of the above Acts, if such orders affect beneficial interests in Māori freehold land, and it is likely that these restrictions will be increased in the future.

The court has the power to order any provision that it thinks fit for proper maintenance or support for any person who can claim under the Act.

In these comparatively depressed times, it remains to mention that a person who could have brought a claim under the Family Protection Act, but has failed without good and sufficient reason to do so, may possibly have their eligibility for a benefit affected.

In summary, we can now see that, although the basic principle remains paramount, a person may by their will dispose of their property in any way they see fit and may change their mind by altering or revoking their will. Considerable inroads have been made into the effect of this principle. The courts will have due regard for any promises made by the deceased as to how they will dispose of their property, whether these promises take the form of enforceable contracts or not, and they may revise the deceased's will to make some provision for the deceased's dependants in cases where the deceased has ignored a moral obligation to do so.

Law: Law Reform (Testamentary Promises) Act 1949, ss 3, 5, 5A
Family Protection Act 1955, ss 2–4A, 11, 12, 15

1.6 Changes proposed by Law Commission

On 15 December 2021 Te Aka Matua o te Ture | Law Commission issued its Final Report in the Review of Succession Law project: He arotake i te āheinga ki ngā rawa a te tangata ka mate ana | Review of succession law: rights to a person's property on death.

The Commission noted that the law relating to who gets a person's property when they die is important law that affects all New Zealanders. The Commission concluded that new law is needed to keep up with social change and meet New Zealanders' reasonable expectations.

The report recommends that Pt 8 of the Property (Relationships) Act 1976, the Family Protection Act 1955 and the Law Reform (Testamentary Promises) Act 1949 be repealed. In their place, the Commission recommends that there be a new Inheritance (Claims Against Estates) Act to be the principal source of law regarding entitlements to and claims against estates. This new Act should:

- weave new law that reflects tikanga Māori and other values shared by New Zealanders
- provide that tikanga Māori determine succession to taonga
- continue a surviving partner's rights to a division of relationship property when their partner dies
- provide for when certain family members can claim further property from an estate despite what the will says or the intestacy rules say
- restate a revised testamentary promises cause of action
- give courts greater powers to access property outside an estate to meet awards made against an estate, and
- support efficient and effective dispute resolution both in and out of court.

In addition, the Commission recommends that the rules under the Administration Act 1969 governing the distribution of intestate estates should be reformed.

The Commission's Report and other information about the Review of Succession Law project can be found on the Commission's website: lawcom.govt.nz/our-projects/review-succession-law.

1.7 Changes in a will

A will is the sole evidence of how a person wishes their estate to be disposed of after their death. It is, therefore, very important that there should be no possibility of fraudulent alteration of a will. To avoid this possibility of fraud, strict rules about alterations to wills have been laid down by statute and by the courts.

Section 15 of the Wills Act provides that a valid will may be changed if the change is made in writing on the will and the change is signed and witnessed on the paper next to or beside the change or the change is in a note written on the will and witnessed or the words are obliterated or the High Court declares a change valid. Changes can be made informally by a military or seagoing person.

However, if a codicil referring to the alteration is subsequently executed, this will make the alteration effective.

An alteration made before the will is executed will be effective and the attestation clause should confirm that it was made before the execution and should be initialled by the will-maker and by the witnesses.

If part of the will has been obliterated so that the words cannot be read in any ordinary inspection of the paper, this will be effective.

Law: Wills Act 2007, s 15

1.8 Revocation of wills

It has already been stated that an essential feature of a will is that it shall be freely revocable by will-makers at any time before their death. However, even though there may be clear evidence that a will does not represent the will-maker's wishes at the time of their death, their property will nevertheless be disposed of as directed by the will, unless it has been effectively revoked by one of the methods prescribed by law.

1.8.1 Revocation by operation of law

1.8.1.1 Total revocation

The will-maker marrying or entering into a civil union after they make their will automatically revokes the will. No legislation deals with the effect of the commencement and termination of a de facto relationship on existing wills.

However, if a will is expressed to be made in contemplation of a particular marriage or does not expressly say that it is in contemplation of a particular marriage or civil union, but the circumstances existing when it was made show clearly that it was made in contemplation of a particular marriage or civil union, it is not revoked by the contemplated marriage. Such a will will usually begin like this: "This is the Last Will and Testament of me, AB and so on, made in contemplation of my marriage to CD, and this will is conditional on the marriage taking place".

It is important that the will contain some phraseology as strong as this, as, in New Zealand,[10] wills merely containing dispositions to "my fiance" [so and so], have been held to be revoked by the will-maker's subsequent marriage to

10 Unlike some other Commonwealth countries.

[so and so]. To bring the will within the exception, there must be, as Mahon J said in *Public Trustee v Crawley* [1973] 1 NZLR 695, "an unequivocal declaration of the will-maker" — they must "express in the will the fact that it is made in contemplation of marriage".[11]

For a will to survive the will-maker's subsequent marriage, the marriage must be the one contemplated in the will. If A were to make a will expressed to be in contemplation of A's marriage to B, and B subsequently married C, the will would be revoked.

Unless the will is made conditional on the marriage taking place (as in our example), it will be effective even if the contemplated marriage is not celebrated; in other words, it will not be revoked if the marriage fails to take place.

1.8.1.2 Partial revocation

It is now possible for provisions in a will to be revoked by the dissolution of a marriage or a civil union or a separation order applying to a marriage or a civil union. In the absence of an express provision to the contrary in the will or in a codicil executed after the dissolution of a marriage or a civil union, such a dissolution renders null and void (to the extent that it affects the former spouse) any provision in the will:

- appointing the former spouse or partner as executor, trustee or advisory trustee,[12] and
- making any disposition other than a power of appointment exclusively in favour of the former spouse or partner's children.

(A codicil made by the deceased between the date of the will and the date of the dissolution of a marriage would, of course, form part of the will itself.)

The will must be read as if the spouse or partner died immediately before the will-maker, without prejudice to the possibility of a claim under the Family Protection Act.

1.8.2 Revocation by voluntary act of the will-maker

Before we get into the details of this topic, we should mention that will-makers, as well as needing testamentary capacity at the time that they make their wills (as was covered in Subsection 1.3.2 — *Who may make a will?*), also need it at the time of a voluntary revocation.[13]

11 Similar conclusions were reached in *Burton v McGregor* [1953] NZLR 487, and *Re Whale (dec'd)* [1977] 2 NZLR 1, with the same result, that is, the will was held to be revoked by marriage.

12 The substitute executor, if there is one, is entitled to probate — *Re Jackson* [1991] 3 NZLR 125.

13 In *Brunt v Brunt* (1873) LR 3 P & D 37, the will-maker, drunk and in a state of delirium tremens, tore up his will. The Court accepted that he was "in an unsound state of mind" at the time, and that he was "not capable of exercising any judgment in the matter". The act of

It, therefore, follows that the will of a will-maker who has lost testamentary capacity permanently will be irrevocable by the will-maker.

The Wills Act provides that, apart from revocation by marriage or civil union, a will may be revoked only in the following ways:

1. *Making a later valid will or codicil* — We saw in our sample will that it is usual to include a clause expressly revoking all prior wills, whether or not the will-maker has, in fact, made any. Such a clause will always be effective, unless it was included without the knowledge of the will-maker. But even without any express revocation clause, an earlier will will be implicitly revoked by a later one if it is clear from the terms of the later will that this was the intention of the will-maker. This will obviously be so where the later will disposes of all the assets of the will-maker; but, where a later will leaves undisposed assets, and such assets were the subject-matter of gifts in the earlier will, the court may hold that revocation was not intended, and the 2 wills will both be effected as far as this is possible. The court leans against implied revocation, unless this was clearly the intention of the will-maker.
2. *Writing a document making clear an intention to revoke* — Will-makers may effectively revoke their wills by making clear their intention to do so in writing, or by doing anything else in relation to the will that satisfies the High Court that the will-maker intended to revoke the will, such as giving written instructions to the person holding the will to destroy it. The writing must be executed and attested with the same formalities that are required for executing a will; otherwise, the revocation will not be effective.
3. *Destruction* — It is possible for a will to be partially revoked by destruction if the will-maker destroys only a part of the will with the necessary intention. For a will to be revoked by destruction, it, or a part of it, must be destroyed intentionally, for example, by burning, tearing, or complete mutilation, or the will-maker, with the intention of revoking the will or part of the will, directs another person to destroy it in the will-maker's presence. A merely symbolic destruction will not revoke the whole will. It will not be revoked by writing "Cancelled" on it, nor will it be partially revoked by drawing a pen through some lines, leaving the words quite legible, and writing on the back "All these are revoked", unless the revocation is declared valid under s 14 of the Wills Act.[14] The will-maker must destroy the will personally, or someone must do so at his or her direction and in his or her presence.

---

destruction therefore had no effect on the instrument that he attempted to destroy, and the reconstructed pieces were admitted to probate.

14 *Cheese v Lovejoy* (1877) 2 PD 251.

To be revoked, the will, once made, must be destroyed animo revocandi (with the intention of revoking it). If it can be proved that a will was destroyed by mistake, or merely lost, *provided* that there is adequate evidence before the court that the will was in fact made,[15] it will not be revoked, and a draft or copy will be admitted to probate. As James LJ said in the English Court of Appeal in *Cheese v Lovejoy* (1877) 2 PD 251, "It is quite clear that a symbolical burning will not do, a symbolical tearing will not do, nor will a symbolical destruction. There must be the act as well as the intention. ... All the destroying in the world without intention will not revoke a will, nor all the intention in the world without destroying: there must be the two".

This point is emphasised in s 16 of the Wills Act, which states that the will-maker must have the intention of revoking the will.

1.8.3 Conditional revocation

Revocation of a will may be conditional. If the condition is not fulfilled, the revocation fails and the will remains operative. In particular, revocation (or partial revocation) of a will may be conditional upon the making of a later will, with the will-maker not intending the revocation to be operative if they, in fact, do not make the later will. This is known as dependent relative revocation, and the application of this principle to alterations in a will have already been stated. If, for any reason, the later will does not take effect, the revocation is inoperative.

An example makes the principle clear. X made a will in 1992 and, in 1993, made a second will expressly revoking the 1992 will. In 1994, X said that X intended to revoke the 1993 will and revive the 1992 one. To effect this, X destroyed the 1993 will by burning it. As we shall see in the next section, a revoked will cannot be revived by the will-maker simply stating that it shall be revived, but X did not know this. The court would accept evidence that X destroyed the second will only on the assumption that this would revive the

---

15 In *Palmer v Smedley* [1974] 1 NZLR 751, a case of an alleged lost will, the deceased's widow failed to obtain a grant of Letters of Administration with Will Annexed (see Chapter 7 — *Administrators* for the meaning of this term). Mahon J said:

> "In order to obtain letters of administration with the reconstructed will annexed the plaintiff [the widow] had to establish the following facts:
>
> (1) That the deceased had executed a will.
>
> (2) That it was duly subscribed and attested by witnesses ...
>
> (3) That the contents of the last will was in accordance with the epitome [reconstructed summary] presented.
>
> (4) That if the loss of the will raised the presumption that it had been destroyed by the deceased animo revocandi [will in the custody of the deceased] then that presumption was rebutted ... In the present case the only evidence before me is a narration of oral post-testamentary declarations on the part of testator [the deceased]".

He held that these were insufficient evidence, and ordered that the estate be distributed as on an intestacy.

earlier one. As the intended revival failed, so too would the revocation of the second will, and a copy or draft of the second will or other indisputable evidence of its contents would be admitted to probate.

However, to return to our general discussion, the courts must be satisfied that the will-maker's intentions in revoking the will were exclusively referable to the condition. In other words, it appears that the condition that the will-maker had in mind must be their sole reason for revoking the will. In *Re Jones (dec'd)* [1976] Ch 200; [1976] 1 All ER 593, the testatrix revoked her will by cutting off the signatures at a time when she had the intention of making a new will the next week, but was, by her untimely illness and death, prevented from ever carrying this intention into effect. All 3 judges in the English Court of Appeal, reversing the decision of the court below where dependent relative revocation had been applied, drew a distinction between:

- revoking the will, and having the intention of making a new will, and
- revoking the will conditionally upon the making of a new will.

They held that the correct inference to be drawn from the facts was that the testatrix had intended to revoke her will forthwith and be intestate in the meantime, even though she had the intention of making a new will to replace it.

Law: Wills Act 2007, ss 10, 14, 16, 18, 19

1.9 Revival of a revoked will

A revoked will cannot be revived merely by the will-maker stating their intention to revive it, even if the intention is set down in writing. It can be revived only by the will-maker re-executing it with the usual formalities under s 11, or, presuming it is still in existence, by the execution of a codicil expressing the intention to revive the will or it can be done informally by a military or seagoing person. If it is revived by re-executing it, the will is then treated as though it was made on the date it was re-executed; but, if it is revived by codicil, it is treated as though it was made on the date on which it was first made.

Law: Wills Act 2007, s 17

1.10 The effect of contracts relating to wills

It has already been stressed that an essential feature of a will is that it remains revocable by the will-maker and does not come into operation until their death. Consistent with this basic principle, people cannot, by contract, deprive themselves of the power to alter their wills. They cannot, by contract, convert their wills into irrevocable instruments; nor can they bind themselves irrevocably to make certain gifts under their wills. But note that this is not the same thing as saying that a person cannot enter into a valid contract of this type.

The position is that will-makers, who have contracted to include certain provisions in their wills, or not to revoke a will already made, may, notwithstanding the contract, alter or revoke their wills. By so doing, they may make themselves or their estates liable to an action for breach of contract, but the important point for us is that the alteration or revocation of the will is valid. Again, a contract not to make a will does not prevent a person from making a valid will, though, in so doing, they may become liable for a breach of contract. In all of these cases, the contract itself may be valid; but it does not make a will that is made in contravention of the contract invalid, nor a revocation ineffective.

1.11 The effect of property relationships legislation on wills

The Property (Relationships) Amendment Act provided a new procedure for resolving issues relating to the division of relationship property after death. The intent is to provide a codified regime for the division of matrimonial, civil union and de facto property after the death of one partner, which is similar to the outcome should the property be divided while both partners are still alive. The presumptions of equal sharing will apply, as will the discretion to make orders to redress economic disparities. If the income and living standards of one spouse or partner are likely to be significantly higher than the other spouse because of the effects of the division of functions within the relationship while the parties were living together, the court may award lump sum payments or order the transfer of property.

1.11.1 Election

If one of the spouses or partners has died and no proceedings were issued under the Property (Relationships) Act prior to death, the surviving spouse or partner must elect either:

- Option A — to make an application under the Property (Relationships) Act for a division of the relationship property, or
- Option B — not to make an application under the Act, but, if the spouse or partner is a beneficiary under the will of the deceased spouse or partner, to receive that property; or, if the deceased spouse or partner died intestate, to receive a beneficial interest on the intestacy.

1.11.2 Time limits for making election

If a surviving spouse or partner wishes to choose Option A or Option B, the following time limits apply:

- In the case of a "small estate" that can be administered without grant of administration, application to the court must be made within 6 months of the date of death. A "small estate" is one where the deceased's property does not include land and where the value of any personal property does not exceed $15,000.

- In any other case, the choice must be made no later than 6 months after administration of the estate of the deceased spouse is granted in New Zealand.

The court may extend the time for making the choice after hearing the applicant and other concerned parties, but only if the application for the extension is made before the final distribution of the estate of the deceased spouse or partner. This is to avoid a situation in which distribution or partial distribution has taken place before the application for extension of time. The following time limits apply:

- An application made after a de facto relationship has ended must be made no later than 3 years after the de facto relationship ended.

- An application relating to married couples or civil union partners must be made within 12 months of dissolution of the marriage or civil union.

If distribution of any part of the estate has taken place before the personal representative of the deceased spouse or partner receives notice that an application has been made to the court, the distribution cannot be disturbed.

1.11.3 Making the election

A surviving spouse or de facto partner may not apply under the Act for a division of the relationship property, unless they have first chosen Option A. However, a surviving spouse or partner may apply without having made an election if there was a separation order in force in relation to the marriage or civil union or the deceased spouse or partner dies intestate or the marriage or civil union was dissolved prior to death. In both these situations, the former spouse would be obligated to issue proceedings.

1.11.4 How the choice is to be made

The election is made by completing and signing a written notice in the prescribed form, which contains a solicitor's certificate stating that the solicitor has advised the surviving spouse, civil union partner or de facto partner of the effect and implications of the choice. The form and the solicitor's certificate must be lodged with the administrators of the estate or, if made before probate or letters of administration have been granted, in the High Court Registry in which the application for probate or letters of administration would be filed.

1.11.5 Notification

Various people must be notified of the choice of option. These include other shareholders and company directors if the deceased owned shares in a company, and the final managers of any superannuation fund or life insurance policy. Any beneficiary under a life insurance policy other than the applicant must also be notified.

1.11.6 No choice made

If no choice is made, the Act provides that the surviving spouse or partner is deemed to have elected to take under the will or on intestacy. Once a choice has been made, the surviving spouse or partner cannot withdraw their choice. However, the court can set the choice aside.

Law: Property (Relationships) Act 1976, ss 15, 62–68, 74

1.12 The court's power to set the choice aside

The court has the discretion to set aside the choice of option if it is satisfied that:

- the choice of option is not freely made
- the surviving spouse or partner did not fully understand the effect and implication of the choice
- the surviving spouse or partner has become aware of relevant information after the choice was made
- since the election was made, some other person has made an application under the Law Reform (Testamentary Promises) Act or the Family Protection Act.

In addition to these factors, the court must also be satisfied that it would be unjust to enforce the choice of option. In deciding whether or not to set aside the choice, the court must have regard to:

- the circumstances in which the choice was made
- the length of time since the choice was made, and
- any other matters that the court thinks relevant.

However, the court may not set aside the choice of option, unless the application to set aside is made before the final distribution of the estate.

The effect of these provisions is that the advice a solicitor gives to a spousal partner that leads to the making of the choice should be carefully recorded.

Law: Property (Relationships) Act 1976, ss 69–70

1.13 Distribution of estates

No part of the estate can be distributed until either:

- 6 months after the grant of administration or the date of death in the case of small estates, or
- the surviving spousal partner chooses Option A or Option B, or
- disposal of any claim in respect of the estate, including a claim for property division under the Property (Relationships) Act or from the estate as a consequence of a Family Protection Act claim or Testamentary Promises claim.

Distribution is restricted until proceedings are finally determined or withdrawn, including time for appeal. However, distribution can take place if the surviving spousal partner consents or if there is court approval for the distribution.

Law: Property (Relationships) Act 1976, ss 62(1), (2), 71, 73

1.14 Effect of election

If the surviving spousal partner chooses Option A, every gift in the will to the surviving spousal partner is revoked. The will is treated as though the surviving spousal partner predeceased the other. However, if the deceased's will states that the deceased intended the other partner to take gifts under the will, even if an election is made, those gifts will still be effective. If the spousal partner died intestate, the surviving spousal partner has no entitlement under Pt 3 of the Administration Act. However, the court does have the power to order that the surviving spousal partner takes under the will if that is necessary to avoid injustice.

Law: Property (Relationships) Act 1976, ss 76–77

1.15 Surviving spouse or partner

The Property (Relationships) Act makes special provisions for a surviving spouse or de facto partner. Any property or payment entitlement arising from a court order or agreement made under the Act has priority over beneficiaries under the will of the deceased or any beneficial interest arising as a consequence of intestacy. It also has priority over an order made under the Family Protection Act or the Law Reform (Testamentary Promises) Act and costs payable, apart from properly incurred estate administration costs and funeral expenses.

All property owned by the deceased partner at the time of death is presumed to be relationship property (Property (Relationships) Act 1976, s 81). Anyone who wishes to rebut this presumption bears the burden of proof. In addition, the Act presumes that all property acquired by the estate of the deceased partner is relationship property. This presumption is also rebuttable.

Any property that passes to the surviving partner by survivorship will not necessarily be treated as separate property. The decision as to whether such property is relationship property or separate property is determined as if the deceased spouse or de facto partner had not died. Any property acquired by a surviving partner after the death of the other is presumed to be separate property, although the court retains a discretion to treat such property as relationship property if justice requires it (Property (Relationships) Act 1976, s 84). This does not, however, apply to property acquired by the deceased by inheritance, under a trust, or by gift from a third party.

Law: Property (Relationships) Act 1976, ss 10(2), 78, 81, 83, 84

1.16 Death of a partner in a relationship of short duration

Generally, marriages or de facto relationships where the parties have been together for less than 3 years are relationships of short duration, although they may include longer relationships, if the court, in all the circumstances, considers this just. If one marriage spouse dies and the relationship is one of short duration, the surviving spouse's share of the relationship property is to be determined as if the marriage were of long duration, unless to do so would be unjust. The presumptions of equal sharing of relationship property, such as the family home and the family chattels, apply. The treatment of short de facto relationships is the same, whether the relationship ends during the lifetime of the partners or as a result of the death of one partner. The court cannot make an order for the division of relationship property, unless satisfied that there is a child of the de facto relationship or that the claimant has made a substantial contribution to the de facto relationship, and it is necessary to make such an order to avoid serious injustice. In such a case, the share of the partners is determined in accordance with the contribution of each de facto partner to the de facto relationship.

Law: Property (Relationships) Act 1976, ss 2E, 11, 12, 85

1.17 Priority of competing claims

In some situations, more than one partner of the deceased may have competing claims for a share of relationship property after death. There may have been a marriage followed by a de facto relationship or a series of relationships. The will may provide for the last partner alone but make no provision for other potential claimants. If there has been no property division relating to the earlier relationships or only partial division, there may be grounds for such claims.

It will be necessary to establish the extent of the relationship property attributable to each relationship. The Act provides the priority if competing claims are made for relationship property, and one claim relates to a marriage and the other a de facto relationship, and there is insufficient property to satisfy the property orders under the Act.

The relationship property is divided as follows. If a marriage and a de facto relationship are successive, irrespective of the order in which they occur, relationship property is to be divided in accordance with the chronological order of the relationship. If the marriage and the de facto relationship were at some time contemporaneous, property is to be divided as far as possible from the property that is attributable to the particular relationship. If it is not possible to determine whether a particular item of property is attributable to the marriage or to the de facto relationship, the property is divided in accordance with the contribution of each partner to the acquisition of that property. The marriage and de facto relationship are successive if the de facto relationship begins during the marriage but after the husband and wife cease to live together as husband and wife.

Where two de facto relationships are involved, the approach is similar. Where the relationships were at some time contemporaneous, then, to the extent possible, the property orders must be satisfied from the property that is attributable to each de facto relationship. To the extent that it is not possible to attribute all or any of the property to either de facto relationship, the property is divided in accordance with the contribution of each relationship to the acquisition of the property.

Law: Property (Relationships) Act 1976, ss 52A, 52B

Chapter 2
Commorientes

2.0 Introduction

This is a specialised topic. We intend here merely to introduce it, and to provide information on where to look for answers to relevant questions.

When two or more people die in circumstances in which it is impossible to determine the order in which they died, for instance, in a car accident, they are referred to as "commorientes". When one person is named as a beneficiary under another's will or would succeed to the estate on intestacy if they had survived the other, the court must first determine which of the two died first. The following example illustrates this:

> A by A's will leaves all A's property to B, and B by B's will leaves all B's property to C. If A survives B, A's property on A's death will go to A's next-of-kin under the rules of intestacy, the gift to B having failed. But if B survives A, then A's property will go to B, and on B's death it will go under B's will to C.

With commorientes, as it is impossible to determine who died first, the law has always laid down certain rules or presumptions. Formerly, it was legally presumed that the younger survived the older, but the practical results of this presumption were often inequitable. For instance, in the above example, if A and B were commorientes, whether A's property went to A's next-of-kin or to C would have depended merely on whether or not A was older than B.

The law in New Zealand was altered and made much fairer with the passing of the Simultaneous Deaths Act 1958. This Act laid down that, in deciding how commorientes' estates should be distributed, each is deemed to have survived the other. Thus, again in the above example, A by will left A's property to B, but as B would be deemed to have predeceased A, A's property would go to A's next-of-kin as an intestacy, instead of to B, and thence, under B's will, passing to C (who may have been unknown to A). B's property alone would go to C.

Over and above the main rule in the Act, and speaking a little more generally now, it is possible for people to make their own express provision in their wills for a commorientes situation, or for a party to show by evidence that one person in fact survived the other, but the burden of proof rests on the person who asserts this.

The Act also sets out a number of other rules that can be important in specific commorientes applications. These rules are more detailed and subsidiary to the main rule, from which they do not detract, and they are not discussed here. In total, they comprise a code covering all the questions to which they relate and, it is submitted, covering virtually all of the situations that can arise. Finally, the old presumption is preserved to the extent that none of the rules in the Act are applicable. As we have implied, the old presumption's operation is now extremely limited.

The term "next-of-kin" is sometimes used loosely in everyday speech to mean close relatives. Legally, unless a contrary intention is expressed in the will (if any), the term means those persons who would, on intestacy, be entitled to the deceased's estate under the rules of intestate succession set out in the Administration Act 1969. Such persons will take in the shares set out in that Act, unless a contrary intention is expressed in the will.

Law: Simultaneous Deaths Act 1958, s 3

Chapter 3
Gifts under Wills

3.0 Legacies

Legacies, bequests, and devises are all types of gifts under a will. Here, legacies and bequests will be dealt with first.

Legacies are general, specific, demonstrative, or residuary.

A *general legacy* is a gift in general terms of personal property to be provided out of the will-maker's estate, no particular part of the estate being indicated as intended to satisfy the legacy. The most common general legacy is a gift of money (*a pecuniary legacy*), for example, "$20,000 to my wife". Or it may be an unspecified diamond ring "worth $800"; in which case, if the will-maker at their death did not own such a ring, their personal representative would have to buy one either out of the estate's cash or out of the sale of assets not specifically bequeathed.[1]

(Note that different rules would apply to a gift of "*my* diamond ring valued at $800", as we will see below.)

A *specific legacy* or *bequest* is a gift of a specified part of the will-maker's personal estate, so described that it can be exactly identified and set apart from the rest of the estate, for example, "my 2017 Mercedes-Benz car", or, as mentioned above, "my diamond ring valued at $800", or "the money in my Kiwibank Account". (Statutory provisions exist by which a client of a bank, for example, Kiwibank, may nominate that amounts not exceeding $6000 in any one bank account, shall pass on their death to a designated person or persons. Such "Nominations of Accounts" take effect as though they were specific legacies in the deceased person's estate, and the instrument of nomination is subject to much of the law relating to wills.[2] The provisions are infrequently used.)

A *demonstrative legacy* is one that falls between a general legacy and a specific legacy. It is a general gift of a certain sum, to satisfy which the will-maker has

1 In this instance, the beneficiary can demand the cash instead of the ring.

2 However, a nomination is not in a better position than a specific legacy, as it is subject to any claims that can be made against specific legacies in the deceased person's estate. For example, the nomination could be abated to satisfy outstanding debts in the estate.

A nomination can be revoked in any manner in which a will or codicil can be revoked — including revocation by operation of law. Also, a later will containing a clause revoking all former testamentary dispositions will include and revoke a nomination(s), unless the nomination is expressly preserved. The same result follows, without a revocation clause, in the case of a later general testamentary disposition of the whole estate of the nominator, or of the whole of the residuary estate.

indicated a particular fund, for example, "$20,000 to my wife, to be paid out of the proceeds of the sale of my shares in XYZ Ltd". If the fund indicated by the will-maker is not large enough to meet the gift, the remainder of the legacy will be paid out of the general estate.

For a legacy to be demonstrative, the gift must be construed as a general gift of a certain sum, but it must also be directed that it be paid out of a particular fund if the fund is available. This fund must be intended to be the primary source, and not the sole source, from which the gift is to be satisfied. On the other hand, if the will-maker appears to have intended the indicated fund to be the sole source for satisfying the gift, it will be a specific legacy; and, if the fund is not available or is not enough to meet the gift in full, the legacy will be adeemed or partially adeemed accordingly. Ademption is discussed in Subsection 3.3.1 — *Ademption*.

The following examples distinguish a general pecuniary legacy, a specific pecuniary legacy, and a demonstrative legacy:

- A gift of "the sum of $20,000 to my wife" is a general legacy. No particular fund is indicated, and there can be no ademption unless there is no general estate from which it can be satisfied.
- "The sum of $20,000 on fixed deposit in my account at the ANZ Bank to my wife", is a specific legacy. A particular fund is identified and given and, if at the will-maker's death, there is no such sum on fixed deposit at this bank, the gift is adeemed.
- "The sum of $20,000 to my wife, to be paid out of the moneys in my account at the ANZ Bank", is a demonstrative legacy. If there are no moneys or not enough money in the bank account to meet the gift, it will not be adeemed, but will be paid out of the general estate. It can, therefore, be seen that, with ademption, a demonstrative legacy is much better than a specific legacy. (It is also better than a general legacy in abatement discussed below.)

A *residuary legacy* is a gift of what remains of a will-maker's personal estate after all other legacies have been met and after all debts and expenses have been paid.

Law: Administration Act 1969, ss 68A–68D

3.1 Abatement

Sometimes, when an estate is to be distributed, there are not enough assets in the estate after payment of expenses and debts to satisfy all the gifts that the will-maker has made in the will. This means that some beneficiaries must go short or receive smaller legacies. Such a reduction is known as "abatement". The distinction among the various classes of legacy is very important here, because there is a definite order of abatement, and the order in which legacies abate depends on the category into which they fall.

We intend, at this point, merely to introduce the topic of abatement, to define it, and to illustrate the relevance of the distinction between the various classes of legacy. What is said in the next paragraph does not fully cover abatement. A complete summary of the topic of abatement is made later in Chapter 10 — *Application of Assets in Payment of Debts*.

In distributing the estate, testamentary expenses and debts must be paid first. Then, if the estate is too small to satisfy all gifts, legacies will abate in the following order: residuary legacies abate first, then general legacies, and finally specific legacies. Within each class, the legacies abate rateably. A demonstrative legacy is treated as a specific legacy if the fund from which it is to be met is available at the will-maker's death. If the fund is not available, or if the fund is too small, the demonstrative legacy will sink, wholly or partially, to the rank of a general legacy, and will abate proportionally with the other general legacies.

A demonstrative legacy has, therefore, the particular advantage of a specific legacy, which does not abate until after residuary and general legacies, if the fund is available. If the fund is not available, it has the particular advantage of a general legacy, which is not dependent on the continued existence of any particular asset in the estate, as it will not be adeemed, but will be satisfied out of the general estate.

The following example shows how abatement and ademption operate:

By his will, Adam makes the following gifts:

1. "My 2020 Mitsubishi car to my son Brian"
2. "$200,000 to my daughter Celia, to be paid out of the moneys in my Kiwibank account"
3. "$500,000 to my wife Dina", and
4. "The residue of my estate to my son Eamon".

At his death, Adam's assets are:

1. A 2020 Mercedes-Benz car worth $200,000
2. $100,000 in a Kiwibank account, and
3. Other assets worth $200,000.

Assuming that provisions have already been made for the payment of debts and so on, the estate will be distributed as follows:

As Adam does not now possess a 2020 Mitsubishi car, the gift to his son Brian is adeemed — Brian receives nothing. The Mercedes-Benz car will go into the general estate, which, with both the car and the other assets valued at $200,000, will amount to $400,000.

As this sum of $400,000, together with the $100,000 in the Kiwibank account, is the total amount available to meet the general legacy of $500,000 to wife Dina and the demonstrative legacy of $200,000 to daughter Celia, these legacies will be abated according to the rules set out above.

The demonstrative legacy cannot be abated until the indicated source of payment has been exhausted. Daughter Celia will, therefore, receive the $100,000 from the Kiwibank account. This will leave $400,000 to meet the $100,000 balance of the demonstrative legacy, which will now be treated as a general legacy, and the general legacy of $500,000 to the wife.

With only $400,000 to pay $600,000, each legacy will abate by 33⅓%, the daughter receiving a further $66,666.66, and the wife $333,333.33. As there is no residuary estate, his son Eamon will receive nothing. (Note, however, that both sons, who received nothing, may have a claim under the Family Protection Act 1955.)

3.2 Devises

A devise is a *gift of land* and may be of 3 kinds:

1. A *general devise* is a gift of land described in a general manner, for example, "all my real property to X".
2. A *specific devise* specifies and identifies the land concerned, for example, "my property at 123 Main Road, Wellington, to X".
3. A *residuary devise* is a gift by general description of lands that have not otherwise been disposed of by the will. (Note that the residuary clause in the specimen will in Section 1.2 — *The form of a will* of this text would include all the remainder of the will-maker's property, both real and personal, not otherwise disposed of. This is a common clause.)

3.3 Failure of gifts by will

Apart from the possibility of abatement already mentioned, a gift left by a will may fail in a number of circumstances.

3.3.1 Ademption

A couple of examples of this have already been given in the immediately preceding pages. A gift is "adeemed" when the will-maker no longer has the power to make it because the property involved no longer forms part of the will-maker's estate.

Ademption is an important principle that applies principally to specific legacies (bequests) and *specific* devises. It means that, if the subject-matter of a gift no longer exists or forms part of the will-maker's estate at their death, the gift fails. The beneficiary will not be entitled to any substituted gift or compensation from the rest of the estate. The item, for instance, may have been sold or given away by the will-maker, it may have been destroyed, or it may, in more difficult cases, have altered location. In the first two groups of cases, the gift is said to have been *adeemed*, and the beneficiary receives nothing under it. Section 27 of the Wills Act 2007 provides that, if a will-maker makes a will and later disposes of an interest in property disposed of in the will, the will applies to any interest in the property to which the will-maker is entitled when the will-maker dies, unless the will-maker made it clear that the disposition in the will was intended to be void.

The principle is clear, but it can be difficult to apply. For example, is the beneficiary entitled to shares in a company that has undergone a reconstruction or other transformation since the date of the will?[3]

As we have already said, the principle applies equally to specific devises.

If a will-maker leaves to their spouse "my residential property situate at 84 Brougham Street, Wellington" and, at the time of will-maker's death, has sold this property and now owns a property at 22 Evans Bay Parade, Wellington, the latter property will fall into the residuary estate and will not go to the spouse in substitution for the property sold. To avoid this, a phrase such as "the principal residential property owned by me at the date of my death" is usually used.

3.3.2 Lapse

A gift lapses if the beneficiary dies before the will-maker. In other words, the descendants of the beneficiary normally receive nothing in these circumstances. But remember that, when will-makers leave a gift to their child or children who predecease them leaving a child or children, such a child or children will take the parent's gift (Wills Act 2007, s 23).

A will-maker may leave a gift to several persons in succession, the first person (the "life tenant") to take a life interest, and the second person (the "remainderman") to take an absolute interest on the death of the life tenant. If the life tenant predeceases the will-maker, only the life interest lapses, and the remainderman receives an immediate absolute interest. If the remainderman predeceases the will-maker, the gift lapses after the death of the life tenant.

3.3.3 Non-fulfilment of condition

A donor can make a gift subject to any lawful[4] condition and, for this reason, gifts are either absolute or conditional. If the gift is conditional, it may fail

3 In this area, the cases conflict.

4 The word "lawful", as used here, has a meaning a little narrower than just "not infringing the criminal law". The courts have traditionally (not only in the law of succession but also in the law of contract) regarded some objectives as undesirable, and have refused to assist in their attainment.

A condition must also be certain, to the extent that the court must be able to ascertain from the beginning the events upon the happening of which it will be fulfilled. For example, in *Re* because the condition is not fulfilled. Conditions may be either conditions precedent or conditions subsequent.

- The fulfilment of a *condition precedent* is necessary before the beneficiary can take a vested interest in the gift.
- The non-fulfilment of a *condition subsequent* brings to an end an interest in a gift already taken by a beneficiary.

When a gift is not subject to a condition, it is said to be absolute or vested indefeasibly. It cannot be taken away. When it is subject to a condition precedent, the beneficiary's interest is contingent. When it is subject to a condition subsequent, the interest is said to be vested, subject to being divested.

A leaving a gift to "B on B getting married" is an example of a condition precedent. The gift is contingent on B's marrying, and, if B does not marry, B gets nothing.

A condition subsequently attached to a gift will often at the same time constitute a condition precedent to a further gift. When it refers to the same gift to a second person, for example, a gift to "A, but if A does not marry within 6 months, then to B", A receives a vested interest subject to being divested if A fails to marry within 6 months. This constitutes a condition subsequent. At the same time, A's failure to marry is the condition precedent to B receiving a vested interest. In the meantime, B's interest is merely contingent.

3.3.4 Disclaimer

A gift will fail if the beneficiary "disclaims" it. Beneficiaries are always entitled to refuse a gift if they choose to do so. However, there is a presumption that a beneficiary will accept a gift and this, of course, is normally the case. The only types of gift that are disclaimed with any frequency are gifts of leasehold property, and gifts of company shares encumbered with liability for calls.

When a gift fails for any reason, the property involved falls into the general estate, and, thus, becomes available to satisfy general legacies or will go to the residuary legatee. If the residuary gift fails, there is an intestacy as regards the residue.[5]

Lichtenstein [1986] 2 NZLR 392, a condition subsequently divesting the widow's right to income should she remarry was held valid, while a further condition having the same effect should she "enter into a de facto relationship" was held void for uncertainty. The effect, on the gift, of a void condition varies but, *sometimes*, when a condition precedent is unlawful and void, the gift itself will also fail — in other words, the *whole* disposition is void.

5 *Re Pugh's Will Trusts* [1967] 3 All ER 337.

3.4 Gifts subject to a charge

The property involved in a gift may be subject to a mortgage or charge, securing moneys owing at the will-maker's death. Who pays off the charge? The law on this matter has been taken over by legislation.

With respect to the estates of people who died on or after 1 February 2002, "spouse" includes a surviving de facto partner of the person. It also includes a civil union partner. With the exception of "personal chattels" passing to a spouse, charges existing at the date of death on interests in property of a deceased person pass with such interests in property. In other words, such interests pass to the beneficiaries, respectively, *subject to the charge*, and the satisfaction of the charge becomes the responsibility of the beneficiary or beneficiaries.

The term "personal chattels" is defined in the Administration Act 1969 and, although it means what you would expect it to mean, it nevertheless does not include all types of personalty. In addition to s 34, the term is also important in s 77, which sets out the rules of intestate succession, and an explanation of its meaning is given in Chapter 9 — *Succession on Intestacy*. If "personal chattels" passing to a spouse are subject to a charge, the spouse can have the charge paid off if there is enough money in the general estate.

The operation of the main rule in the legislation can be prevented if the deceased person has, in their will, or by deed or other document, expressly or by necessary implication referred to the charge itself and made plain that it is their intention that the beneficiary or beneficiaries take free of the charge.

The legislation, which applies to both testate and intestate estates, clarifies the position regarding chattels held under hire-purchase agreements. The above rules apply to such chattels — including the rule that "personal chattels" passing to a spouse do not pass subject to charges. Hence, as between beneficiaries, "personal chattels" passing to a spouse are taken free of liability from any hire-purchase instalments due or to become due.

In the case of wills made before 1 January 1971, the old law still applies, which can be summarised by saying:

- personalty passes free of the charge or charges
- in the absence of contrary provision in the will, real property passes subject to the charge.

Law: Administration Act 1969, ss 34–36

3.5 The executor's year

An executor is given a year to bring in the will-maker's assets and pay the legacies, and this is referred to as the "executor's year". Beneficiaries who do not receive their legacies within the executor's year are usually entitled to interest thereafter. There are, however, exceptions to this rule, for instance, a will-maker may direct that the legacy shall bear interest from the date of their death.

3.6 The meaning of per capita and per stirpes

When a will-maker leaves a gift to be shared among a group of people, the share each will receive may depend on whether the will-maker has directed the distribution to be made per stirpes (by stocks or families) or per capita (by heads).

Suppose, at the time of her death, Ann has 2 married sons, Bruce and Chris. Bruce has one child, and Chris has 4 children. In her will, Ann made the following gift:

"$1000 to be divided among my grandchildren per *capita*". Each of the 5 grandchildren would receive an equal share — $200.

But, if the gift was "$1000 to be divided among my grandchildren per *stirpes*", each family or stock would take an equal share, and that share would be subdivided equally among the members of the family taking it. Here, there are 2 stocks, those of Bruce and Chris, each of which takes $500. As Bruce has only one child, he will receive the full $500, and as Chris has 4 children, each will receive $125.[6]

3.7 Satisfaction by advancement

The most important instance of satisfaction by advancement arises when people by their will leave their estate, or part of their estate, to be divided among their children and, during their lifetime, make a substantial gift to one of those children. It is presumed that the gift was intended as an advancement of the child's share or part of their share in the estate. In such cases, the amount of the gift will be notionally brought back into the estate so that each child's share can be estimated.

For example, if A by A's will nominates $500,000 to be divided equally among A's 3 children, Xero, Yani, and Zac; and, during A's lifetime, A gives the sum of $100,000 to Xero, it will be presumed that A intended the gift of $100,000 to be an advancement of part of Xero's share in the estate.

On A's death, the $100,000 will be notionally added to the $500,000, making a total of $600,000. Each child is then entitled to a third — $200,000. Xero, having already received $100,000, will then receive $100,000 from the estate, and Yani

6 The meaning of per stirpes, and what it involves, is further elaborated in *Re Te Huango* [1993] 3 NZLR 77 — a case raising a rather difficult question of interpretation, which is not reproduced in this text.

and Zac will each receive $200,000. When this happens, the advancement to Xero is said to be brought into *hotchpot*, and Xero's legacy is said to be partially satisfied by the advancement.

The presumption of satisfaction by advancement will be rebutted if it was clearly not the will-maker's intention. In particular, the presumption will usually be rebutted if the will was executed after the gift was made. For instance, in the above example, if A had executed A's will *after* making the gift of $100,000 to Xero, A could have adjusted A's will by specifically providing that Xero should receive $100,000 and Yani and Zac should receive $200,000 each. As A did not do so, A appears to have intended each child to take a third of the $500,000, notwithstanding the gift of $100,000 already made to Xero.

Sometimes, when a will-maker leaves a sum to be divided among a number of beneficiaries, they will specifically direct in the will that any gift made during the will-maker's lifetime to one of the beneficiaries must be taken into account in calculating each beneficiary's share. Such a provision in a will is called a hotchpot clause.

3.8 Powers of appointment

Will-makers may, in their wills, authorise another person to direct how and to whom the estate or part of it is to be distributed. By so doing, the will-maker is in effect transferring to another their right to decide how their assets will be disposed of. Such a provision is called *a power of appointment*. It may be a general power or a special power.

- A general power of appointment gives the person nominated (the "donee" or "appointor") complete freedom to choose the beneficiaries. The donees may even make themselves the beneficiary and, hence, a general power of appointment is almost tantamount to a gift of the property to the donee.
- A special power of appointment restricts the donee in the choice of beneficiaries. The donee must appoint the beneficiaries from the group or class named by the will-maker. For example, will-makers may leave their estate to their spouse for life, and, thereafter, to such of their children, and, in such proportions, as they shall by deed or by their will appoint.

Chapter 4

Protection of Personal and Property Rights Act 1988

4.0 Introduction

The Protection of Personal and Property Rights Act 1988 assists adults who, because of incapacity, are no longer able to make or communicate decisions or manage their own affairs. Many people incorrectly believe that a spouse, parent or next of kin can legally make decisions on behalf of a "mentally incompetent" relative without that relative's specific authorisation.

If a person is incompetent, decisions must be made by a legally authorised representative such as a Welfare Guardian appointed by the Family Court or if the person themselves while still competent had appointed an Enduring Power of Attorney. If there is no representative, health and disability services may be provided under Right 7(4) of the Code of Health and Disability Services Consumers' Rights:

> "Right 7
>
> Right to Make an Informed Choice and Give Informed Consent
>
> . . .
>
> (4) Where a consumer is not competent to make an informed choice and give informed consent, and no person entitled to consent on behalf of the consumer is available, the provider may provide services where —
>
> (a) It is in the best interests of the consumer; and
>
> (b) Reasonable steps have been taken to ascertain the views of the consumer; and
>
> (c) Either, —
>
> (i) if the consumer's views have been ascertained, and having regard to those views, the provider believes, on reasonable grounds, that the provision of the services is consistent with the informed choice the consumer would make if he or she were competent; or
>
> (ii) if the consumer's views have not been ascertained, the provider takes into account the views of other suitable persons who are interested in the welfare of the consumer and available to advise the provider."

4.1 Objects of the Protection of Personal and Property Rights Act

The primary objectives of the court are to make the least restrictive intervention in the person's life having regard to their incapacity and to enable the person to exercise and develop their capacity as much as is possible.

4.2 Who is covered by the Act?

The Act can apply to a wide range of people including the mentally ill, infirm elderly, intellectually disabled, people who are paralysed and victims of head injuries. The Act deals separately with personal and property rights. It allows for the appointment of welfare guardians and property managers in two separate circumstances:

- Any competent person can choose to grant another person an enduring power of attorney to look after their personal affairs or property should they become incompetent in the future.
- If a person lacks the capacity to manage their own affairs, an application can be made to the Family Court to make personal or property orders for their benefit. Alternatively, an application can be made to appoint a welfare guardian or a property manager.

4.3 What does the Court have to consider?

In making decisions under the Act, the Family Court must protect and promote the personal and property rights of people needing protection. In making any orders, the Court considers the following:

- that the order causes the least interference with the person's life
- that the person is encouraged to use and develop their capacity to the greatest extent possible
- that the welfare and best interests of the person subject to the order are paramount.

This Act operates alongside the Mental Health (Compulsory Assessment and Treatment) Act 1992 and the Intellectual Disability (Compulsory Care and Rehabilitation) Act 2003.

4.4 Enduring powers of attorney

4.4.1 What is an enduring power of attorney?

The Protection of Personal and Property Rights Act enables people to authorise another or others to act on their behalf to manage their affairs.

An enduring power of attorney may relate to the person's property or to their personal care and welfare or both.

Only **one** personal care and welfare attorney can be appointed at a time.

More than one property attorney can be appointed.

4.4.2 How can an enduring power of attorney be completed?

People wishing to make an enduring power of attorney should ask a lawyer for advice and help.

There are 2 forms that are used for appointing an enduring power of attorney. They are:

1. Enduring Power of Attorney in relation to Property, and
2. Enduring Power of Attorney in relation to Personal Care and Welfare.

The Protection of Personal and Property Rights (Enduring Powers of Attorney Forms) Regulations 2008 set out the content of the forms for appointing an enduring power of attorney. The forms must be completed, signed and witnessed by a lawyer, registered legal executive or officer of a trustee organisation.

The Statutes Amendment Act 2016 provides that if two people appoint each other as attorney, the witness to the signature of one person as donor (**witness A**) does not fail to be independent by reason only that the witness to the signature of the other person as donor —

(a) is a lawyer or legal executive in the same firm, or an officer or employee of the same trustee corporation, as witness A, or

(b) is the same person as witness A, if, the witness is satisfied that witnessing both signatures does not constitute more than a negligible risk of a conflict of interest.

The witness must complete a certificate similar to the following:

> **CERTIFICATE OF WITNESS TO DONOR'S SIGNATURE ON ENDURING POWER OF ATTORNEY**
>
> Section 94A(7), Protection of Personal and Property Rights Act 1988
>
> I, May Elizabeth Bloggs of Hightown, Legal Executive, certify that—
>
> 1. I witnessed the signature of the donor, Enid Brown of Hightown, retired, on the attached enduring power of attorney form.
>
> 2. I am a legal executive and I—
>
> - am a member of the New Zealand Institute of Legal Executives Inc; and
> - hold a current annual registration certificate issued by the Institute; and

- have at least 12 months' experience as a legal executive; and
- am employed by, and under the direct supervision of, a lawyer who holds a current practising certificate as a barrister/barrister and solicitor issued by the New Zealand Law Society.

3. I am independent of John Smith of Lowtown, Accountant, who is appointed as attorney under the enduring power of attorney.

4. Before the donor signed the enduring power of attorney form, I explained the effects and implications of the enduring power of attorney to the donor and advised the donor of—

- (a) the matters referred to in the notes to the prescribed form of power of attorney; and
- (b) the donor's right to suspend or revoke the power of attorney; and

5. I have no reason to suspect that the donor was or may have been mentally incapable at the time she signed the enduring power of attorney form.

6. I believe that the donor understands the nature of the instrument; understands the potential risks and consequences of the instrument; and is not acting under undue pressure or duress.

Date:

Signature of witness:

____

Notes

1. This certificate is required to be attached to the enduring power of attorney form.

2. The term *trustee corporation* means the Maori Trustee, Public Trust, and every trustee company within the meaning of the Trustee Companies Act 1967.

The witness to the donor's signature may give the explanation by —

(a) giving a copy of the form to the donor, and

(b) following any instructions in the form for giving a verbal explanation to the donor, and

(c) if the form and the instructions do not cover all of required matters, using other appropriate means to fulfil all of the requirements.

4.4.3 Who can be an attorney?

An attorney does not have to be a lawyer.

An attorney must be at least 20 years old, not bankrupt and not subject to a personal or property order or subject to compulsory treatment or a special patient under the Mental Health (Compulsory Assessment and Treatment) Act 1992, or otherwise becomes incapable of acting.

A trustee corporation cannot act as an attorney for personal care and welfare matters.

4.4.4 When does an enduring power of attorney take effect?

A property enduring power of attorney may come into effect at the point it is created and while the person has his or her capacities, or may come into effect when capacity is lost.

A personal care and welfare enduring power of attorney can only take effect when capacity is lost.

4.4.5 Medical certification of incapacity

The person will be "mentally incapable" if he or she lacks the capacity to:

- make a decision, or
- understand the nature of decisions, or
- foresee the consequences of decisions or foresee the consequences of failure to make such decisions, or
- communicate decisions about matters relating to personal care and welfare.

(Protection of Personal and Property Rights Act 1988, s 94)

The previous forms of enduring power of attorney referenced the phrase "if I become mentally incapable". The concern was always as to who would decide the issue of mental incapacity.

Previously the law required certification of incapacity to be by a medical practitioner on a prescribed form. The Statutes Amendment Act 2016 amended the requirement to use the prescribed form to provide that a certificate of the donor's mental incapacity must contain the prescribed information, but no particular form is required (s 99D).

The donor may specify in the enduring power of attorney the type of medical practitioner to make such a medical assessment.

4.4.6 Disclaimer by attorney

The donor, whilst mentally capable, can revoke the enduring power of attorney at any time. If the donor still has mental capacity, the attorney can disclaim directly to the donor to terminate the appointment as attorney.

If the donor lacks mental capacity, the attorney must file the disclaimer with the Family Court together with a report outlining whether, in the opinion of the attorney, there should be a property manager and/or a welfare guardian appointed for the donor and the reasons for the attorney's opinion.

4.4.7 What if an attorney needs directions about what to do?

An attorney may apply to the Family Court for directions relating to the exercise of their powers under an enduring power of attorney.

A Family Court can also be asked to consider if a document is actually an enduring power of attorney, or if the person the enduring power of attorney relates to has become mentally incapable.

4.4.8 What if there are concerns about the decisions that an attorney is making on behalf of the person that it relates to?

An application can be made to the Family Court to review any decision made by an attorney.

Section 103(1) and (2) of the Protection of Personal and Property Rights Act provides that this type of application can be made by:

- the person who the enduring power of attorney relates to
- a relative of the person the enduring power of attorney relates to
- an attorney of the person that the enduring power or attorney relates to (not being the attorney acting under the enduring power of attorney)
- a social worker
- a medical practitioner
- a trustee corporation
- the principal manager of a place providing hospital care/rest home care/residential disability care to the person
- a welfare guardian appointed for the person
- a person authorised by a body or organisation contacted by the Government to provide elder abuse and neglect prevention services
- a person granted leave by the Court to make the application.

A Family Court can revoke the appointment of an enduring power of attorney if it is satisfied that the attorney is not acting in the best interests of the donor, or is failing to comply with their obligations.

4.5 Personal orders

4.5.1 What is a personal order?

If a person becomes incapacitated and unable to make decisions, the Court can make a personal order for their protection.

A personal order is an instruction given by a judge requiring an action to be taken to look after a specific part of an incapacitated person's care and welfare.

4.5.2 Who would the Court make a personal order for?

The Court can only make personal orders for people who ordinarily live in New Zealand.

Personal orders can be made for anyone who is 18 or older, but can also be made for 16- and 17-year-olds if they are or have been married, in a civil union or in a de facto relationship.

The person must either:

- lack, wholly or partly, the capacity to understand the nature, and to foresee the consequences, of decisions in respect of matters relating to their personal care and welfare, or
- have these capacities, but totally lack the capacity to communicate decisions about their personal care and welfare.

The Court will not make a personal order for a person who has granted someone an enduring power of attorney, unless the enduring power of attorney is not working properly to protect their best interests.

4.5.3 Who can apply for a personal order?

The following people can apply:

- a person who lacks capacity
- a relative or attorney of the incapacitated person
- a social worker
- a medical practitioner
- a representative of any non-profit group that provides services and facilities for the welfare of the people covered by the Act
- the superintendent, licensee, supervisor or person in charge, if the person is a patient or a resident of a hospital, home or other institution
- the manager of a person's property if the person is subject to a property order
- any other person with the Court's permission.

4.5.4 Who is considered a relative?

The following people are considered a relative:

- a spouse or de facto partner of that person
- a parent or grandparent of that person or of his or her spouse or de facto partner
- a child, stepchild or grandchild of that person or of his or her spouse or de facto partner
- a brother or sister of that person or of his or her spouse or de facto partner

- an aunt or uncle of that person or of his or her spouse or de facto partner
- a nephew or niece of that person or of his or her spouse or de facto partner.

To apply for a personal order, an application must be filed with the Family Court.

4.5.5 What will the Family Court do?

The Family Court will consider the evidence and decide whether the order is necessary. The Court must decide:

1. that the person concerned either:
   - lacks, wholly or partly, the capacity to understand the nature, and to foresee the consequences, of decisions in respect of matters relating to their personal care and welfare, or
   - has these capacities, but totally lacks the capacity to communicate decisions about their personal care and welfare
2. that a personal order should be made
3. what kinds of orders should be made.

The Court does not have the power to make an order just because the person under consideration makes decisions that the average person would not make.

The Court may recommend what it thinks should be done, instead of making an order. Applicants and people who lack capacity can then decide if they want to follow the Court's recommendations.

4.5.6 What kinds of personal orders can the Court make?

The Court can make a range of personal orders including:

1. an order requiring someone to pay an incapacitated person for work they have performed or are going to perform
2. an order requiring a parent or parents to make suitable arrangements for their child's personal care after their death
3. an order requiring that arrangements made for the personal care of the incapacitated person after the parent's death be observed, or varied
4. an order requiring that an incapacitated person be provided with specified residence and living arrangements, not including psychiatric hospitals or licensed institutions under the Mental Health (Compulsory Treatment and Assessment) Act
5. an order for medical advice or treatment
6. an order for educational, rehabilitative, therapeutic or other services
7. an order requiring an incapacitated person not to leave New Zealand without the permission of the Court, or only on specified conditions

8. an order appointing a representative or guardian ad litem for an incapacitated person in any District Court proceedings
9. an order appointing someone to administer any item of specified property that is worth $5,000 or less, or any income or benefit that is worth $20,000 or less a year
10. under s 12 of the Protection of Personal and Property Rights Act, an order appointing a welfare guardian for the person.

The Court may make an interim order, for example, when urgent medical treatment is required.

4.5.7 When does a personal order expire?

A personal order expires at the time set in the order.

If no time is set, the order stops when all tasks set in the order are completed, or 12 months after the order was made, whichever comes first.

The Court may also specify a date to review the order.

4.6 Review of personal orders

4.6.1 What is the purpose of a review?

At the review, the Court must determine whether the order is still necessary.

The Court will review the person's capacity to:

- understand the nature of decisions about their own personal care and welfare
- foresee the consequences of such decisions, and
- communicate such decisions.

For welfare guardianship orders, the Court should also ensure that the reason the application was made still exists.

4.6.2 Who may seek a review?

An application for review of a personal order may be made by:

- the person themselves
- the welfare guardian
- the manager
- any other person with leave of the Court.

4.6.3 When must reviews take place?

For orders appointing a welfare guardian, the Family Court must set a date for the order to be reviewed within three years.

The welfare guardian is responsible for applying for the review before the term of the order expires.

A renewal of an order can be made for 5 years.

For any other personal order, the Court may set a date for the order to be reviewed. The Court must specify who is to apply for the review.

4.6.4 Can they occur at other times?

An application for review of a decision of a welfare guardian can be made at any time by the person concerned, or any other person who has the Court's permission.

4.6.5 What can the Court do on a review?

As a result of a review, the Court can:

- vary or refuse to vary an order
- discharge or refuse to discharge an order
- extend the period of the order; in which case, the Court must then set a date for review
- make an order in relation to a welfare guardian's decision, which has been reviewed.

4.7 Welfare guardians

4.7.1 What is a welfare guardian?

A welfare guardian is someone appointed by the Family Court to make and implement decisions on behalf of a person in relation to all aspects of their personal care.

4.7.2 When would a welfare guardian be appointed?

The Court must believe that the appointment of a welfare guardian is the only satisfactory way to ensure that appropriate decisions are made for a person.

The person must wholly lack the capacity to make or communicate decisions about an area or areas relating to their personal care and welfare.

A welfare guardian can be appointed for anyone who is 18 or older. A welfare guardian can also be appointed for a 16- or 17-year-old if:

- the person is or has been married, or in a civil union, or in a de facto relationship, or
- the person has no living parents or guardians, or
- no parent or guardian is in regular contact with the person and the Court thinks it would be in their interests to appoint a welfare guardian.

Welfare guardians may also be appointed if other kinds of personal orders (eg that the person be provided with specified medical treatment) are not carried out.

It is a welfare guardian's role to take all reasonable steps to ensure the order is complied with.

4.7.3 Who can be a welfare guardian?

As far as possible, the Court will find out whom the person lacking capacities wishes to have as their guardian.

The Court can only appoint a person over the age of 20 years who:

- is capable of carrying out the duties of a welfare guardian in a satisfactory manner
- will act in the best interests of a person who lacks capacity
- consents to being appointed
- does not have a conflict of interest with the person who lacks capacity.

Normally only one welfare guardian will be appointed for a person who lacks capacities. In an exceptional case, more than one may be appointed.

4.7.4 What does a welfare guardian do?

A welfare guardian has all reasonable powers to make and carry out decisions for the person, in the areas specified in the court order.

In making and carrying out decisions, the welfare guardian must:

- promote and protect the welfare and best interest of the person for whom they are acting
- encourage the person for whom they are acting to develop and exercise any capacity they have
- encourage the person for whom they are acting to act in their own interest wherever possible
- assist the person to be, as much as is possible, a part of the community
- consult the person, and others that they consider are interested in and competent to advise on the personal care and welfare of that person, including any relevant voluntary welfare agency, and
- consult with the property manager if the person is subject to a property order.

If a welfare guardian needs guidance in exercising or carrying out their powers under an order, they may apply to the Court for directions.

4.7.5 When does the order for a welfare guardian expire?

The Court is required to set a date by which time the welfare guardian must apply for a review of the order.

The date specified by the Court must be within three years from the date of the order.

If the welfare guardian does not apply for a review prior to the expiry of the order, the order and the powers granted under that order will expire.

The powers will also expire if:

- the person for whom the welfare guardian is acting dies
- the welfare guardian dies, becomes bankrupt, or becomes incapable of acting
- the order is discharged by the Court on a review of that order.

4.7.6 What is a representative not able to do?

A welfare guardian or enduring power of attorney may not:

- make any decision relating to marriage or civil union, or dissolution of marriage or civil union, on the part of the subject person
- make any decision relating to the adoption of any child of that person
- refuse consent to the administering to that person of any standard medical treatment or procedure intended to save the person's life or to prevent serious damage to the person's health
- consent to the administering to that person of electro-convulsive treatment
- consent to the performance on that person of any surgery or other treatment designed to destroy any part of the brain or any brain function for the purpose of changing the person's behaviour
- consent to that person taking part in any medical experiment other than one conducted to save the person's life or preventing serious damage to the person's health.

4.8 Property orders

In some cases, instead of applying to the Court, an incapacitated person can apply in writing directly to a trustee corporation and ask the corporation to act as the manager of property or any part of it.

4.8.1 Applications to a trustee corporation

Special conditions apply to this type of application.

The application must:

- Specify the property to be managed and the rights and powers the applicant wishes the trustee corporation to exercise.
- Be accompanied by certificates from two registered medical practitioners (at least one of whom must be a psychiatrist and not otherwise involved

with either the application or the person who lacks competence). The certificates must state the extent of the person's lack of competence to manage their own property affairs.

- Be accompanied by a statutory declaration signed by the person who lacks competence. The declaration must state the person has received independent legal advice about, and understands the nature, purposes and consequences of the application. The declaration must also state the person understands the right to end the trustee corporation's appointment on seven days' written notice.

Where the total value of an incapacitated person's property is less than $100,000, any other person who is eligible to apply for a property order for the incapacitated person, can apply directly to a trustee corporation and ask it to manage the incapacitated person's property.

4.8.2 What happens if the trustee corporation accepts the application?

When the trustee corporation accepts the application, it must file a copy of the application with the Court within 30 days.

4.8.3 Can the appointment be cancelled?

If a trustee corporation is appointed in this way, the appointment can be cancelled by the person the corporation is acting for.

The person can do this by notifying the corporation in writing that they no longer want the corporation to act as property manager.

The appointment is cancelled seven days after the notice is given to the corporation.

4.9 Applications for property orders

4.9.1 Who can apply for a property order?

Any of the following people can apply to the Court for a property order:

- an incapacitated person in respect of themselves
- a relative or attorney of the incapacitated person
- the person who has power of attorney of the person's affairs
- a social worker
- a medical practitioner
- a trustee corporation
- a representative of any non-profit group that provides services and facilities for the welfare of people covered by the Act

- the superintendent, licensee, supervisor of person in charge, if the person is a patient or resident of a hospital, home or other institution, if the person concerned is a patient or resident there
- the welfare guardian of the person concerned, if one has been appointed
- anyone else with the Court's permission.

4.9.2 Urgent application

The Court can make a temporary order appointing a temporary property manager where there is urgent need to protect the property of a person, while a property order application for the appointment of a manager is being determined.

A temporary order cannot last for more than 3 months.

4.9.3 What is a personal order to manage property?

The Court may appoint a person to administer any property, income or benefit belonging to an incapacitated person.

Personal orders to administer property can only be made in relation to any item of property worth less than $5,000, or any income or benefit that is less than $20,000 per year.

4.9.4 What is a property manager?

The Court can appoint a property manager or managers for a person of any age who lacks, wholly or partly, the competence to manage their own property affairs.

In deciding whether to appoint a property manager for a person, the Court may consider whether the person is subject to undue influence in the management of their property affairs.

The Court cannot appoint a property manager just because the person concerned manages their property in a way that the average person would not.

So far as is practicable, the Court must find out the wishes of the person for whom a property order is sought about who should be appointed.

The Court can appoint more than one person as a property manager.

If more than one manager is appointed, the managers will have joint responsibility for management unless the Court decides that each manager can exercise their management powers without having to get the agreement of the other manager or managers.

Property managers can be appointed to manage property of any value.

4.9.5 Who can be appointed to manage property?

A property manager must either be:

- a person of at least 20 years of age, or
- a trustee corporation.

Like welfare guardians, property managers must:

- be capable of carrying out their duties in a satisfactory manner
- act in the best interests of the person for whom they are appointed
- consent to be appointed.

4.9.6 What does a property manager do?

Each property order made by the Court lists the specific rights and powers given to the property manager appointed by the order.

In making the order, the Court must grant only the powers necessary in the circumstances because it has a duty to make the least restrictive intervention possible.

So far as is practicable, the Court must find out the wishes of the person for whom a property order is sought about who should be appointed.

The Court can appoint more than one person as a property manager.

If more than one manager is appointed, the managers will have joint responsibility for management unless the Court decides that each manager can exercise their management powers without having to get the agreement of the other manager or managers.

Several actions by property managers require the consent of the Court. For example:

- buying or selling property worth over $120,000
- making charitable donations over $5,000 a year
- granting a lease of 10 years or more.

Every decision made by a property manager has the same effect as if it had been made by the incapacitated person.

4.9.7 Duties of a property manager

In making and carrying out decisions, property managers must:

- promote and protect the interests of the incapacitated person
- encourage the person to develop and exercise such competence as the person has to manage their own property affairs
- consult the incapacitated person and other competent individuals and/or welfare groups that are interested in the incapacitated person's welfare

- consult on a regular basis with any welfare guardian appointed for the person.

Property managers must also follow the terms of any personal order made for the incapacitated person.

4.9.8 Effect of the appointment of a property manager

When a property manager has been appointed, no one can, without the Court's permission:

- bring or continue proceedings (apart from proceedings under the Act) against the person
- enforce any debt, judgment or order (apart from a judgment or order under the Act) against the person
- foreclose, enter into possession, sell, appoint a receiver or exercise any power under a mortgage, charge or security instrument over the person's property
- determine a tenancy, or enforce any rights under a tenancy agreement.

4.9.9 Controls on the powers of property managers

The property manager must file financial statements containing details of the management of the property concerned in the Court.

The financial statements must be filed at the beginning and end of the managership, and annually during the managership.

The initial financial statement is a summary of the assets and liabilities at the date on which the order was made.

Annual financial statements should include detailed statements of receipts and payments, together with a balance sheet or list of assets and liabilities.

Statements filed by a trustee corporation are examined by Public Trust.

It is an offence to file a false statement or to fail to file a statement.

4.9.10 Can a person make a will if a property manager has been appointed?

Yes, unless the Court directs otherwise, the appointment of a property manager does not affect the power of the person to make a will in the normal way.

The Court can try and find out whether a will that was made before a person became subject to a property order was made when the person was unable to manage his or her own property affairs. If the Court finds out that the will was made in this situation, it can make further inquiries to find out whether the will gives effect to the present wishes of the person.

If the will does not do this, the Court can take steps to find out the person's present wishes and can authorise the property manager to make a new will for the person to give effect to these wishes.

The Court can also direct that a person under a property order can make a will only with the permission of the Court.

In some cases, the Court can authorise the property manager to make a will for the person.

When a will is made by a property manager, the Court will settle the terms of the will on a provisional basis.

It will hear the people who wish to be heard and whom it considers have a proper interest in the matter.

The Court then authorises the property manager to make a will, the terms of which are settled by the Court.

4.9.11 Settlement of a person's property

The Court may order that all or part of the property under management be put into trust for the benefit of the incapacitated person.

It may also order that any of this property be given for the maintenance or benefit of members of the person's family, or to people or purposes that the person might be expected to provide for if he or she was competent to manage his or her own affairs.

4.9.12 When does a property manager's appointment end?

A property manager stops acting if:

- the person for whom the manager is acting dies
- the manager dies
- the manager is adjudged bankrupt
- the manager becomes a special patient or a patient under the Mental Health (Compulsory Assessment and Treatment) Act
- the manager becomes subject to a property order or otherwise becomes incapable of acting
- more than one manager is appointed, and one of them ceases to act in any of the above circumstances, which is only applicable if they have joint responsibility
- the property order is discharged by the Court
- another person is appointed as property manager, in which case, the previous manager will cease to act, unless the Court orders otherwise.

4.9.13 Are property managers paid?

Normally property managers are not paid, but they can apply to the Court for remuneration from the incapacitated person's estate.

Property managers can claim expenses from the estate.

4.9.14 Can a property manager be personally liable?

Property managers are personally liable only when entering into contracts or arrangements without disclosing to the other party that they are acting in their capacity as property manager under the Act, or if they act in bad faith or without reasonable care.

If a property manager does not act in good faith and with reasonable care, they may become legally liable for their actions.

Property managers can ask the Court for directions in relation to exercising their rights and powers.

4.10 Review of property orders

4.10.1 When must reviews take place?

The Court must set a date for the property order to be reviewed within 3 years.

The property manager must apply for the review.

If a trustee corporation has accepted an application to act as property manager, the corporation must file reports not earlier than 2 years or later than 3 years after the date of filing the application in the Court.

4.10.2 Can reviews take place at other times?

Yes, the following people can apply at any time for a property order to be reviewed:

- the person in respect of whom the order was made
- the manager or welfare guardian acting for the person
- any of the people who could have applied to the Court for a property order
- anyone else who is given permission by the Court.

Except where a property order is being reviewed to appoint a new manager, the Court must review the competence of the person subject to the order.

The person concerned or any other person who has the Court's permission can make an application for review of a decision by a property manager at any time.

4.10.3 What can the Court do on a review?

As a result of a review, the Court can:

- vary or refuse to vary an order
- discharge or refuse to discharge an order
- if the Court makes an order extending the original property order, it must specify another date for review being a date at least three years after the last review.

4.11 Application under the Protection of Personal and Property Rights Act

Applications should be filed in the Family Court.

4.11.1 Application for a personal order

To make an application for a personal order, complete the following documents:

- Form PPPR 14 Information sheet to accompany applications under Protection of Personal and Property Rights Act 1988
- Form PPPR 1 Front page for documents filed in Court under Protection of Personal and Property Rights Act 1988
- Form PPPR 3 Application for personal order in respect of applicant

  or
- Form PPPR 4 Application for personal order.

4.11.2 Application for the appointment of a welfare guardian

Where possible, the applicant should name the person to be appointed. The application should also include the consent in writing of the person to be appointed.

To make an application for a welfare guardian, complete the following documents:

- Form PPPR 14 Information sheet to accompany applications under Protection of Personal and Property Rights Act 1988
- Form PPPR 1 Front page for documents filed in Court under Protection of Personal and Property Rights Act 1988
- Form PPPR 7 Application for appointment of welfare guardian for applicant

  or

- Form PPPR 8 Application for appointment of welfare guardian

  and

- Form PPPR 16 Statement of consent to appointment as welfare guardian.

4.11.3 Application for a property order

To make an application for a property order, complete the following documents:

- Form PPPR 14 Information sheet to accompany applications under Protection of Personal and Property Rights Act 1988
- Form PPPR 1 Front page for documents filed in Court under Protection of Personal and Property Rights Act 1988

  and

- Form PPPR 10 Application for property order in respect of applicant's property

  or

- Form PPPR 11 Application for property order

  or

- Form PPPR 5 Application for order to administer property of applicant

  or

- Form PPPR 6 Application for order to administer property.

Applications to the Court must normally be served on the person for whom the order is sought, and are also served on a number of others interested in their welfare, such as their parents.

4.11.4 Applications about enduring powers of attorney

To make an application about an enduring power of attorney, complete the following documents:

- Form PPPR 14 Information sheet to accompany applications under Protection of Personal and Property Rights Act 1988

  and

- Form PPPR 23 Application by attorney for directions

  or

- Form PPPR 24 Application for exercise of Court's jurisdiction in respect of enduring power of attorney

  or

- Form PPPR 25 Application for review of attorney's decision.

4.11.5 Appointment of a lawyer

The Court will appoint a lawyer to represent the person who is the subject of the application if they do not have their own lawyer.

The Court-appointed lawyer must make contact with the person and help them understand the application as much as is practicable.

The lawyer will report on the circumstances of the application and make recommendations to the Court.

The Court will pay the Court-appointed lawyer.

4.11.6 Pre-hearing conferences

Pre-hearing conferences can be held to try to resolve matters by discussion. The person for whom the order is sought must normally be present at the conference and at the hearing.

At the hearing, they may speak to the Court directly and without parents, guardians or lawyers present.

The pre-hearing conference and the hearing are not open to the public.

4.11.7 Specialist report

The Court may request medical, psychiatric, psychological or other reports on the person concerned.

4.11.8 Court hearing

Any evidence may be heard, even if it is not the sort the Court would normally allow.

The person concerned is entitled to be heard and call witnesses.

The Court itself may call witnesses.

4.12 Legal aid

Legal aid is available for protection of personal and property rights matters.

4.12.1 Law Commission to review the law relating to adult decision-making capacity

Te Aka Matua o te Ture | Law Commission has launched a review of the law relating to adult decision-making capacity and published the Terms of Reference that will guide this review: He Arotake i te Ture mō ngā Huarahi Whakatau a ngā Pakeke | Review of Adult Decision-Making Capacity Law (Ngā Huarahi Whakatau).

The Law Commission will consider how issues relating to adult decision-making capacity should be regulated in Aotearoa New Zealand. In particular, it will consider whether our laws strike an appropriate balance between enabling people to make decisions about their own lives (including with appropriate support from whānau, family, caregivers, professionals or the wider community), and safeguarding people from harm.

Geof Shirtcliffe said:

> "The law relating to adult decision-making capacity covers a wide variety of decisions we may all face over the course of our lives. This law affects a significant range of people, and particularly affects disabled communities."
>
> "Key law in this area hasn't been reviewed in decades. There have been significant developments in this time. Our attitudes towards disability have shifted, and Aotearoa New Zealand has committed to implementing the United Nations Convention on the Rights of Persons with Disabilities. In addition, as our population ages an increasing proportion of New Zealanders will require support to make decisions about their lives. Further, our law may not be compatible with perspectives from te ao Māori, te Tiriti o Waitangi and the rights of tāngata whaikaha Māori (Māori disabled people), their whānau, hapū, and iwi."

The Law Commission will conduct public consultation in 2022. In addition, it will work with disabled people and their representative organisations to facilitate accessible consultation processes and maximise the participation of those individuals and communities most directly affected by the law relating to adult decision-making capacity.

The Commission intends to report to the Minister of Justice by the end of 2023.

Chapter 5
Donatio Mortis Causa

5.0 Introduction

This is the name given to the kind of gift that lies between a gift inter vivos and a gift by will, although it is not a gift by will. Because a donatio mortis causa is not a gift by will, it is here made the subject of a separate brief chapter.

The requirements of this type of gift were stated in *Cain v Moon* [1896] 2 QB 283 — a case in which the deceased handed to her mother the deposit note for fifty pounds invested with a London bank. Lord Russell CJ said that:

> Three things must combine:
>
> 1. The gift or donation must have been made in contemplation, though not necessarily in expectation, of death
> 2. There must have been delivery to the donee of the subject-matter of the gift,[1] and
> 3. The gift must be made under circumstances showing that it is to take effect only if the death of the donor follows.[2]

A donatio mortis causa, then, is a conditional gift of personal property made in contemplation of death, for example, when the donor is suffering from a serious and usually fatal illness. The gift must be made by the donor actually handing over to the donee the property itself or the means of access (or control) to it, such as the key to a safe deposit box. We repeat that there must be an actual handing over — there must be some visible act of change of possession. In *National Trustees Executors and Agency Co Ltd v O'Hea* (1904) 29 VLR 814, the deceased, on his death bed, merely told his servant that he was entitled to certain chattels, and it was held that this was insufficient to constitute delivery. The donee must understand that the gift is conditional and does not become absolute until the donor dies. The donor may revoke the gift by repossessing the property at any time if he recovers. As the gift takes effect, though conditionally, when the requirements are met, it is not a testamentary disposition and does not need to be in writing.

1 This requirement has been mitigated in that it does not have to be carried out literally — constructive delivery will suffice (see next paragraph).

2 This case held that there had been a valid donatio mortis causa. It decided that it is not essential that the expressions of points 1. and 3. above be made at the *same time* as the delivery — the delivery can be antecedent. Here, the deposit note was handed to the deceased's mother in 1883, while the expressions of points 1. and 3. above were made during a serious illness in 1885.

On 9 June 2015, the United Kingdom Court of Appeal overturned the High Court judgment in the case of *King v Dubrey* [2014] EWHC 2083 (Ch); [2014] All ER (D) 24 (Jul). This case involved a donatio mortis causa.

This case involved the estate of Ms June Fairbrother ("the Deceased"). It was widely known by the Deceased's family and friends that she loved animals and planned to leave her property in Hertforshire, worth approximately £350,000, to a number of animal charities. The Deceased's will, dated 20 March 1998, was drafted in those terms, providing for legacies of £19,000 to friends and family and leaving her residuary estate to a selection of animal charities.

Mr King, the Deceased's nephew, brought a claim before the High Court, claiming that the Deceased had made a donatio mortis causa of her property to him between four and six months before her death by handing him "the deeds" to the property at a time when she knew her health was failing, saying "this will be yours when I go". There were no witnesses to this conversation and therefore the only evidence in support of this was the testimony of Mr King himself.

The High Court held that there had been a donatio mortis causa by the Deceased to Mr King. The Court considered that the words used by the Deceased were sufficient to suggest a conditional gift on her death; the significant passage of time and absence of serious illness did not prevent the Deceased's contemplation of her death; and that the Deceased handing the deeds for the property to Mr King was sufficient for her to part with possession, despite the deeds remaining at the property owned by her thereafter.

In deciding in favour of Mr King, this in effect removed the most valuable asset from the Deceased's residuary estate which was gifted to the animal welfare charities nominated as residuary beneficiaries in her 1998 Will.

Redwings Horse Sanctuary and Chilterns Dog Rescue Society, two of the seven animal charities set to benefit under the Deceased's 1998 Will, appealed the decision of the High Court. The principal issue before the Court was whether the Deceased's words and conduct months before her death gave rise to a donatio mortis causa.

The Court of Appeal by unanimous decision found in favour of the charities and overturned the High Court judgment, Lord Justice Jackson stated that the three requirements to constitute a valid donatio mortis causa are:

1. the donor contemplates his or her impending death
2. the donor makes a gift which will only take effect if and when his or her contemplated death occurs (until then the donor has the right to revoke the gift), and
3. the donor delivers dominion over the subject matter of the gift to the recipient (for example, handing over the deeds to the property).

The Judge noted that, if the donatio mortis causa claim were upheld, the Deceased's Will would be largely superseded and the majority of her estate would pass to Mr King who was not even named as a beneficiary in the Will. Lord Justice Jackson said the requirements to constitute a valid donatio mortis causa were not satisfied because:

> "It cannot be said that June (Ms Fairbrother) was contemplating her impending death at the relevant time. She was not suffering from a fatal illness. Nor was she about to undergo a dangerous operation or to undertake a dangerous journey. If June was dissatisfied with her existing Will and suddenly wished to leave everything to the claimant, the obvious thing for her to do was to go to her solicitors and make a new Will . . . If June had taken that course, the solicitors . . . would have ensured that June understood the new Will she was making and the intended consequences. One of those consequences was that the animal charities, which June had supported for many years, would inherit nothing on her death".

Chapter 6

Executors

6.0 Introduction

Whether a person has made a will directing how their estate is to be distributed on their death or whether they had died intestate, someone must be entrusted with the responsibility of getting in the assets, discharging the deceased's lawful debts and liabilities, and distributing what remains of the estate to the persons lawfully entitled to it. The person on whom these duties are imposed is known as *the deceased's personal representative*. In the next four chapters, the nature of this office and the rights and duties that attach to it will be considered.

Persons making wills have the right to appoint the person or persons whom they wish to be responsible for administering their estate, although the court is not bound absolutely to endorse the will-maker's choice. It is the almost invariable practice for a properly drafted will to include a clause appointing a personal representative (an executor).

When a person dies intestate or, having made a will, neglects to appoint an executor or appoints a person unwilling or unable to accept the responsibility of administering the estate, the Administration Act 1969 directs the court to appoint a personal representative called the Administrator.

First, the position of the executor will be dealt with, and then that of the administrator. These are similar, but not identical, offices, and certain differences between them will be noted. For the purposes of any wider reading, however, it is important to realise that, when the word "administrator" appears in many texts, the term is being used in a wide sense to refer to both executors and administrators. The Administration Act, which contains the legislation relating to the administration of estates in New Zealand, also defines "administrator" in this wide sense for the purposes of the Act. This definition has not been adopted in this text. Here, the term "personal representative" is used when both executors and administrators jointly are being referred to, because the Wills Act 2007 defines "personal representative" as meaning administrator, executor or trustee.

6.1 Probate

As the executor is appointed under the will, the right to administer the estate begins as soon as the will-maker dies and the will becomes operative. However, to prove their right to deal with the assets of the deceased, executors must apply to the court for a *Grant of Probate*. In other words, they must prove the will and, thereby, prove their appointment as personal representatives.

Probate in New Zealand is normally obtained by the executor filing the will in the High Court at Wellington together with:

- an Application without notice for Obtaining Probate
- an Affidavit for Obtaining Grant of Probate, and
- Probate

Usually, the Notice for Obtaining Probate is made by a lawyer on behalf of the executor[1] and, when this is done, the Application must be certified pursuant to the Rules of Court to be correct and be signed by a partner of the law firm. The Affidavit for obtaining Grant of Probate is a statement made on oath, in which the executor/s swear that:

- they have personal knowledge of the will-maker's death (either by having seen the will-maker's dead body or by having been present at their funeral)[2]
- they believe that the document produced to the High Court is the last will of the will-maker
- they are the person appointed as executor in that will
- they will faithfully execute the will in accordance with the law, and
- if the executor is the spouse or partner of the will-maker, that there has not been any dissolution of the relationship.

They also undertake in the Affidavit that they will provide the court with a detailed statement of the administration of the estate if called upon to do so. The Application without notice for Obtaining Probate is a formal request to the court to grant administration of the estate to the executor appointed in the will. The documents can be referred to a judge, but are usually examined by a Registrar of the Court and, if all appears to be in order, a grant of probate is made. As evidence of this, the court issues to the executor a document under seal of the court known as *the Probate*, which the executor may produce to all concerned as proof of their right to deal with the assets of the deceased. For example, the deceased may have died leaving a large credit balance in a bank account. Before the executor can withdraw the money, they must produce the Probate to the bank. The form of these documents can be varied to meet the circumstances, but typical examples are set out in Appendix 1.

1 Although this is not required by law, and the executors can make the Application themselves. It is not required by law that lawyers be employed to obtain probate of a will.

2 The death of the will-maker must be sworn to by someone who knew the will-maker. If none of the executors can swear to paragraphs 1. and 2. of the sample Affidavit set out in Appendix 1, Rule 27.4 provides that a further affidavit shall be filed by some other person who can.

In most cases, there is no difficulty in obtaining probate of a will. However, if the registrar is not entirely satisfied with the documents, they can call for a further affidavit or affidavits. Registrars sometimes do this if there are pinholes in the will, giving rise to a possibility that pages could have been removed or inserted,[3] or if the signature of the will-maker is very wavering. In this latter instance, the executor would require an affidavit of valid execution that the will-maker did have testamentary capacity. Frequently, the registrar is satisfied by such affidavits. Provided that a will has been properly drawn and correctly executed, the court will usually grant probate on the Application and Affidavit filed by the executor without any appearance in person by the executor or further proof being required. Such a grant is called Probate in Common Form.

A person who objects to probate of any given will being granted can, at any time before it is granted,[4] lodge a caveat with the High Court. For example, a person who has been left out of the will may allege that the will-maker lacked testamentary capacity. However, there are provisions in the relevant legislation under which the court can award costs against a party who has lodged a caveat that the court considers vexatious or frivolous. When there is some doubt about the validity of the will or its due execution,[5] that is, the registrar is not satisfied and the court considers that the will is irregular or suspicious, the executor may have to apply form Probate in Solemn Form. The matter will then be tried in court before a judge, and all parties likely to have an interest in the estate must be served with notice of the hearing. If the judge grants Probate in Solemn Form, this finally resolves all questions about the validity of the will. Apart from cases in which the grant has been obtained by fraud, the grant can be recalled by the court only on proof of a later will or proof that the will-maker had revoked the will, whereas Probate in Common Form can be recalled on other grounds.

3 See *Wills and Succession* 14.14. Normally an affidavit of Plight will be sworn by a person who knows the reason for the damage.

4 Probate cannot be granted until the expiration of at least seven days from the death of the will-maker (except by direction of the court).

5 For example, in *In re Mair (deceased)* [1955] NZLR 1144, the one page will had two complete tears from top to bottom (one of them passing through the signature of the testatrix), and a third partial tear. The will had been restored by pasting a backing sheet onto the original page. The Court wondered whether there had been a revocation and, in view of the lack of explanation, the quite substantial size of the estate, and the fact that not all persons affected may have knowledge of the circumstances, ordered the executors to apply for Probate in Solemn Form.

See also *Wills and Succession*, Chapter 9.13.

The number of applications for Probate in Solemn Form is relatively small but, executors are wise to so apply voluntarily when they have any doubts about the validity of the will, because they can then carry on with the administration without fear of this being questioned later. Such applications are made by filing a Statement of Claim and Notice of Proceeding and, depending upon such matters as what other wills the will-maker may have made and what parties the court has directed to be served, the documentation can be considerable. The executor may be ordered by the court to so apply if anyone lodges a caveat.

Where the estate is a small one, it may not be necessary to apply to the court for a Grant of Probate. We have statutory provisions under which, if no bank account, insurance policy, Accident Compensation, Government Stock, company shares or debentures, etc were valued, respectively, at more than $15,000, the fund-holder can, on application being made to them following the death of the owner, pay out or transfer the funds without sighting the Probate or Letters of Administration. Fund-holders can make such a payment, or transfer, if they regard such evidence as being adequate and, if they make the payment or transfer to a person whom they believe, on reasonable grounds, is entitled to receive it, they are discharged from all liability in respect of it. This, however, is without prejudice to the right of any person who is truly entitled to the money or property to recover it from the person to whom it has been paid or transferred. Everyone to whom money is so paid is liable to apply it in due course of administration, and fund-holders may, if they think fit, require the recipient to give an undertaking or enter into a bond for that purpose. Thus, where a will-maker and their spouse jointly owned their house property[6] and furniture etc, and the will-maker has two bank accounts with $6,800 and $3,600 in them respectively, and a life policy worth $8,500 including bonuses, it would not be necessary for the executor to take out probate, although they could apply for it. However, even if the property passes to the surviving spouse by survivorship, that property is not automatically treated as the separate property of the surviving spouse. The status of the property will be determined as if the deceased relationship partner had not died.

However, if the deceased owned *realty* (other than as a joint tenant), probate must be applied for, even if it was just a section worth $13,000. The probate is required to register the transmission instrument with the Land Information NZ (LINZ).

6 When a joint tenant dies, the surviving joint tenant(s) takes. In other words, the surviving joint tenants just become the owners of the property. What is required (at LINZ), in order to transfer this property into the name of the widow, is a transmission instrument by survivorship supported by a death certificate.

Under the "Nominations of Accounts" provisions mentioned in Section 3.0 — *Legacies,* amounts not exceeding $15,000 per bank account can, by express nomination in writing made by the deceased, be transferred straight into the estate for the nominated beneficiary or beneficiaries as though they were specific legacies in a will made by the deceased. The operation of these provisions is not dependent upon the obtaining of a grant of administration.

Law: Administration Act 1969, ss 5, 6(1)–(4), 60, 61, 64, 64A, 65, 68A–68D

High Court Amendment (Wills Act 2007) Rules 2007

High Court Rules, Sch 1, Forms G 31, PR 1, PR 7

Property (Relationships) Act 1976, s 83

6.2 Types of executor

6.2.1 Appointment of executors

An executor is appointed by:

- *Express appointment* — The executor is usually appointed by express words in the will: "I appoint AB of Wellington, solicitor, to be the executor of my Will".
- *By necessary implication* — Sometimes, although no express appointment is made, it is clear from the general provisions of the will (from its "tenor") that the will-maker wished a particular person to assume responsibility for administering the estate. Such intention is usually gathered from some sort of general direction given to such a person. Such a person, who will be granted probate of the will, is known as the *executor according to the tenor*. Another instance is where the will-maker has directed some person to pay their debts after their death. The situations usually arise when will-makers have drawn up their own will without professional guidance.

A New Zealand example occurred in *McGinley v Woollett* HC Greymouth, A26/83, 8 March 1984. The will-maker, on the eve of his death in hospital just before an operation, made a will, the relevant part of which read, "I Dudley Rathburn hereby authorise my solicitor, McGinley, to take over my estate and to carry on the Dudley Rathburn trust with the Public Trustee". He then signed in the presence of a nurse and the surgeon, in a manner that complied with the requirements of the Wills Act. McGinley, who was the only solicitor in the area of that or a closely similar name, and who had acted for the will-maker and set up a family trust for him, applied for Probate in Solemn Form to be granted to him as executor according to the tenor, and was successful.

6.2.2 General, special, and substitute executors

A *general executor* is one appointed to administer the whole of the estate. Several executors may be appointed to act jointly, and such persons will also be "general executors". However, a will-maker will occasionally appoint more than one executor, each to administer a particular part of the estate. Such persons are known as *special executors*.

A will-maker may also make provision in their will for the substitution of another person as executor in place of one who is unable or unwilling to act or one who has predeceased the will-maker. That person is known as the "substituted executor".

6.2.3 Executors de son tort

When translated into English literally, this term means "an executor by his wrongdoing". It is applied to a person who, without having been appointed executor under the will or granted Letters of Administration by the court, meddles with the assets of the deceased. Even though they do this with the best of intentions, they have no legal right to do so, and, by doing this, they may burden themself with all the responsibilities of an executor without obtaining any of the rights or privileges attached to this office. If their dealing with the assets is inconsistent with the rights of a beneficiary or creditor, they will lay themself open to an action for damages. The term "executor de son tort" has been created by the court, and is one applied by the court for the purpose of holding a person to the liabilities and duties of an executor, although we now have some degree of legislative duplication.

However, it is obvious that, when a person dies, certain things must be done immediately. These things must be done before an executor can obtain probate or an administrator can be appointed. People who, in good faith, take it upon themselves to attend to such matters as arranging for the funeral, paying pressing debts, or collecting and locking up the deceased's goods, will not automatically constitute themself an executor de son tort. "Officious intermeddling" best describes the kind of action that will place a person in this position.[7]

Law: Administration Act 1969, s 52

7 It is similarly possible for a person to make themself a "trustee de son tort". "If one, not being a trustee and not having authority from a trustee, takes upon himself to intermeddle with trust matters or to do acts characteristic of the office of trustee, he may thereby make himself what is called in law a trustee of his own wrong — ie a trustee de son tort, or, as it is also termed, a constructive trustee" — *Mara v Browne* [1896] 1 Ch 199.

6.3 Who may be appointed executor

Any person may be an executor and, in general, will-makers may appoint anyone they choose to be their executor. A will-maker will advisedly appoint someone they can confidently rely on to complete the administration of the estate in a proper and efficient manner. A will-maker will often appoint their spouse or partner jointly with their solicitor, accountant, or a close friend. When the administration is likely to be complex, or the will sets up trusts that will need supervision over a number of years, a will-maker may be advised to appoint a Trust Corporation, which specialises in this kind of work, or the Public Trust. There are, however, some special classes of persons such as unmarried minors, minors who have not entered into a civil union,[8] mentally incapable persons, bankrupts and insolvent persons, and former spouses or partners who cannot be the executor.

Law: Administration Act 1969, ss 6, 9
Wills Act 2007, s 19

6.4 Acceptance or renunciation of executorship

The appointment of an executor in the will does not, of itself, impose liability upon the person appointed. They are free to accept or decline the office as they choose. The position of executor is a responsible and sometimes onerous one, and not everyone is prepared to accept this responsibility. The person appointed will be held to have accepted the office if they intermeddle with the estate even to a small degree, or, as is usually the case, when they apply to the court for probate of the will.

Once a person has accepted the office of executor, they must continue to discharge the duties of that office until they have either completed the administration, or been released or removed by the court.

A person who does not wish to accept the office may simply fail to apply for probate, but they must, of course, be careful to refrain from taking any part in dealing with the assets, or else they may be held to have accepted the office by their actions. This, however, is not very satisfactory, and the court can, generally, direct an executor to either apply for probate or renounce. Although an executor can renounce by conduct, the proper course for an executor who does not wish to act is to file a renunciation in the High Court. The position is then ascertained in black and white, and interested parties can proceed accordingly.[9]

---

8 See Subsection 7.1.4 — *Administration durante minore aetate.*

9 Two of the main instances in which renunciations are filed are:

- Alteration in the composition of legal firms — the firm acting for the deceased will send for signature a renunciation to an ancillary solicitor-executor who has now left the firm, and
- The executor is old, and does not want the responsibilities of office.

We also have more specific provisions. As it is clearly desirable that the administration of an estate be undertaken as soon as possible, and that some person or persons should be made legally responsible for this, executors may be able to retain their options for only three months.

When an executor has done *nothing* for three months, they can, upon application for the purpose made to the court by the other executor or executors, be called on to show cause as to why probate should not be granted to the other executor or executors alone.[10]

Similarly, when none of the executors have applied for probate of the will within three months of the death of the will-maker, the court may grant Letters of Administration with Will Annexed (this term will be explained presently) to any creditor or person interested in the estate who applies, or to the Public Trust (or the Maori Trustee).

Law: Administration Act 1969, ss 19, 53

6.5 The devolution of executorship

When a will-maker has appointed two or more persons as the executors, they will be granted probate jointly and will hold the assets of the estate as joint tenants. With all joint tenancies, on the death of one party, that party's interest devolves upon (or passes to) the survivor or survivors.[11]

Therefore, when one of several executors dies, the other or others will continue to administer the estate.

However, when there is only one executor, or one surviving executor, who dies *after taking out probate* but before completing the administration, the executor's executor (if they have appointed one in their will) will become executor of the original will-maker's will, unless the will expressly provides otherwise. If this executor in turn dies after taking out probate but before completing the administration, that person's executor will take over, and so on, until administration of the estate is completed.

10 Probate will normally be granted to executors jointly. In non-contentious instances, when one or more of the executors alone apply for probate, they must state in their Affidavit the address of the remaining executor or executors and the reason why they have not joined in the Application. If there is adequate reason, probate will be granted to the applicants, with leave reserved to the remaining executor or executors to apply also at any time in the future if they are able and willing. This latter grant, if it eventuates, is known as a "Double Probate".

11 As we have seen in footnote 7 of this chapter, and as we are going to see further in Chapter 7 — *Administrators*.

However, if any executor has failed to make a will appointing an executor,[12] the chain will be broken. A person appointed by the court as administrator of such an executor's estate will not take over and administer the prior uncompleted estates. Instead, the court will appoint other persons to complete administration, such persons being called the administrators de bonis non (short for "de bonis non administratis" — the goods not already administered). The traditional reason for this distinction has been summed up as follows: "Inasmuch as the power of an executor is founded on the special confidence and appointment of the deceased, in the case of a single or sole surviving executor, he is allowed to transmit that power to another in whom he has equal confidence; and so long as the chain of representation is unbroken by any intestacy, the ultimate executor is the representative of every preceding will-maker" (*Inghem on Executors*).

Law: Administration Act 1969, ss 13, 24(3)

12 Or failed to take out probate.

Chapter 7
Administrators

7.0 Introduction

Even if will-makers fail to make a will, following their death, their estate must still be administered, even though, in dying intestate, they have left no directions on how they wish their assets to be distributed. In the absence of such directions, the law steps in by setting out in the Administration Act 1969 persons who will succeed to the estate and the respective share each will take. This aspect will be dealt with in Chapter 9 — *Succession on Intestacy.*

The above Act also provides for the appointment of an *administrator* when no effective executor has been appointed by the deceased. Just as an executor will require a grant of probate as proof of their right to deal with the assets of the deceased, similarly a grant of *Letters of Administration* will be made to the administrator as evidence of their appointment to the office and of their right to deal with the estate.

7.1 Types of grants of administration

7.1.1 General administration

This is the kind of administration that will usually be granted when the deceased has died without making a will (has died intestate). Anyone may apply to the court for Letters of Administration, but the court will regard certain persons as having priority over others. However, the court does not regard itself as rigidly bound by these priorities, and so the selection of the person who is appointed remains in the discretion of the court — no one has an absolute right to a grant of Letters of Administration. Any person applying must normally secure the written consents of others having higher priority or equal priority, or satisfy the court that those people are dead or incompetent or that the applicant has given notice of the application to them, but these requirements may be dispensed with in special circumstances.[1]

The order of priority is:

1. the surviving husband, wife, civil union partner (who can be disqualified if a separation order is in force) or de facto partner
2. children (or grandchildren, if their relevant parent has predeceased the deceased)
3. parents

1 See *Re Akamoeau* [1989] 3 NZLR 325.

4. brothers and sisters
5. grandparents
6. uncles and aunts
7. the Attorney-General, if they claim *bona vacantia* on behalf of the Crown,[2] and
8. creditors.[3]

Also entitled to apply (under statute), and not ranking anywhere specific in the order of priority, are Trustee Companies,[4] and the Public Trust, and indeed, when no person has applied for administration of the deceased's estate, Letters of Administration will usually be granted to the Public Trust.

7.1.2 Administration with will annexed (cum testamento annexo)

This grant is made when the deceased left a will but:

- failed to appoint an executor
- appointed someone who predeceased the deceased or died before taking out probate
- appointed a person unable or unwilling to assume the office
- appointed a person who cannot be found, or
- appointed an executor or executors none of whom have applied for probate within 3 calendar months of the will-maker's death.

The person appointed is an administrator and not an executor, but they must administer the estate as if probate had been granted to them as an executor, and distribute the assets according to the provisions of the will and not according to the rules of intestate succession. The priorities of entitlement to a grant of Letters of Administration with Will Annexed are different from those applying in an intestacy and, broadly speaking, follow the persons having the greatest interest in the estate. In similar manner as in an intestacy, the applicants must secure the written consents of those having priority (or of equal priority), or satisfy the court that they are dead or incompetent or that notice of the application has been given to them.

When the deceased left a will, but no person has applied for probate or Letters of Administration with Will Annexed within 3 months of the date of death, the Public Trust may apply and, failing satisfactory explanation by other

2 This refers to cases where the government (as it is entitled to do) asserts a claim to property for which there are no claimants under the Administration Act 1969.

3 A person holding an enduring power of attorney (under Pt IX of the Protection of Personal and Property Rights Act 1988) from a person having priority, will not automatically be granted Letters of Administration — see *Re Dennis* [1993] 3 NZLR 86.

4 The New Zealand Guardian Trust Company Limited, Trustees, Executors, and Agency Company of New Zealand (Limited), AMP Perpetual Trustees Company NZ Limited, PGG Trust Limited, and New Zealand Permanent Trustees Limited.

applicants, the court is directed to appoint it. In practice, as in the case of intestate estates, the Public Trust, to obtain the knowledge to act, is largely dependent upon the deceased's relatives.

The following types of grants of administration are limited in their scope or duration:

- Administration de bonis non administratis
- Administration durante minore aetate
- Administration durante dementia
- Administration pendente lite
- Administration durante absentia.

7.1.3 Administration de bonis non administratis

This kind of grant, which is made when the sole or last surviving executor dies without themself having appointed an executor, has already been referred to. It may also be made when the executor disappears, or has been removed from office. It will also be made in cases of intestacy when the administrator dies or disappears without having completed the administration or has been removed from office. This type of grant is sometimes shortly called administration de bonis non.

The purpose of a grant of administration de bonis non is to ensure that administration of an estate will not remain incomplete, when, for any reason, the person who began the administration is unable to complete it.

7.1.4 Administration durante minore aetate

This is a temporary grant of administration during the minority of a sole executor. The age of majority under the Administration Act is 18 years so when one of several executors is a minor, probate is granted to the adult executors, but not to the minor, until the minor attains 18 years of age.[5]

When a minor is the sole executor, the above Letters of Administration are granted to an adult during the period of incapacity of the minor-executor. The executor cannot act until they meet the requirements that we have noted.

7.1.5 Administration durante dementia

This is also a temporary grant of administration and is closely analogous to administration *durante minore aetate.* It is a grant of administration to another during the period of the mental incapability of a sole executor.

5 At the age of 16, minors can marry with the consent of their parents or the Family Court — ss 17–20 Marriage Act 1955.

7.1.6 Administration pendente lite

This is another temporary grant of administration pending the outcome of legal proceedings relating to the validity of the will or to the obtaining or recalling of any grant of probate or Letters of Administration. It is analogous to administration *durante minore aetate*. The powers of an *administrator pendente lite* do not extend to distributing the estate.

7.1.7 Administration durante absentia

This is another usually temporary grant of administration given during the absence of a sole executor. It is also analogous to administration *durante minore aetate*.

We also have specific provisions enabling, among other things, the court to grant:

- Letters of Administration to a person who is residing outside New Zealand
- Letters of Administration to the attorney of such a person on behalf of such person,[6] and
- "Special Administration" (with such powers as the court approves) in cases where an executor, or administrator, has taken out a grant but has ceased to reside in New Zealand.

Law: Public Trust Act 2001, s 77

Trustee Companies Act 1967, s 4

Administration Act 1969, ss 2, 4A, 5, 6, 7, 8, 9

Family Proceedings Act 1980, s 26(1)

High Court Rules 2016, Part 27, rr 27.17, 27.25, 27.35, 27.36

Age of Majority Act 1970, s 4

7.2 Security for grant of administration

This topic is not now as important as it was, but a little background is useful.

When will-makers appoint an executor in their will, it can be assumed that they do so with confidence that the person appointed will carry out their duties faithfully and, consequently, the court does not require any security for due performance of the executor's duties. But when there is no executor, and the court appoints an administrator, it cannot necessarily be assumed that the deceased person would have chosen this same person as one in whom they had confidence to administer the estate faithfully.

6 Where the estate is not a simple one, the overseas executor should appoint an attorney to act for them. A power of attorney will need to be prepared, signed and filed, and the application for probate will need to be appropriately worded.

Therefore, except in the case of the Public Trust and Trustee corporations, as a prerequisite to the granting of Letters of Administration, the Administration Act formerly required the person applying for the grant to file in the court a bond as security against their failure to properly administer the estate. The bond was, in effect, a binding promise, enforceable at law, to forfeit a sum of money if maladministration resulted in a loss to those interested in the estate. The amount of the bond required was the value of the estate up to a maximum of $20,000, but the court had power to reduce the amount or dispense with the requirement altogether if it thought fit. Two sureties (guarantors) of the bond had also to be obtained, but the court could also dispense with this requirement, and sometimes did, when it was clear that no harm could come to the estate, for example, when the administrator was also the sole interested party and there were no creditors.

The requirement of security for a grant of administration was considerably relaxed by the amended Administration Act and, under this legislation, the *general requirement* of an administration bond was abolished. However, an administration bond may still have to be supplied on the granting of Letters of Administration as, in defined fairly wide circumstances, the court may still require such a bond of an amount that the court considers appropriate. The court is thus left with a discretionary power to require security to be given for a grant of administration in some circumstances, although the general requirement of an administration bond was abolished as of 1 January 1980.

Law: Administration Act 1969, s 6(5)–(7)

7.3 Retirement and removal of personal representative

In former times, it was difficult for a personal representative, once having accepted office, to retire before the administration of the estate was completed. It was also difficult for a personal representative to be removed from office because of misconduct. We now have an adequate provision to cater for these contingencies.

Persons who do not wish to continue in office may now, among other things, apply to the court for its consent to their retirement. Personal representatives may also be removed from office if the court considers that this is desirable.

In such cases, the court will give such directions as it considers appropriate, and it may appoint a new personal representative, or an administrator de bonis non, to complete the administration.

Law: Administration Act 1969, s 21

7.4 When title to the deceased's property vests in the personal representative

When Letters of Administration are granted to an administrator, the title to all the assets of the deceased, both realty and personalty, vests in the administrator, and this vesting dates back to the date of the deceased's death. This enables the administrator to deal with the assets, and also ratifies their actions in dealing with the assets from the date of death up to the date of the grant. In the period between the date of death and the date of the grant, title to the deceased's property vests in the Crown, thus enabling any claims against the estate to be served in that period.

The position is a little different when the deceased has made a will appointing an executor. In this case, the will itself vests the title to all the deceased's personal property in the executor at the time of death, and the grant of probate is merely confirmation or proof of the right to deal with those assets. But, for historical reasons, which will not be discussed here, the will itself does not vest title to the deceased's real property in the executor, and probate must be obtained and a Transmission Instrument registered with Land Information NZ (LINZ), not just as confirmation, but to vest title to real property in the executor. As with Letters of Administration, the grant of probate relates the vesting of the title in the real property back to the date of the will-maker's death, so as to ratify any dealings by the executor before the grant.

However, as we mentioned in Chapter 6 — *Executors*, when any real property, and personal property, is owned by the deceased jointly with another person, it is not necessary to apply for probate or Letters of Administration in respect of it, although it may be necessary to apply because of other assets. Property held under a joint tenancy passes on the death of one of the joint tenants to the survivor or survivors, irrespective of the provisions of the will or, if there is no will, the provisions of the Administration Act relating to intestate succession. However, remember that such property may still be treated by the court as relationship property if justice so requires and so may be subject to a claim by a relationship partner. This is in contrast to property held under a tenancy in common, shared ownership, where the share of the deceased passes to their estate.

Although the assets are said to vest in the personal representatives, they do not own them, as they do their own property, but hold them in trust for the beneficiaries under the will or the persons entitled to succeed on intestacy.

Law: Land Transfer Act 1952, ss 41(1), 122, 123
Administration Act 1969, s 24
Property (Relationships) Act 1976, s 83

Chapter 8
Functions of a Personal Representative

8.0 Introduction

In the final stages of the last chapter, we made a start in considering topics that relate to both administrators and executors. In this chapter, we will consider important general matters that are common to both administrators and executors.

8.1 The basic duties of a personal representative

In the course of this text, brief reference is frequently made to the duties of a personal representative. These duties have been summed up by saying that the personal representative must gather in all the property of the deceased, pay the deceased's debts, and distribute what remains to those entitled to succeed — either under the terms of the will or according to the rules of intestate succession.

Estates vary considerably in size and complexity and in what is involved in their administration. Although it is not possible to list easily all the duties that a personal representative may be expected to carry out, the main duties of a personal representative are set out below, and correspond with the typical situation. It is not put forward as being absolutely correct in every possible instance.

8.1.1 Burial of the deceased

The personal representative has the duty of seeing to the burial or cremation of the deceased, although, in fact, this is often taken care of by the deceased's immediate family. Legally, although no one has property in a dead body, the body of the deceased passes into the custody of the personal representative, who should make the arrangements for the proper disposal of it that they consider fit, subject to any express directions left by the deceased. However, note that these directions are not binding, even though most personal representatives abide by them. The role of the executor was considered in *Takamore v Clarke* [2012] NZSC 116 in which a majority of judges in the Supreme Court reinforced the view that, at Common Law, the personal representatives have both the right and duty of disposal of the body. However, Māori burial customs are relevant considerations to be weighed among others in deciding how to exercise those rights. It remains to be seen how competing views are to be weighed.

The funeral expenses are a debt chargeable against the estate, and rank first in priority over all other debts. Where the personal representative engages the funeral director, the estate will be liable for reasonable funeral expenses but, where some other person arranges the funeral, that person will be primarily liable for the funeral expenses.

In *The Public Trustee v Loasby* (1908) 27 NZLR 801; 10 GLR 548, the first wife of a distinguished Māori chief obtained from Loasby provisions for a tangi following the death of the chief. The Court held that most of the expenses were reasonable and were, in accordance with Māori custom, to be regarded as the funeral expenses of the chief. Loasby (in the then Magistrate's Court) sued the Public Trustee as personal representative for the expenses. Later, the then Supreme Court held that the action failed, and that the first wife was liable for the expenses. She, however, had a right to proceed against the Public Trustee for their recovery if there were sufficient assets in the estate, which in this case there were.

The amount spent on the funeral must be reasonable in relation to the deceased's circumstances and station in life and, if the estate is insolvent, the cost of the funeral should be kept strictly to a minimum.

8.1.2 Inventory of assets

Personal representatives should make a full list of the assets in the estate, which list they could be called upon to file in the High Court.

In the Affidavit for obtaining Grant of Probate,[1] or to precede Letters of Administration,[2] the personal representatives will have attested that they will "when required by the court so to do, to file in the court and verify by affidavit a true and perfect inventory of the estate of the deceased", and also "a true and perfect account of the estate of the deceased . . .", which would be filed at the conclusion of the administration. In practice, it is unusual for the court to require an inventory or an account to be filed, but personal representatives should make an inventory of the assets so that they can comply if required to do so.

8.1.3 Application for probate or Letters of Administration

Personal representatives must complete the necessary papers to obtain the grant of probate or Letters of Administration as evidence of their right to deal with the assets of the deceased. Applicants for Letters of Administration must satisfy the court that they have made reasonable inquiries to ascertain whether or not there are any persons who are entitled to take under the provisions of the Status of Children Act 1969.

1 See Appendix 1.

2 *Wills and Succession*, at [1013].

The Act removes the former legal disabilities of children born out of wedlock, and any natural child or parent of the deceased is entitled to take under the Act. The applicant must have:

1. searched the register of births and deaths[3] and ascertained whether or not the existence of any such claimant is revealed in the register, and
2. looked through the papers of the deceased and ascertained whether or not the existence of any such claimant is revealed in those papers, or

satisfied the court that:

1. no useful purpose would be served in the particular case by making such inquiries (such as where the net estate is below $155,000, so it will all pass to the spouse), or
2. the making of such inquiries would unduly delay the grant of administration, or
3. the getting in or preservation of the assets of the estate requires an immediate grant of administration.

Somewhat oddly, it is submitted, trustee companies,[4] and any applicants for a grant of Letters of Administration jointly with a trustee company, are exempted from the above requirements.

To obtain the usual grant of probate, an executor must file in the High Court:

1. an application without notice for obtaining probate
2. an affidavit or affidavits
3. probate partially completed, and
4. the will.

What is involved was discussed in Section 6.1 — *Probate*.

8.1.4 Effect of Property (Relationships) Act 1976 on administration procedures

From 1 February 2002, the following procedures have been required to be followed by personal representatives:

- Check the will and inquire of the next of kin whether the deceased:
  - was married at the date of death
  - was in a civil union at the time of death
  - was in a de facto relationship at the date of death
  - had been in a de facto relationship that had ceased prior to death.

  Note that it is possible for a person to have more than one of these applying, for example, a person could be married and also in a de facto relationship at the same time.

3 Set up under the Births, Deaths and Marriages Registration Act 1995.

4 See Chapter 7 — *Administrators*, footnote 4.

- Check at the High Court Registry whether a notice of election has been lodged by any relationship partner.
- If there was a marriage, civil union or de facto relationship, observe the 6-month time limit before any distribution, unless:
  - — an election notice electing Option B is received, or
  - — a written consent is received from the potential claimant.
- If the administration of the will or intestacy may result in the potential claimant not receiving an amount equivalent to their entitlement under the Property (Relationships) Act 1976, they should be advised to obtain independent legal advice.
- Obtain any elections required within the stipulated time of six months from the date of death or grant of administration.
- If Option A is elected, obtain the written consent of the claimant before making any interim distribution pending the outcome of the claim.

8.1.5 Getting in the property of the deceased as far as possible

Personal representatives are under a duty to get in the assets of the deceased as soon as possible, and this means that they must take control and possession of the deceased's property as soon as they can.

At this stage, personal representatives are unlikely to be able to get their hands on all the deceased's assets, because it is the established practice that people holding funds belonging to the estate do not pay out until production and sighting of probate or Letters of Administration. When probate, or Letters of Administration, are applied for, the formal grant is partially completed and filed in the High Court by the solicitors acting in the estate and, after it has been completed and sealed by the court, it is returned to the solicitors acting.

However, personal representatives are usually able to take possession of some of the deceased's assets immediately, and it is their duty to do this. Moreover, remember that, under the Administration Act 1969 (as amended in 1994), the personal representative, and indeed some of the beneficiaries, are entitled to request, without production of probate or Letters of Administration, payment of certain funds if such funds do not individually exceed $15,000. Under the provisions, from the complementary point of view of the fund-holders, most bodies or persons holding funds of the deceased may, without fear of incurring legal liability, pay out funds not individually exceeding $15,000 in value, without requiring a grant of administration if they are satisfied on such evidence that everything is in order. These exemption figures are likely to be increased from time to time.[5]

5 The relevant statutory references were given in Section 6.1 — *Probate*, where this topic was covered, and they are not repeated in this subsection.

The personal representative should furnish the necessary evidence in small estates where it is not proposed to take out a probate or Letters of Administration.

Also, the Public Trust and trustee corporations can elect to administer an estate, or the unadministered balance of an estate in New Zealand, without obtaining a grant of administration, if the estate, or unadministered balance thereof in New Zealand, does not exceed $120,000 in value, and no one has obtained a grant of administration in New Zealand.

An executor, administrator or trustee may now be registered as a shareholder in a company *in their capacity of executor, administrator or trustee* of a deceased person. This, however, of itself, does not constitute public notice of the trust.

Generally, as far as funds are concerned, the personal representative will find it most desirable at this stage to get in enough monies to pay the funeral expenses, tax owing, and the debts of the estate. In former times, to enable the payment of estate duty, probate or Letters of Administration sometimes had to be conditionally released by Inland Revenue under special limited arrangements, but this is now all in the past.[6]

---

6 However, it is still of interest because of the possibility that estate duty may be reintroduced at some time in the future. With regard to the estates of persons who died prior to 17 December 1992, the date as from which the National Government retrospectively suspended estate duty by means of the Estate Duty Abolition Act 1993, the following applied, and an outline of the old position is given here.

Where an estate was clearly dutiable, the personal representative had to complete forms known as the *Administrator's Statement and Schedules*, which set out all the assets and liabilities of the deceased and their respective values. In order to complete these forms, it was usual to employ professional valuers to value, for example, the deceased's furniture and personal chattels, their car, and so on. The government valuation was usually taken, initially, as the value of the deceased's residential property and any other realty.

These forms, together with copies of all bank statements, including savings bank's passbooks, for the 3 years preceding the date of death, had to be filed with Inland Revenue within six months from the date of the grant of administration. All large entries and recurring entries in the bank statements had to be explained by notation or covering letter to Inland Revenue. The schedules described each item of property and gave a valuation of it, while the Administrator's Statement contained summarised particulars of the various classes of property and gave a total picture of the estate.

However, where an estate's value, after deduction of allowable debts, was less than the amount at which estate duty started to become payable ($450,000 for a person dying after 31 March 1984), an abbreviated form of Administrator's Statement could be used, and the schedules could be dispensed with although, especially where the value was approaching the figure at which duty became payable, the use of schedules was recommended. These abbreviated forms of Administrator's Statement had to be completed by the solicitor acting, or Trust Company officer, as the case may be.

The estate duty was assessed by Inland Revenue on the basis of the information in the Administrator's Statement and Schedules, but the personal representative and their solicitor did not always agree with Inland Revenue's assessment. Inland Revenue was not, of course, bound to accept the information in the above forms, and it sometimes brought additional assets into the estate, challenged valuations, and disallowed deductions. In such cases, Inland Revenue and the personal representative would eventually agree on the amount of

Another possible source of funds for such payments could be a loan from one or more of those beneficially interested in the estate; this will depend both on willingness and ability to lend.

8.1.6 Meeting Inland Revenue requirements

Personal representatives have an obligation to:

- File a tax return to date of death. They should also advise Inland Revenue of the name and address of the firm acting in the estate (for notices and assessments), and file an application for a tax number for the estate.
- Ensure that there are no arrears of tax owing in the deceased's lifetime.
- File further tax returns — including a final return as at the date of distribution of the estate. (If the estate is ongoing for some years, for example, because of a life interest and infant beneficiaries, several tax returns will be required.)

In a simple estate able to be mainly distributed on 15 June 2022 where the deceased died on 1 December 2021, the personal representative would have to:

- file a tax return as at 1 December 2021
- ensure that there were no arrears of tax owing in the deceased's lifetime
- file a tax return as at 31 March 2022, and
- file a tax return as at 15 June 2022.

It is prudent for the personal representative to hold back an appropriate amount from the main distribution to allow for any tax payable on the above returns when all the assessments are to hand; the personal representative has to bear in mind that there may be a discrepancy between a return's figures and Inland Revenue's assessment. This is all the more so if the tax aspect is not so simple, for example, if the deceased was running a business, in which case the personal representative should consult the deceased's accountant. Any refund or refunds can be amalgamated with the money held back for a final distribution. Also note that, if the funds are placed on call during the administration, they will continue to earn interest.

---

estate duty payable. When the assessment of the estate duty had been accepted by the personal representative, it was their duty to pay it. Interest at 5% was payable on unpaid estate duty after six months from the date of the deceased's death and, in addition, a penalty could be charged if duty was not paid within three months of the notice of assessment.

It went without saying that a personal representative who supplied deliberately false information to Inland Revenue was liable to prosecution.

When the estate duty, if any, had been paid, Inland Revenue would certify accordingly on the probate or Letters of Administration, and send it to the personal representative (or their solicitor).

8.1.7 Payment of funeral and testamentary expenses and debts

If personal representatives do not have sufficient monies to pay the estate's debts, possession of the probate or Letters of Administration, and the ability to produce it, enables them to get in the required monies.

The personal representative must pay, out of the monies of the estate, the funeral expenses, tax owing, the deceased's debts, and testamentary expenses that are the cost of and incidental to obtaining the grant of administration and getting in the assets.

The task of paying the deceased's debts may often be simplified pursuant to the Trusts Act 2019 and, incidentally, as we are going to see in Subsection 8.2.1 — *Some of the statutory powers of a personal representative*, the Act also gives them wide discretion as to how they act in that regard. Quite frequently, personal representatives will be in some doubt as to who all the creditors of the deceased are, and, in this situation, it is most desirable for them to act under a particular provision, which will avoid their having to halt distribution of the estate to the beneficiaries on account of possible unknown creditors. Although the provision (cited below) does not apply to every possible claim, it applies to all normal business debts. It provides, in effect, that, upon the expiration of a period of not less than one month,[7] specified in a newspaper advertisement calling upon creditors to make known their claims and published at least once in the localities where the deceased resided or carried on business, the personal representative may distribute the estate. Under the provision, once the specified period has expired, personal representatives are not personally liable for debts of which they are unaware, but any rights that the creditors may still be able to exercise against the deceased's property are preserved. In short, the provision relieves a personal representative from liability for failure to take into account the debts of unknown creditors if such creditors did not respond to public advertisement.

There is no need for the work of personal representatives to be delayed for long because they receive claims that they are not happy about. Such claims can be brought to a head under another provision of the Trustee Act, which will force the alleged creditor to take court action to prove their claim within 3 months. (When it appears that the assets of an estate will not be sufficient to pay all the debts, the personal representative may apply to the court to have the estate administered under the Insolvency Act 2006, or the court may make an order to this effect on the application of a creditor. When this happens, the court may direct that the insolvent estate be administered by the Public Trust, the Maori Trustee, or some other person. In such cases, the debts of the estate will be paid in the order of priority laid down in the Act, which order is much the same as for a bankrupt person whose affairs are being administered by an Official Assignee.

7 Two months in the case of a newspaper circulating mainly outside New Zealand.

If the Public Trust or the Maori Trustee is acting as personal representative, or is entitled to so act, respectively, because of the insolvency, they can elect, respectively, to administer the estate under the Act after merely filing a certificate in the appropriate Court Registry.)

The above two paragraphs have been bracketed because the administration of insolvent estates is dealt with in more detail in Chapter 17 — *Administration of Insolvent Estates.*

8.1.8 Getting in all remaining assets

Fortunately, however, the usual estate is solvent, not insolvent.

As the personal representative now has the probate or Letters of Administration, they have the recognised means of proving their office to all those still holding property of the deceased (now property of the estate). They can now compel a transfer of all such property to themself in their official capacity.

In most estates of any size, the probate or Letters of Administration now does the rounds, so to speak. It is forwarded, successively, by the personal representative to each person holding property of the estate — bank managers, company secretaries, registrars of stock, life insurance managers, and so on. Each such person returns the probate or Letters of Administration, after noting it, and transfers the asset concerned to the personal representative. Most, but not all, asset holders in New Zealand will accept a copy of the grant certified by the solicitors acting in the estate.

The general rule, existing by virtue of case law, is that the personal representative has one year, "the executor's year", in which to get in the assets and distribute the estate, but this is not a hard and fast rule. The realisation of assets that are required to be converted into money may be postponed when the personal representative considers it to be in the best interests of the beneficiaries. For example, they may decide to postpone the sale of shares during a temporary slump on the stock market.

If the will does not direct immediate distribution of the estate to the beneficiaries, that is, if the will sets up a continuing trust, the personal representative will not only have to get in the assets, but may have to "*convert*" them to "authorised investments". A person who has been appointed executor and trustee under a will, changes from an executor to a trustee[8] when they have completed their duties as an executor. The law of trusts requires a personal representative who has become a trustee to hold

8 Trusts are dealt with in Chapter 11 — *Introduction to Trusts* to Chapter 16 — *Trustees* of this text. (Executors and administrators, as we have mentioned in Chapter 6 and Chapter 7, respectively, are similar, but not identical offices, and the principal differences between them are covered in Section 8.4 — *Summary of the differences between executors and administrators*).

only "authorised investments" on behalf of the trust estate. Authorised investments are now a very wide category and include any property nominated as such in the will and, failing such nomination, any investments that a prudent businessperson would take out on behalf of others. A trustee's duty to take out authorised investments is dealt with in more detail in Subsection 16.5.4 — *Investment of trust funds*.

If the will sets up a trust, the personal representative will have to sell any items in the estate that do not constitute authorised investments and, with the sale monies, take out authorised investments instead. Such "*conversion*" should likewise be done within the executor's year.

8.1.9 Distribution of the assets to the beneficiaries

In the abstract, the meaning of this important duty is clear. Nevertheless, exactly what it involves may not be clear in particular cases, and a considerable volume of law that is beyond the scope of this text falls under this heading.

Let us merely say that, in the usual simple estate, the personal representative must distribute the assets according to the deceased's will. If the deceased did not leave a will, the personal representative must distribute the assets according to the rules of intestate succession, which we will consider in Chapter 9 — *Succession on Intestacy*.

The Trustee Act contains a provision entitled, "Distribution of shares of missing beneficiaries", which is of considerable assistance to personal representatives and trustees. In short, it provides that, when a personal representative or a trustee does not know the whereabouts of any possible beneficiary or whether or not the beneficiary is in existence, they can publish advertisements (in New Zealand or elsewhere, and under the direction of the court if need be) calling upon such beneficiaries to come forward within a period of not less than 2 months. If the personal representatives or trustees receive responses that they are not happy with, they can take action to bring them to a head (similar to those that we have alluded to in Subsection 8.1.6 — *Meeting Inland Revenue requirements* in the case of debts). After the advertisements, and being informed of the results, the court may order that the personal representative (or trustee) may distribute the estate[9] to such persons and upon such basis as it thinks fit — including the basis that the possible beneficiary or beneficiaries are not in existence. Distribution of the estate, in accordance with the court's order, exonerates the personal representative (or trustee) from liability to such possible beneficiary or beneficiaries, but preserved are the rights of any such beneficiaries to pursue any claims that they may be able to exercise against the property.

9 After such notice of the proposed order as the court may determine.

A personal representative must keep proper accounts of their administration and, as we have seen,[10] be prepared to produce them if required to do so, as the court may require production of the accounts on the application of an objecting party.

Another important aspect that should be borne in mind when the stage has been reached at which distribution of assets may be made is whether 6 months have passed since the date of the grant of probate or Letters of Administration. If they have not and the assets are distributed, the personal representative is personally liable if a claim is brought, and succeeds, under the Property (Relationships) Act, the Family Protection Act 1955 or the Law Reform (Testamentary Promises) Act 1949.[11]

Personal representatives who receive written notice of an intention to make a claim under any of these Acts, cannot distribute any part of the estate, except that which, if they have not been served with the appropriate court documents within a year from the grant of administration,[12] they may distribute. If they are so served, the estate is frozen until the claim is disposed of by the court or by settlement.

A similar consideration now applies in respect of a large and controversial statute — the Child Support Act 1991.[13]

That Act imposes a sizeable liability on parents,[14] not having day-to-day care of their children, to contribute towards the support of those of them who are unmarried and under 19 years of age.[15]

Personal representatives who distribute prior to six months from the date of the grant of probate or Letters of Administration are not protected against claims under the Act, even if they had no notice of them. However, normally, the personal representative would have notice of such claims as a result of the inquiries that they are bound to make under the Status of Children Act, dealt with next.

Also, the Status of Children Act is still not yet dead as far as our imaginary estate is concerned. The relevant provisions require reasonable inquiries to be made in terms of that Act before any distribution of any estate is made. In addition to carrying out the identical steps that were required in connection

10 Subsection 8.1.2 — *Inventory of assets.*

11 These Acts were dealt with in Section 1.5 — *The implementation of the will-maker's intentions.*

12 Two years in the case of a Family Protection claimant not of full age or mental capacity.

13 The Act was not dealt with in Section 1.5 — *The implementation of the will-maker's intention,* because it does not involve varying the will-maker's will.

14 According to a fairly rigid formula.

15 The Act, which contains 273 sections, is administered through Inland Revenue, and the liability of the parent is a debt due to the Crown. Central to the general scheme of the Act are the following sections: ss 4–6, 8(1), 9, 23–25, 29–30, 67–69, 72, 88–89, 128–129, 131, 141, 154, and 178 (as amended).

with applications for Letters of Administration as seen in Subsection 8.1.3 — *Application for probate or Letters of Administration,*[16] the personal representative must:

- in cases where an adviser, who the personal representative believes may have relevant knowledge, can be located, inquire from at least one such adviser about the existence of any ex-nuptial children and obtain, if the adviser or advisers are willing to make it, a statutory declaration concerning the matter
- inquire from the solicitor, if any, last known to have acted for the deceased, whether the solicitor knows of the existence of any such claimant.

These provisions are much wider in scope than the provisions that we examined in Subsection 8.1.3 — *Application for probate or Letters of Administration*. They apply to estates where probate has been granted to an executor, as well as to estates where Letters of Administration have been granted to an administrator. They also apply to all distributions of any property held upon trust.

A personal representative or a trustee is not personally liable to a claimant under the Act if the personal representative or trustee has complied with the provisions of the Act acting in good faith and has no knowledge of the claimant. The court is also given a discretion to relieve a personal representative or a trustee, wholly or partly, from personal liability for failure to comply with the provisions of the Act, if they have acted honestly and ought fairly to be excused.

Note that the Property (Relationships) Act prevents distribution while proceedings are pending or after an election has been made but before proceedings have been commenced, unless the surviving relationship partner consented in writing or the court has approved the distribution.

Law: Status of Children Act 1969, ss 5A, 6, 6A, 6B

Property (Relationships) Act 1976, ss 62, 71–73

Public Trust Act 2001, s 77

Trustee Companies Act 1967, ss 36, 37

Companies Act 1993, s 79

Administration Act 1969, ss 47, 65, 82

Trustee Act 1956, ss 14(1)(c), 35, 75, 76

Law Reform (Testamentary Promises) Act 1949, s 6

Family Protection Act 1955, ss 2(5)(b), 9

Child Support Act 1991, ss 5, 6

16 The first numbers 1. and 2.

8.2 The powers, rights, and liabilities of a personal representative

To carry out the duties of their office, personal representatives must have the power to deal with the assets of the estate. As in all matters relating to the estate, the intention of the will-maker is dominant and, hence, the initial source of an executor's powers is the will. Thus, if the deceased had made a will, they could have, by express provision in the will, given the executor any powers in relation to the assets of the estate.

In addition to any such powers, certain powers are given by statute to a personal representative, unless will-makers make express inconsistent provision in the case of their executor. Personal representatives may also gain further powers by way of agreements made between themselves and all the beneficiaries.

8.2.1 Some of the statutory powers of a personal representative

8.2.1.1 Power of sale

Personal representatives may enjoy the facility of having available to them more than one statutory power of sale, depending upon the circumstances, as there are several statutory powers of sale in existence. Some of these powers are more specialised than others, and the principal ones are set out below.

The most general, and the most important, of these statutory powers of sale is that contained, among other things, in s 56 of the Trusts Act. Under s 56, a trustee has all the powers necessary to manage the trust property and all the powers of an absolute owner of the property.

In intestate estates where the deceased leaves a surviving spouse, the personal chattels may not be sold without the consent of the court or the surviving spouse, unless the sale is required for the purposes of administration as a consequence of lack of other assets.

Note, as is stated in Section 16.8 — *Liability of trustees*, that a provision giving power to a personal representative or trustee does not necessarily mean that they are immune from liability at the suit of the beneficiaries — they must still meet their duty of diligence and prudence.

8.2.1.2 Power to compound liabilities

As is mentioned in Subsection 16.6.2 — *Statutory powers of a trustee*, legal action to recover a bad debt is sometimes unsuccessful and only adds to the amount of the loss. Personal representatives are given a wide statutory discretion as to how they deal with debts owing to, or by, the estate, and are not liable for any resulting loss provided that they took action when necessary and acted in good faith. Among other things, they may:

- accept any composition or any security for any debt owing to the estate
- allow any time for payment of any debt owing to the estate
- pay any debt owing by the estate on any evidence that they think sufficient, or
- abandon, adjust, submit to arbitration, or otherwise settle, any debt or claim owing by or to the estate.

8.2.1.3 Power to appropriate assets

A personal representative has the power, with the agreement of the beneficiaries concerned, to appropriate or set aside particular assets to satisfy a legacy.

8.2.1.4 Power to carry on business

A personal representative has the power to carry on the deceased's business for the purpose of winding it up, and has the power to use in the business any part of the estate that is subject to the same trusts. Moreover, because it may be in the interests of the beneficiaries that the business should not be wound up immediately, the personal representative is empowered to carry it on for a period of two years or such longer period as the court may approve. This topic is dealt with in a little more detail in Subsection 16.6.2 — *Statutory powers of a trustee.*

8.2.2 Rights of a personal representative

Personal representatives have much the same rights as trustees. These are dealt with in Chapter 16 — *Trustees.*

Personal representatives also have some rights of a very general nature. As mentioned,[17] when it appears that the assets may be insufficient to pay the debts, personal representatives may apply to the court for the estate to be administered as an insolvent estate under Pt 6 the Insolvency Act.

In similar manner to trustees, when personal representatives are in any doubt as to how they should perform any of their duties, they can apply to the court for directions, and are protected when acting pursuant to such directions.

When an action is brought against the estate, personal representatives may plead any defence that would have been available to the deceased when alive. In addition, in defence of actions generally, they may plead "*plene administravit*", which means that they have disposed in the proper course of administration of all the assets and have nothing left to satisfy the claim. If

17 And as will be shown in more detail in Chapter 17 — *Administration of Insolvent Estates.*

they have not disposed of the assets, they may plead that there are only enough assets to meet claims having priority.

When an action is brought personally against personal representatives,[18] they can apply to the court for relief under the Trusts Act. That Act, in effect, gives the court a general discretion to relieve personal representatives from personal liability if the court considers that this is warranted in the circumstances of the case.

8.2.3 Liabilities of a personal representative

8.2.3.1 Devastavit

This term embodies most of the liabilities of personal representatives. A devastavit is to personal representatives what a breach of trust is to trustees. Any maladministration is a devastavit, for example, paying legatees without providing for creditors, misappropriating the assets, failing to get in monies owing to the estate, or paying beneficiaries out of the proper order when there are insufficient assets. Whenever personal representatives act improperly, they can, if loss follows, be made liable either to the trust estate or to some person who is entitled to look to the trust estate for satisfaction of their claim.

8.2.3.2 Liability for acts of co-representative

A general principle expressed in the Trusts Act is that personal representatives are liable only for their own acts and responsible only for the assets that come into their own hands, but this must not be carried too far. Personal representatives are expected to take part in the administration of the estate, and they are expected to keep an eye on their co-representatives. They are not entitled to assign to themselves the role of a sleeping partner and then be immune to the consequences of what has been done.

8.2.3.3 Liability to account

As has already been noted, personal representatives are under a duty to keep proper accounts and to produce these if required.

Law: Administration Act 1969, ss 26 and 27
Trusts Act 2019, ss 4, 5, 81, 82

8.3 When a personal representative is entitled to commission

As the reader will now appreciate, a personal representative's position is a responsible one and may involve considerable work on the part of the person appointed.

18 "Devastavit" — see Subsection 8.2.3.1 — *Devastavit*.

The general rule applying to all trusts and estates is that a trustee, and a personal representative, must not make a profit out of their positions, and so, personal representatives are expected to perform their duties gratuitously. However, the court is given wide discretion by s 139 the Trusts Act to award, at any time, payment of a commission as remuneration for the work done or to be done.

A personal representative will also be entitled to charge for their work when they have been expressly authorised to do so in the will, or when there is a definite agreement to this effect between the personal representative and all of the beneficiaries or persons who will succeed to the estate. When the solicitor drawing up a will is also appointed executor, it is the invariable practice to include a clause authorising them to charge for their work as executor. Solicitors who neglect to include such a clause may pay dearly for their omission because, under the general rule, they will not be entitled to remuneration.

Note that such a clause is deemed to be a legacy in favour of the solicitor and, hence, the solicitor must not witness the will. Because of the rule, which we saw in Subsection 1.3.3 — *Who may take under a will*, that a witness cannot take a gift under the will, a solicitor-executor who has witnessed the will is unable to charge for their work as executor.

Trustee Corporations and the Public Trust are expressly authorised by statute to charge for work done in administering the estate, according to a set scale of charges.

Law: Trusts Act 2019, s 139

Trustee Companies Act 1967, ss 18, 19

8.4 Summary of the differences between executors and administrators

Although the office of executor and that of administrator are basically very similar in that both are appointed for the purpose of administering the estate of a deceased person, there are certain differences between them which may be summarised as follows:

1.

(a) Executors are appointed by the will, that is, they are appointed by the will-maker. Administrators are appointed by the court.

(b) Probate granted to executors is not by appointment of the court. It is merely the official recognition by the court of an appointment made by the will-maker. The granting of Letters of Administration is the actual appointment of an administrator by the court.

2. The title to personal property vests in the executors on the death of the will-maker by virtue of the will itself, and the title to real property is vested in the executors pursuant to the grant of probate and subsequent registration of an Application for Transmission at the Land Titles Office.[19]

   The title to both real and personal property is vested in the administrators pursuant to the grant of Letters of Administration.
3. Under s 6 of the Administration Act, the court may require administrators to give security for their due administration of the estate if the court is satisfied that this would be expedient having regard to the matters set out in that section. Executors, because of the confidence presumably reposed in them by the will-maker, do not have to give security for their proper administration of the estate.
4. Executors must administer the estate according to the terms of the will. This also applies to administrators with will annexed, but the usual type of administrators appointed on an intestacy must administer the estate according to the rules of intestate succession, which is dealt with in the next chapter.
5. If, before administration is completed, a sole executor dies after taking out probate having left a will appointing a further executor, the further executor will take over and complete the administration of the original will-maker's estate. On the other hand, if a sole administrator dies before completing the administration, that person's personal representative will not take it over, but instead the court will appoint an administrator de bonis non.

Law: Land Transfer Act 1952, ss 122, 123

Administration Act 1969, ss 6(5), 6(6), 13, 24, 25

19 For the position regarding real property held jointly (joint tenancy), see Chapter 6 — *Executors* footnote 7.

Chapter 9
Succession on Intestacy

9.0 Introduction

When a person dies without leaving a valid will, that person is said to die "intestate". An "intestacy" will also result when the deceased has left a will but all the gifts fail as, for example, when the beneficiaries have all predeceased the will-maker.

There will be a partial intestacy when the deceased has left a will, but has failed to dispose effectively of the whole of the estate. This will occur when the will-maker has left specific gifts, but has not included a residuary clause to cover those assets not specifically bequeathed and gifts that fail, or when the residuary disposition itself fails. In such cases, the deceased will be deemed to have died intestate for that part of their estate not effectively disposed of under the will.

When a person has died intestate, either wholly or partially, their assets must still be disposed of. The law in New Zealand governing succession on intestacy is contained in the Administration Act 1969, which, in Part III, sets out the rules of intestate succession.[1]

The amendments in the Administration Act apply only in respect of the estates of persons who die on or after 1 February 2002.

For the purposes of these rules:

A. In similar manner to what we saw in Subsection 7.1.1 — *General administration* in connection with grants of Letters of Administration, a husband or wife does not qualify as such when a separation order is in force.[2]

B. "Personal chattels" do not correspond exactly with "personal property". Not only do "personal chattels" exclude leaseholds, but they also exclude any chattels, including cars, used principally for business purposes, and money and securities for money, for example, mortgages and company shares.

C. "Issue" means children of the intestate, plus the children of any child who has predeceased the intestate, such grandchildren (or great

1 Where a Māori person has died intestate, and the estate includes a beneficial interest in Māori freehold land, see the Maori Land Act 1993, s 109.

2 Even though such a "spouse" is not entitled to succeed under the rules of intestate succession, they can still bring a claim under the Family Protection Act 1955, see Subsection 1.5.2 — *The Family Protection Act 1955*. See Family Proceedings Act 1980, s 26.

grandchildren, as the case may be) taking per stirpes the share that their parent would have received.

D. "De facto relationship" has the meaning in s 2 of the Property (Relationships) Act 1976 and "surviving de facto partner" means a person who was living in a de facto relationship with the deceased at the date of their death.

The main rules of intestate succession are as follows:

1. The husband or wife or surviving de facto partner (the spouse) of the intestate gets the personal chattels,[3] plus $155,000 plus interest.
2. The spouse of the intestate also gets one-third of the balance of the estate. The other two-thirds go to the issue of the intestate.
3. If the intestate left no issue, the spouse gets two-thirds of the balance of the estate. The other one-third goes to the parents (or surviving parent) of the intestate. The spouse gets the personal chattels.
4. If the intestate left no issue and no parents, the balance of the estate goes to the spouse.
5. If the intestate left no spouse, the whole of the estate goes to the issue.
6. If the intestate left no spouse and no issue, the whole of the estate goes to the intestate's parents (or surviving parent).
7. If the intestate left no spouse, no issue, and no parents, the whole of the estate goes to the brothers and sisters of the intestate.[4]
8. If the intestate left no spouse, no issue, no parents, no brothers or sisters, and no nephews or nieces, the estate is divided into two halves to cater for the mother's and father's sides of the family, respectively:
   (a) The first half of the estate goes to the maternal grandparents (or the surviving one).
   (b) The second half of the estate goes to the paternal grandparents (or the surviving one).
   (c) However, if the intestate did not leave a maternal grandparent, the first half of the estate goes to the maternal uncles and aunts.
   (d) If the intestate did not leave a paternal grandparent, the second half of the estate goes to the paternal uncles and aunts.

3 Remember that, if personal chattels are subject to a hire-purchase agreement, the spouse will, as between successors, take them free of liability for instalments due or to become due. This topic was covered this in Section 3.4 — *Gifts subject to a charge*, and the relevant statutory references are not cited again in this chapter.

4 With respect to the estates of persons who died before 1 February 2002, if a sibling predeceased the will-maker, the estate is passed to the issue of the sibling. The Administration Act 1969 deletes the reference to "issue" in relation to nephews and nieces and cousins.

9.

(a) If, in addition to the foregoing defaults, the intestate left no maternal grandparents, no maternal uncles or aunts, the first half of the estate goes to the other side of the family and is distributed, along with the second half, in accordance with 8. (b) and (d) above and, likewise

(b) Vice versa, in the case of the second half of the estate, if the intestate left no paternal grandparents, no paternal uncles or aunts.

10. If nobody qualifies under 1.–9. above, the estate goes to the Crown as *bona vacantia* (literally, "goods without any apparent owner"). The Act provides that the Crown may, out of the whole or any part of the property, provide for any dependants of the intestate, whether kindred or not, and other persons for whom they might reasonably have been expected to make provision.[5]

When any children or grandchildren of the deceased are unmarried and are under the age of twenty, their share of the estate, although vested, does not become payable immediately, but will be held upon what are known as the "statutory trusts" until the children or grandchildren become of age (now twenty) or marry under this age. In the meantime, the administrator is empowered by the Trustee Act 1956 to make available such portions of the child's share in the estate as may be necessary for the child's proper maintenance or education.

Adopted children, by virtue of the order of adoption, have the same rights of succession as if they had been the natural children of their adoptive parents. They cease to have any rights of succession through their natural parents, except when, before the date of the adoption order, they have acquired a vested interest in property under a will or intestacy by virtue of their relationship to their natural parents.

By virtue of the Status of Children Act 1969, an ex-nuptial child takes on the same basis as a legitimate child provided that, in the case of a claim against the intestate estate of a man, the ex-nuptial child (or their representative) is able to establish paternity in accordance with the provisions of that Act.

In those cases of *partial intestacy* where the spouse receives a benefit under the deceased's will as well as being entitled to take under the rules of intestate succession, the statutory legacy of $155,000 is reduced to the extent of the benefit received under the will. However, in all other cases of this type, that is, when a person is entitled to a benefit under the will of the deceased and is also entitled to an interest in the intestate part of the estate, they take both ways.

Persons entitled under the rules of intestacy to a share in an estate are not compelled to accept their interest. They may disclaim their interest, provided

5 A de facto spouse may bring a claim under the Family Protection Act as amended by the Family Protection Amendment Act 2001.

they comply with certain conditions. The whole interest must be disclaimed, and so people cannot disclaim onerous property while accepting what will be of benefit to them.

The effect of a disclaimer is to pass the property direct to the issue of the person disclaiming or, failing such issue, to those entitled to succeed next under the rules of intestate succession.

Law: Property (Relationships) Act 1976, ss 52A, 52B, 77
Administration Act 1969, ss 2, 77, 77B, 78, 79, 81
Family Proceedings Act 1980, s 26
Adoption Act 1955, s 16(2)(a)–(2)(d)
Trusts Act 2019, ss 62–66
Status of Children Act 1969, ss 3, 7, 8

9.1 Intestacy and de facto spouses

If there is a surviving spouse and one or more surviving de facto partners, or two or more surviving de facto partners, the statutory "spousal" share is divided equally between the surviving partners (Administration Act 1969, s 77).

If the relationship is of short duration, it is treated in the same way as short duration relationships in the Property (Relationships) Act. A de facto partner of a short duration relationship is entitled to receive a statutory share, provided the court is satisfied that:

- there is a child of the de facto relationship, or
- that the partner made a substantial contribution to the relationship, and
- the court is satisfied that not being entitled to succeed on intestacy would result in serious injustice to the partner (Property (Relationships) Act 1976, s 77).

Where there are two or more surviving partners (or a spouse and de facto partners), s 77C of the Administration Act provides that the surviving partners share equally in the statutory share. A spouse or partner can elect to make a claim under the Property (Relationships) Act, Option A under s 61 rather than receiving the share of the statutory entitlement under the Administration Act. If any surviving partner makes an election in an intestate estate, the court must assess the competing claims and apply the approach to priority of entitlement under ss 52A and 52B.

Law: Property (Relationships) Act 1976, ss 52A, 52B, 77
Administration Act 1969, ss 77, 77C

Chapter 10

Application of Assets in Payment of Debts

10.0 Introduction

When a person dies with a valid will (testate) and solvent (which, fortunately, happens more commonly than not) and the estate is large enough to pay all debts and expenses and still leave assets for distribution to the beneficiaries, it is necessary to decide which of the assets are to be used in payment of the debts and expenses. As we stated in Section 3.2 — *Devises*, sometimes, when an estate is to be distributed, there are not enough assets in the estate, after payment of debts and expenses, to satisfy all the gifts the will-makers make in their will. This chapter deals with which beneficiaries are to receive less and in what order. The question does not arise in relation to intestate estates, because the rules of intestate succession refer to the balance of the estate after all debts and expenses have been paid.

Estate duty (now suspended) was in a special position, but this is now of only academic interest.[1]

The sum required for payment of debts and expenses in a testate estate will not necessarily be spread rateably over all the assets of the estate, but instead its source will be determined either by the terms of the will or by certain recognised rules. This will be of great importance to the beneficiaries, because the amount received by a beneficiary may be considerably reduced if the assets left to them are charged with payment of debts.

Similar comments can apply to the payment of pecuniary legacies, where assets may have to be sold to pay the legacies.

1 By the Estate Duty Abolition Act 1993, estate duty is suspended in the estates of persons who died on or after 17 December 1992 (see Subsection 8.1.5 — *Getting in the property of the deceased as far as possible*). The rules relating to payment of debts, which have been built up largely by case law, did not apply to payment of estate duty. Estate duty was in a special position. Prior to 1993, the will-maker could, and frequently did, direct that a specific part of their estate (usually the residuary estate) be charged with payment of estate duty, or they directed that certain bequests or devises should be taken free of estate duty. Such directions were effective.

However, if the will did not include directions on the payment of estate duty, or if the provisions for the payment of estate duty made by the will-maker were insufficient, under the provisions of ss 54 and 55 of the Estate and Gift Duties Act 1968, duty, or the remainder of duty, respectively, was payable out of the gifts received by each beneficiary in proportion to the value each gift bore to the total value of the estate. In other words, each person who succeeded to property had to pay a proportionate share of the outstanding estate duty.

The attention of this text is focused on the rules for determining which assets are to be applied in the payment of debts. The salient points may be summarised as follows:

1. When will-makers have left specific gifts of real or personal property (or a residuary gift of real property) without making provision for payment of debts and legacies, it can be assumed that they did not intend the specific gifts to be charged with such payments so long as there are other assets in the estate not specifically bequeathed or devised. In other words, it may be assumed that the will-maker intended that the beneficiaries should receive their specific gifts intact, so far as this is possible.

   The law proceeds on this assumption and, consequently, it is the residuary estate that is first charged with payment of debts and pecuniary or general legacies. The law favours real property at the expense of personal property, and so it is the *residuary personal estate* that is looked to as the primary source for payment of debts and legacies. This will be of practical importance if will-makers leave their residuary real estate to one person, and their residuary personal estate to another. It will then be the residuary legatees who suffer a reduction in what they receive, and not the residuary devisee.

2. Will-makers may direct that a particular part of their personal estate shall be charged with the payment of debts and legacies, for example, the proceeds of a particular life insurance policy. In such case, this will be the primary source, but only if the residuary personal estate has been effectively disposed of under the will. If the residuary personal estate has not been disposed of, or if the disposition fails, the residuary personal estate will be regarded as the primary source, and particular assets of the personal estate that have been specifically bequeathed, but have been charged with payment of debts and legacies, will not be resorted to unless the residuary personal estate is inadequate.

3. Will-makers may charge their real estate or some part of it with payment of debts and legacies, but this will not be effective unless also the residuary personal estate is specifically exempted, and effectively disposed of, by them.

4. The presumption favouring real property at the expense of personal property will be negated if the will-makers have clearly created in their will a "mixed fund" of realty and personalty by directing that certain parts of the real and personal property be sold and the resulting fund applied in payment of debts and legacies. Such a specific direction is quite effective.

5. If the residuary personal estate, or the particular part of the estate designated as the primary source as described in 2, 3, and 4 above, is inadequate, other assets in the estate must be drawn upon. If necessary, the whole estate can be made available in set categories of priority. Very briefly, these remaining categories of priority are:
   (a) real estate undisposed of by will, in other words, real estate (if any) in respect of which there has been an intestacy
   (b) real estate (devised but) charged with payment of debts, in cases where the will-maker did not also specifically exempt, and effectively dispose of, residuary personal estate
   (c) general legacies
   (d) devises and specific legacies
   (e) real estate and personal estate appointed by will under a general power of appointment
   (f) donatio mortis causa.

Within each category gifts abate rateably.

Chapter 11
Introduction to Trusts

11.0 What essentially is a trust?

The law of trusts had its beginnings in the Middle Ages, and although its historical development is beyond the scope of this text, a brief summary should help in an understanding of the present law on the subject.

Obviously there are situations in which it is desirable that the legal title to property should be vested in one person, while the right to the benefits arising out of ownership should belong to someone else. For example, when people die leaving property to their infant children, although they should not be deprived of the benefits of ownership, the legal title should not be vested in them until an age when they may be presumed to have attained some degree of maturity and the ability to manage their own affairs.

In the Middle Ages, there were stranger practical reasons for the separation of "legal" and "equitable" ownership. People soon realised that some of the incidents of feudal tenure, by which the King exacted payments from his subjects, could be avoided by transferring the legal ownership of property to another person, on the understanding that the transferor or their children would continue to enjoy the beneficial (equitable) use of the property. And, certain religious bodies that were not permitted to own land could, by a similar arrangement, obtain all the benefits of ownership. Another, and less worthy, objective was achieved by this method, whereby debtors could avoid having their property seized by their creditors, by transferring the legal ownership to another while retaining the beneficial use of it.

Such an arrangement, known as a "use", was never countenanced by the Common Law Courts. These courts recognised no such arrangement as the legal title being conveyed to X on the understanding that X was to hold the property for Y. As far as the Common Law was concerned, either the legal title was conveyed to Y or Y had no claim to the property. The person to whom the legal title was transferred became the owner, and no other person was recognised as having any right to the property. However, the Courts of Equity, which developed under the jurisdiction of the Chancellor, recognised such an arrangement, and protected the rights of persons who had an "equitable", as distinct from a "legal", interest in property.

One of the effects of the widespread employment of uses was to deplete the King's income, which was largely derived from the incidents of feudal tenure. To reverse this situation, a statute that prohibited uses was passed in the time of Henry VIII. But, with the breaking down of the feudal system in the seventeenth century, equitable interests in property again came to be recognised by the Courts of Equity, and this time they came to stay. They are now known not as uses, but as "trusts". Since that time, the basic concept of a trust has remained unchanged, and has become of fundamental importance in our law.

The idea of a trust — that the legal ownership and the beneficial ownership of property may be vested in different persons — is a simple one, but this basic concept has been expanded to cover a great variety of situations, and an extensive body of rules has grown up that regulates the creation and administration of a trust and the rights, duties, and liabilities of the parties concerned.[1]

It is these rules that must be considered in most of the remainder of this text.

Because there are now many types of trust, it is generally acknowledged that the legal concept of a trust defies an adequate and exhaustive definition. Stated very simply, a trust arises when one person (the "settlor") transfers property to a second person (the "trustee") to be held on trust for the beneficial use and enjoyment of a third person (the "beneficiary" or "cestui que trust"). This does not by any means profess to be a definition.

Dr GW Keeton has suggested defining a trust as:

> "The relationship which arises whenever a person, called the trustee, is compelled in Equity to hold property, whether real or personal, . . . for the benefit of some persons (of whom he may be one and who are called 'cestuis que trust') or for some object permitted by law, in such a way that the real benefit of the property accrues, not to the trustee, but to the beneficiaries or other objects of the trust".

This attempt at definition goes further than some to include "objects" as well as persons. It covers, for example, charitable trusts,[2] where the purpose of the trust may be to benefit some charitable cause and not individuals.

Note that, although the trust relationship is a three-fold one, involving settlor, trustee, and beneficiary, one person may occupy more than one of these positions at the same time. X, the owner of certain property, may declare that they will hold the property on trust for Y. In such a case, X is both settlor and trustee. Or, X may transfer property to Y to be held on trust for X for life, and thereafter for X's children, A and B. Here, X is the settlor and a beneficiary.

However, a person cannot be sole beneficiary and sole trustee. If there is to be a trust, the legal and beneficial interests in the property must be split up. Also, as is implied in our discussion, the settlor cannot be sole beneficiary.

1 For a trust distinguished from a bailment, an agency, a debt, a contract, a power, and the office of personal representative, respectively, see *Nevill*, at 4–10.

2 See Subsection 11.1.4 — *Private and charitable trusts [classification (B)]* later in this chapter.

11.0.1 Reform of Trust Law

The new Trusts Act 2019 (the Act) took effect on 30 January 2021. The Act updated and improved the law governing trusts for the first time in more than 60 years. It applies to all existing trusts in New Zealand, as well as any trust created on or after 30 January 2021.

11.1 Types of trusts

There are various classifications of trusts each of which is exhaustive (in that it includes all trusts under its various heads). Trusts can be divided up in these various ways depending upon the aspects that the classifier has in mind. The 3 main classifications are those that divide trusts according to:

- Classification A — the basic manner in which they came into existence (this classification consists of express, implied, and constructive trusts)
- Classification B — their general purpose (this classification consists of private and charitable trusts), and
- Classification C — whether they were created separately or as an incident of the creator's estate after their death (this classification consists of trusts inter vivos and trusts arising under wills).

11.1.1 Express or declared trusts [classification (A) 1]

These trusts are occasionally created by statute,[3] but usually come into existence through the adequately expressed intention of the settlor. They are by far the most common and important type of trust in this classification. Basically, all that is necessary to create an express trust is *the adequately expressed intention of the settlor* to create an arrangement that amounts to a trust. There are no formal requirements, that is, it is not essential for the settlor to use legal terms appropriate to the law of trusts. It is the substance of what they have done that counts.

Most express trusts are created in wills and take effect on the death of the will-maker. A typical example would be a will in which X devises X's farm to X's trustee upon trust to carry on the farm, to pay the income to their spouse during their life, and after their death, to sell the farm and divide the proceeds equally among their children.

A trust intended to take effect during the lifetime of the settlor (a trust "inter vivos") is usually made in the form of a deed although, under the basic law of trusts, any declaration in writing, or even by word of mouth, will suffice.[4]

3 For example, as we have seen in Chapter 9 — *Succession on Intestacy*, when any unmarried minors are entitled to take, s 77 of the Administration Act 1969 provides that their shares will be held for them, respectively, upon the trusts set out in s 78 of that Act.

4 But see Subsection 11.1.5 — *Trusts inter vivos* [classification (C) 1] later in this chapter.

Oral transactions are, however, unsatisfactory in practice because of the difficulty of producing adequate evidence of them.

So-called "precatory trusts" are also unsatisfactory because they arise where the settlor has not directed what is to be done, but has used words expressing what the settlor desires or recommends, for example, "To Mary hoping she will use the funds for our children". It is often difficult in such cases to determine whether or not an express trust has been created. The term is usually used to refer to cases where an express trust has not been created, that is, to cases where the expression of the will-maker is held to be too weak and indefinite to amount to an express trust. One or two examples are mentioned in Subsection 12.2.1 — *The three certainties*.

11.1.2 Implied or presumed trusts [classification (A) 2]

In this subsection, and that which follows, we will consider trusts arising under judge-made law, that is, implied or presumed trusts, resulting trusts, and constructive trusts. A reader of the cases is not helped by the courts' sometimes imprecise use of these terms,[5] although, in modern times, the distinctions between these various types of trust are breaking down. A conventional classification follows.

11.1.2.1 Implied or presumed trusts generally

Implied or presumed trusts are not to be confused with inadequate expressions of trust, of which precatory trusts are an example.

An "implied trust" is *not a badly-expressed express trust*, even though there may be some overlap between the beneficiaries under a failed express trust, and those under an implied trust. Such beneficiaries take by operation of law under the implied trust, not under the failed express trust.

An implied trust is one that is deemed by the court to arise not from the express declaration of the settlor, but from the conduct of the parties and the surrounding circumstances. In an implied trust, the settlor has made *no expression of the terms of the trust*, but the court considers that, nevertheless, in the circumstances, the settlor must have intended that the property involved be held on trust.

The court discovers and gives effect to the presumed intention of the parties. For example, it is well-established that, if A purchases property, or contributes towards it, but directs that it be transferred into the name of B, it will be presumed that B holds the property, wholly or partially, in trust for A who provided the purchase moneys.[6]

5 For example, the courts will sometimes hold that the defendant holds the property on a "resulting or constructive" trust and today, as we are going to see, in some cases the two terms overlap. The writer will submit that a resulting trust is a type of implied trust.

6 In *Hussey v Palmer* [1972] 1 WLR 1286, Lord Denning MR said at 1290:

Such a presumption may be rebutted on the production of evidence that no trust was intended, and that A intended to make a gift of the property to B. There will be no presumption of trust when the property is purchased in the name of a child of the purchaser, or in the name of a person in relation to whom the purchaser stands "in loco parentis" (in the position of a parent) — the law presumes a gift in these instances. If one spouse purchases property in the name of the other spouse, and the couple cease living together, the position is governed by the provisions of the Property (Relationships) Act 1976, as we will outline under the next sub-heading.

One instance of implied trust is called a "resulting trust". **Resulting trusts** occur when a transferor of the property can be presumed not to have intended the recipient of the legal title to be the beneficial owner. As a result, the recipient of the legal title must retain the property for the transferor, in the absence of any contrary intention. There are in 2 categories of resulting trusts: "apparent gifts", which cover voluntary conveyance and purchase of property in the name of another person, and "failing trusts", which cover express trusts that fail because of uncertainty and other invalidating reasons, and incomplete disposal of a beneficial interest.[7]

In *In Re Walsh, Keenan v Brown* (1911) 30 NZLR 1166, the will-maker in his will, which was made in 1907, appointed as trustee a minister by the name of Keenan, but the will did not say what the terms of the trust were. Three years later, on his deathbed, the will-maker attempted to give the necessary instructions to Keenan by way of a testamentary disposition, but died before the latter's notes were properly executed. The trust failed as a secret trust under the law relating to secret trusts (which we are not concerned with), and it did not succeed as a testamentary trust because Keenan's notes were not validly executed. The Court held that Keenan held the property concerned on a resulting trust for the next of kin of the will-maker.

> "Thus we have repeatedly held that, when one person contributes towards the purchase price of a house, the owner holds it on a constructive trust for him, proportionate to his contribution, even though there is no agreement between them, and no declaration of trust can be found, and no evidence of any intention to create a trust".

As well as providing authority for our proposition, this statement illustrates the confusing terminology to which we have already alluded (although, as we are going to see in Subsection 11.1.3 — *Constructive trusts [classification (A) 3]*, today there is considerable overlap between resulting trusts and constructive trusts).

7 In this case, the fund was not treated as a *charitable* fund (see the discussion of Certainty of Object in Subsection 12.2.1 — *The three certainties*) — two-thirds of the subscribers were content to leave their subscriptions in the society concerned, and the law relating to charities was not raised. Nowadays, such a fund would be dealt with under Part 4 of the Charitable Trusts Act 1957 (Schemes in Respect of Charitable Funds Raised by Voluntary Contribution), which sets out the steps to be taken when it becomes impossible, impracticable or inexpedient etc to carry out the charitable purpose for which the money has been raised, and the money has not been entirely applied for the purpose after the expiration of one year from its receipt.

11.1.2.2 Ownership of the family home when a de facto couple have split up

From 1 February 2002, it was no longer necessary to make a distinction between married couples and unmarried couples. Similarly, from 26 April 2005, the Civil Union Act 2004 included civil unions. The Property (Relationships) Act applies instead of common law and equity. Consequently, no resulting or constructive trust will arise as between relationship partners. Instead, the Act provides that assets are classified according to a mixture of ownership and use. The Act applies to de facto heterosexual relationships, same-sex relationships, marriage and civil unions. The details of the Property (Relationships) Act relating to the division of property when a relationship ends is beyond the scope of this text. Suffice to say that, if the relationship has existed for over 3 years, all property that comes within the definition of relationship property is divided equally between the parties, unless a court considers that there were extraordinary circumstances that make equal sharing repugnant to justice.

However, if a de facto relationship ended before 1 February 2002, the situation set out below will apply. Additionally, if two people share property but they are not in a relationship, such as friends or relatives, implied or constructive trusts may still be relevant.

The problem for the courts[8] was that the partners, when they acquired and occupied property, frequently did not direct their minds to the consequences of a break-up in the relationship. When the home, which, more often than not, was mortgaged, had been acquired in the name of only one of the partners, the other, upon their ceasing to live together, often claimed an interest in it, and it was to the law relating to implied (or constructive[9]) trusts that we turned to for resolution. It is useful to give a short account of the evolution of the law. The *old* position (now regarded as outdated) was set out in *Burns v Burns* [1984] 1 All ER 244, which will be considered next.

The home, in which the couple had lived for seventeen years, had been acquired with the man's money with the aid of a mortgage, and had been purchased in his name. The woman, who did not work for most of the period, and who changed her name by statutory declaration to be the same as that of the man, and who masqueraded as his wife, brought up their 2 children and decorated the home, but made no significant *financial* contribution towards it or to the partnership. The couple split up, and the woman claimed an interest in the home — to be more explicit, she claimed that the man held the home on a resulting trust for both of them in such shares as the court might determine.

8 Who have taken the view that "the mere existence of a de facto relationship (however defined) does not raise a presumed entitlement to share" — Richardson J in *Gillies v Keogh* [1989] 2 NZLR 327 at 348.

9 These cases are presently regarded as being also cases of constructive trusts — see footnote 14.

The judge at first instance declined her claim, and the English Court of Appeal, after a careful review of the relevant law, upheld the judge — essentially because the woman had made *no financial* contribution towards the acquisition of the home or to the partnership. The argument centred around whether there was in existence an implied trust from the common intention of the parties, which requirement became more liberally interpreted in the 1970s.

May LJ noted at 264 that "there is of course an air of unreality about the whole exercise", referring to the fact that the inquiry is retrospective. Nevertheless, it had to be attempted, and, at 259, he quoted a passage from Lord Denning MR's judgment in *Falconer v Falconer* [1970] 3 All ER 449; 1 WLR 1333, which laid down that whether or not a home which stands in the name of [one partner] alone is, nevertheless:

> "... held to belong to them both jointly (in equal or unequal shares) [depends] not so much [on] an agreement, express or implied, but rather [on] a trust which is *imposed* by law".

Lord Denning MR explained:

> "The law imputes to [the partners] an intention to create a trust, the one for the other. It does so by way of an *inference* from their conduct and the surrounding circumstances, even though the parties themselves made no agreement on it. This inference of a trust, the one for the other, is readily drawn when each has made a financial contribution to the purchase price or to the mortgage instalments. The financial contribution may be *direct*, as where it is actually stated to be a contribution towards the price or the instalments. It may be *indirect*, as where both go out to work, the one pays the housekeeping and the other the mortgage instalments. It does not matter which way round it is. It does not matter who pays what. So long as there is a substantial financial contribution towards the family expenses, it raises the inference of a trust. But where it is insubstantial, no such inference can be drawn ...".

May LJ denied that the court had power "to do what is fair and reasonable in all the circumstances", and later said at 265:

> "Finally, when the house is taken in the man's name alone, if the woman makes no 'real' or 'substantial' financial contribution towards either the purchase price, deposit or mortgage instalments by means of which the family home was acquired, then she is not entitled to any share in the beneficial interest in that home even though over a very substantial number of years she may have worked just as hard as the man in maintaining the family, in the sense of keeping house, giving birth to and looking after and helping to bring up the children of the union".

This decision would not have been reached if Valerie Burns and Patrick Burns had been *married*. In this event, Valerie Burns would (in New Zealand) have been basically entitled to a one-half share in the home, under the provisions of the Matrimonial Property Act 1976.

A seminal case of some importance, more liberally regarded, occurred in New Zealand in *Hayward v Giordani* [1983] NZLR 140 (CA).

Miss Sanders and Mr Hayward, the plaintiff, lived happily together in a bach at Orewa, purchased in Miss Sanders' name with her money, until her unexpected death in 1978. The plaintiff worked full-time for the first half of that period, and as an art tutor for the balance of it earning then about $2,500 per annum. He gave to Miss Sanders (whom he affectionately referred to as "the exchequer") most of his earnings, and by his own labour effected very considerable improvements to the property, both inside and out. The evidence established (to the satisfaction of the Court of Appeal, although not to that of Moller J in the court below) that it was the common intention of the parties that both owned the property, although the property was never transferred into their joint names. Miss Sanders had offered to do this, but such offers had been brushed aside by the plaintiff as being unnecessary and inconvenient. There was no solicitor at Orewa, there would be some cost involved, and anyway Miss Sanders was 20 years younger than the plaintiff and would thus survive him, making such a course of action unnecessary. After Miss Sanders' death, a will, unknown to the plaintiff and obviously forgotten by Miss Sanders, was found leaving the property to the defendant. The plaintiff claimed a trust in his favour as to a one-half share in the property.

The Court of Appeal held that:

1. In the case of implied and constructive trusts, the requirements of writing laid down by s 7 of the Statute of Frauds 1677 United Kingdom [then still in force in New Zealand] have been regarded as inapplicable[10] as, indeed, has been recognised by the modern English legislation [and now by the modern New Zealand legislation[11]].
2. The requirement of common intention of the parties was met by necessary inference from the conduct of the parties, and that the defendant held the property upon an implied trust for the plaintiff as to a one-half share.
3. Although, in view of 2. above, it was not necessary to do so, the Court was prepared to hold that a constructive trust arose for the plaintiff as to a one-half share. Cooke J (as he then was) quoted earlier authority foreshadowing the "reasonable expectations" test that we are shortly going to encounter, and then said at 148:

10 *Gissing v Gissing* [1971] AC 886. The actual decision reached by the House of Lords in this case would not be reached today. In New Zealand, upon dissolution of marriage (or separation), the former spouses share equally in the matrimonial home unless, having regard to the contribution of each spouse to the marriage partnership, equal sharing would be repugnant to justice.

11 See Subsection 11.1.5 — *Trusts inter vivos [classification (C) 1].*

> "For the reasons outlined I would have been disposed to hold that a constructive trust arose here, flowing from the joint efforts of the parties and reasonable expectations, even if they had not applied their minds to the precise question".

A similar result to *Burns v Burns* (supra) was reached in *Pasi v Kamana* [1986] 1 NZLR 603, where *Burns v Burns* was referred to, but it is significant that Cooke P suggested the "reasonable expectations" test. He said at 605:

> "... the test is to ask whether a reasonable person in the shoes of the claimant would have understood that his or her efforts would naturally result in an interest in the property".

In *Pasi v Kamana,* a de facto couple, who had no children of their own, split up after 10 years of living together. The home, which was *not* heavily mortgaged, had been purchased in the man's name and paid for by him primarily out of the proceeds of a successful damages claim brought as a result of his motor accident. The woman (who had worked throughout most of the period, but had not made any improvements to the property) claimed in her favour a trust in the home as to a one-half share, based on the common intention of the parties. The Court of Appeal (affirming the decision of the court below) denied her claim because she had made no significant *financial* contribution, direct or indirect, to the purchase of the home. The Court was of the view that it was not the common intention of the parties that the home be owned jointly, that nothing from the woman "can be identified as a contribution, direct or indirect, to the property", and that she had contributed to the partnership no more than she had received in accommodation and domestic benefits.

The more liberal approach heralded in *Hayward v Giordani* (supra) was developed in *Oliver v Bradley* [1987] 1 NZLR 586, where it was apparent that the New Zealand Court of Appeal was prepared to put the entitlement of a de facto spouse on a wider basis than that enunciated in *Burns v Burns* (supra). *Oliver v Bradley* concerned a de facto couple who split up after four years of living together — the break-up being attributable to the woman. Cooke P spoke of the expectations of "a reasonable person" in the shoes of the plaintiff and the defendant, respectively, and, at 590, said that:

> "contributions may include housekeeping or looking after children, if the other party has been enabled to earn or acquire assets. In principle I would not exclude anything that has formed part of the consortium provided by one or other partner".

At 593, Henry J said that:

> "The continued possession of the property and its enjoyment was due to the financial contributions of the appellant, and to the general household contributions of by the respondent as well as the continuing availability of the advances made to her. It seems to me impossible to make a distinction between them other than on a basis of equality".

It was held that the woman had a trust in the home as to a one-third share, even though most *of the financial* contributions towards it and towards the partnership had come from the man.

In the leading case of *Gillies v Keogh* [1989] 2 NZLR 327, inessential facts of which are omitted, a de facto couple split up after 3 years of living together. The man claimed an interest in the home, which had been bought in the woman's name with her money, by virtue of the considerable physical work that he had done in improving it. The Court of Appeal considered that whether or not a (implied or constructive) trust existed depended primarily on the reasonable expectations of the parties — would a reasonable person, in the shoes of the man, consider that he had an interest in the property, and would a reasonable person, in the shoes of the woman, consider that she had ceded an interest in the property. At 331, Cooke P said that:

> "Whatever legal label or rubric cases in this field are placed under, reasonable expectations in the light of the conduct of the parties are at the heart of the matter".

At 333, he said:

> "The practical position now reached in de facto union cases by all the various routes appears to me to be that the Courts have regard to the reasonable expectations of persons in the shoes of the respective parties ...".

The Court did not consider that it could decide the matter merely on the arbitrary notion of fairness or justice. The Court denied the existence of the (constructive) trust in the man's favour found to exist in the court below, because it held on the evidence that the woman had made it plain throughout that she did not intend to cede an interest in the home and that she regarded it as hers alone. There was thus no basis on which a reasonable person, in the shoes of the man, could have expected that he was acquiring an interest in the property; and the case is authority for the proposition that a (implied or constructive) trust will not be applied when this is contrary to the clearly-expressed intention of the partner who purchased the property and who holds legal title. As Cooke P said at 334:

> "The principle of freedom to stipulate against any trust or obligation is consistent with all the theories. ... Counsel for the appellant was on sound ground in submitting that the sole legal owner can protect his or her position simply by making it clear to the other party that, while the use of the property is shared, ownership is not".

He said at 330:

> "Put shortly ... an interest or monetary right by way of constructive trust or otherwise cannot arise if a reasonable person in the claimant's position would have understood that he or she was not to receive one".

The case also made it clear that domestic services may be as significant as, or more significant than, financial contributions; and we have now departed from *Burns v Burns* (supra).

Gillies v Keogh and the "reasonable expectations" test were affirmed in dicta in the Court of Appeal in *Phillips v Phillips* [1993] 3 NZLR 159, and the reasoning in *Gillies v Keogh* was adopted and applied by the High Court in *Daly v Gilbert* [1993] 3 NZLR 731, and by the Court of Appeal in *Lankow v Rose* [1995] 1 NZLR 277 (followed in *McMahon v McMahon* [1996] 3 NZLR 334).

In summary, the individual facts of these de factos' cases were particularly important in determining the property rights of the partners on the break-up of a relationship. The Court basically had regard to the following factors and worked its way through the following steps:

- Factor 1 — The starting point was the legal title.
- Factor 2 — Any unequivocal expression of intention as to ownership made by the partner who had disposing power over the property. If such an expression has been made, it is paramount — *Gillies v Keogh* (supra).
- Factor 3 — In the absence of Factor 2, the unequivocally expressed, or necessarily inferred, intention of both partners, *Hayward v Giordani* (supra). (Subjective intention has no legal effect at this point.)
- Factor 4 — In the absence of Factor 2 and Factor 3, the respective financial contributions of the partners to the purchase of the property and their respective contributions to mortgage payments and other outgoings (resulting trust — *Pasi v Kamana* (supra), *Cossey v Bach* [1992] 3 NZLR 612.[12]
- Factor 5 — Factor 4 could be *varied* by the reasonable expectations of the parties, and this was the basic test where the partners had made no expression as to ownership, *Oliver v Bradley* (supra). This is a constructive trust based upon what a reasonable person, in the shoes of the claimant, would have expected was their entitlement. Factor 5 was particularly important in stable relationships of long standing.

11.1.3 Constructive trusts [classification (A) 3]

This is an area of the law that is large and rapidly developing. A constructive trust is a fiduciary obligation imposed by the court. Traditionally, it arises when no trust has been created but when it would, according to the principles

12 In *Cossey v Bach* (supra), which had unusual facts raising questions (under the Matrimonial Property Act 1976) beyond the scope of this text, Fisher J examined the New Zealand law on the division of de facto marriage property. He adopted *Gillies v Keogh* (supra), and the "reasonable expectations" test in it, and also made clear that domestic (in addition to financial) contributions of a partner can now be taken into account. His judgment contains a two-page "Summary of principles for the common law division of de facto marriage property".

of equity, be improper for the court to allow the person on whom it imposes the trust to assert beneficial ownership.

In these cases, the court deals with the property involved as though it was subject to a trust, even though no trust had in fact been created by the person holding the property. A constructive trust differs fundamentally from the other types of trust in that there is no intention to create a trust on the part of such a person. A constructive trust is something imposed on the person by the court for equitable reasons.

When, for example, fiduciaries derive a profit from property held by them on behalf of someone else, they are deemed to hold such profit as trustee for the other. Such a position will clearly arise when people, such as solicitors, are holding money in trust for another, and make use of the trust moneys to make a profit for themselves. Equity compels them to hold the profit as trustee for the other person. It will also arise in the case of any other persons in a fiduciary position, such as agents or partners, who are entrusted with the property of others, and may be in a position to derive some personal gain or profit from its use.

Constructive trusts were fully developed in company law with regard to directors, who have been treated as standing in a fiduciary position in relation to the company. These developments have been partially codified in the Companies Act 1993, but the basic position remains unchanged. Directors of a company are in a fiduciary position and cannot, at the expense of the company, make a profit for themselves out of that position. For example, in *Clayton v Chambers* (1912) 32 NZLR 65, three men formed a company for the purpose of obtaining in the Gisborne district, and selling in London, (primarily) oil prospecting concessions. They had previously contracted that any concession obtained by any of them should be held jointly in trust for all of them, but Clayton alleged that he alone was entitled to certain concessions obtained by him. There was a conflict of evidence on whether or not the contract had been discharged by agreement, but the Court of Appeal held that this did not matter — after the company was formed, Clayton, as a director of the company, "stood in a fiduciary position", and he could not thereafter "obtain for his own benefit [and through the use of company connections] concessions which it was in the interests of the company to obtain". He held the concessions concerned as constructive trustee for the company.

For a further traditional example, in *Morrin v Kissling* (1878) 4 NZ Jur (NS) CA 1, Kissling, a land agent, was engaged for commission to purchase for the plaintiffs a certain block of land[13] (which he must, in view of the subsequent court proceedings, have thought a very attractive purchase). The plaintiffs,

13 In the converse situation, a real estate agent cannot, without the consent of the principal on the prescribed form, purchase any land that the agent is commissioned by the principal to sell — Real Estate Agents Act 1976, s 63 (stated briefly).

from the outset, were prepared to pay the commission, and they remained prepared to pay it throughout the proceedings. Kissling obtained a purchase of the land concerned in his own name and then refused to accept payment of his commission and to re-transfer the land to the plaintiffs. As regards the points now under our consideration, the Court held that Kissling was in the same position as a purchaser with notice of an equity, and that he held the land as a constructive trustee for the plaintiffs.

A broadly similar situation arose in *Dickie v Torbay Pharmacy (1986) Ltd* (1995) 5 NZBLC 103,918; [1995] 3 NZLR 429, dealt with in Appendix 2.

In recent years, there has been an explosion of constructive trusts, and it is trite but correct to say that this is now a difficult, confused, and developing area of the law. Also, it now appears that the categories of "resulting trust" and "constructive trust" are not entirely separate and distinct and that, in joint enterprise property cases, there is overlap between the two.[14]

Constructive trusts are being applied to an increasing variety of situations — including the allied fields of banking and commerce but, because of the lack of unanimity, it is impossible to say what is the underlying basis. Former detailed rules are being regarded merely as guidelines. Modern cases reveal:

- a lack of uniformity in the approach taken in different parts of the Commonwealth[15]
- that the New Zealand courts are not committed to any one approach, and
- a considerable degree of imprecision in the principles to be applied.

All that we can do is to discuss some examples and, to avoid encumbering the text, these examples appear in Appendix 2. Thus, in the discussion that follows, when a case name is followed by an asterisk, a summary of the case is to be found in Appendix 2. General observations:

- *Wide cases* — For many years, constructive trusts were, as we have said, determined by the principles of equity, but there have now been some very wide cases. Denning MR in *Hussey v Palmer* [1972] 1 WLR 1286*, abandoned the principles and put the determination of constructive trusts upon a wider basis. He said there that constructive trusts are

14 This comment has relevance to the previous law relating to ownership of the family home when a de facto couple split up. Trusts allowed under this heading were treated by modern judges as being both resulting and constructive trusts, and the terms were used almost indiscriminately. (This is consistent with *Hayward v Giordani* (supra) where the Court of Appeal, having held that the defendant held the property on an implied trust, proceeded to express its willingness to hold that the defendant held the property on a constructive trust, but stated that it did not wish to resolve this fully as it was not necessary to do so in that case.)

15 As Richardson J said in *Gillies v Keogh* (supra) at 341:

> "In both Canada and Australia the highest Courts have taken the matter further by invoking, in Canada, the doctrine of unjust enrichment and, in Australia, the principle of unconscionability".

founded upon large principles and are to be applied "whenever justice and good conscience require it", and this has been applied quite extensively in Canada. In *Stratulatos v Stratulatos* [1988] 2 NZLR 424*, McGechan J declined to specifically commit himself on this, but clearly favoured the imposition of a constructive trust upon a wide basis, while in *Powell v Thompson* [1991] 1 NZLR 597*, the constructive trust rests upon the sole notion of unconscionability. These wide cases, in effect, give the judge power to make a decision on the basis of what she or he considers to be fair and just in the circumstances of the particular case, but the New Zealand courts have, on more than one occasion, denied that the judge has this power. In other words, these wide cases have not been without criticism, and they have not been universally accepted.

- *"Knowing receipt" cases* — *Powell v Thompson* (supra)*, *Elders Pastoral Ltd v Bank of New Zealand* (1989) 2 NZBLC 103,667; [1989] 2 NZLR 180 (CA)*, and *Lankshear v ANZ Banking Group (New Zealand) Ltd* (1992) 4 NZBLC 102,770; [1993] 1 NZLR 481 (HC)*, fall into this category. To the extent that the old rules required a recipient of trust property to stand in a fiduciary relationship to the claimant, this is no longer so. Also, these cases confirm that *constructive knowledge* of an adverse interest is sufficient. Thus it now appears that, if anyone receives property with constructive knowledge of the claimant's interest, a constructive trust will be imposed on him if it is unconscionable for him to retain the property as against the claimant, although the principles require elaboration.
- *Liability of bankers (bankers' cases)* — While a banker is not under any general duty to inquire into the circumstances of the deposit and payment of a cheque, and will not be held to be a constructive trustee of the funds merely because the depositor is not entitled to them, *Lankshear v ANZ Banking Group (New Zealand) Ltd* (supra)* indicates that the bank, if it obtained an advantage out of the dealing, will be held to be a constructive trustee if it has constructive knowledge of the claimant's interest. At the first instance hearing in *DFC New Zealand Ltd v Goddard* [1992] 2 NZLR 445 (CA)*, a bank had been held to be a constructive trustee just because a term deposit had been kept on call for a few extra days while instructions were sought, rather than being repaid in accordance with original instructions. However, a measure of moderation and relief for bankers came when this decision was reversed in the Court of Appeal, as it did with the decision in *Nimmo v Westpac Banking Corporation* [1993] 3 NZLR 218* (HC).

In conclusion, this area of the law is still developing and has *not crystallised*. Typical of its state is *Liggett v Kensington* (1992) 4 NZBLC 102,574; [1993] 1 NZLR 257 (CA), which arose out of the collapse of the Goldcorp companies. Goldcorp Exchange Limited published advertisements inviting members of the public to buy gold bullion (primarily from itself), and represented that the total of gold so purchased, although not individually allocated, would be held by the company for the respective purchasers, who could call up their respective purchase at any time. The company undertook to maintain at all times sufficient reserves of gold to meet its commitments to purchasers. As Gault J said in NZBLC at 102,597; NZLR at 282:

> "2. In the state of public knowledge of bullion dealing in New Zealand, the significance of references by the company to bullion purchased as 'non-allocated' would not have been understood by most private purchasers who were quite justified on the information disseminated by the company in believing that the gold or silver they had purchased was owned by them and stored on their behalf".

However, the actions of the company did not match its representations — reserves of gold equalling the amount purchased were not retained, and the purchase moneys were just paid into the general funds of the company. When the company, insolvent, went into receivership, both the purchasers, and the Bank of New Zealand as a secured creditor, respectively, claimed what reserves of gold the company was holding. The Court of Appeal in a *majority* decision, held that the purchasers of gold had priority as they held the reserves upon a constructive trust. The reserves were impressed with the constructive trust before they passed to the Bank of New Zealand under its security. The Court was *not explicit* on the underlying basis of the constructive trust, but presumably it arose from the Court's finding that the company stood in a fiduciary position in relation to members of the public who had purchased gold, and Gault J spoke of it being "unconscionable for the party into whose hands the property came to retain it against the claimant". He said in NZBLC at 102,596; NZLR at 281:

> "No general principle or principles yet have emerged of which these cases may be said to be particular examples. In some the dominant factor appears to have been that an equitable interest in moneys was regarded as not having been relinquished and in others it appears to have been unconscionability in retaining moneys against claimants. In this developing field which is one in which the principles of law and equity are being melded in many jurisdictions, it would be unwise and conducive of inflexibility to attempt any general judicial formulation".

The case went to the Privy Council,[16] which took a different view of the facts and ruled against a constructive trust, finding that there was no specific property to which a constructive trust could attach.

16 *Re Goldcorp Exchange Ltd (In Receivership): Kensington v Liggett* (1994) 5 NZBLC 103,453; [1994] 3 NZLR 385. See also *MacIntosh v Fortex Group Ltd* (1997) 6 NZBLC 102,141; [1997] 1 NZLR 711 (HC).

In *Murrell v Hamilton* [2014] NZCA 377, the Court of Appeal said that a constructive trust can be imposed over the assets of an express trust.

In *Vervoort v Forrest* [2016] NZCA 375 (4 August 2016), the Court of Appeal stated:

> "... the reality of a trustee's ability to give a third party expectations ... over trust property ... must be recognised. There is no misappropriation of property in that the beneficiaries of the express trust have no claim in conscience to the increases in value resulting from the contributions. Beneficiaries cannot expect trustees to retain for them an unearned benefit, extracted by expectations engendered by the trustees. ...". [70]

The facts of the *Vervoort* case were that Ms A lived with Mr B for 12 years. He had formed a trust before he met her and the trust bought a property while they were together. Ms A said she helped to find the property, decorate it, maintain it, maintain its garden, and do other such things to preserve or enhance its value. When the relationship ended, she made a claim of a constructive trust against the property.

The Court of Appeal held that:

- The trust was not a sham even though Mr B "intended to control it". [28]
- "[Mr B] undoubtedly exercised de facto control of the Trust ...". [36]
- The trust was not an illusory trust.
- The fact that a trustee "in breach of his obligations as a trustee, left the management of the Trust to [Mr B] did not make the Trust expire". [39]

In such circumstances, the Court held (at [39]) that Ms A could make:

- a claim for breach of trust
- a claim of negligence, and
- a claim based on constructive trust.

The judgment is important not only for the fact that it is authority that a constructive trust can be imposed over the assets of an express trust, but also for the Court's acceptance of effective control.

The Court stated:

> "Where one partner has de facto control of the trust and ... contributions and expectations have arisen the non-controlling partner may be forced to claim against the trust ...". [48]

In *Vervoort*, the Court of Appeal has established that a constructive trust can and should be imposed over the assets of an express trust if equity requires it and that it is not necessary that all trustees must have known of the facts that have given rise to a constructive trust over the trust's assets.

The continuing development of this area of the law is of particular interest to persons in positions of power and advantage, such as solicitors, accountants and professional advisors, who can be made accountable for gains that they have made improperly by virtue of their position or their relationship with others.

11.1.4 Private and charitable trusts [classification (B)]

A further classification of considerable importance is the division into private trusts and charitable trusts. All trusts are private, except public trusts, which are recognised as coming within the legal meaning of "charitable". It is not easy to give a definition of what the law regards as a charitable object. Although the modern tendency is towards a more liberal interpretation, some objects that would be regarded by most people as charitable are not recognised as such by the law, and others that come within the legal meaning would not generally be regarded as charitable in the popular sense.

The courts have regarded the list of objects set out in the preamble to the Statute of Elizabeth I (Charitable Uses Act 1601) as the starting point for determining whether or not any trust is for a charitable object and, although the language is archaic, this list of objects[17] is still important. This, however, is not a closed list, and other objects which by analogy have been deemed to come within the "spirit and intendment" of the preamble have also been held to be charitable. What must be regarded is not the wording of the preamble itself but, as we are going to see in the briefest degree, the effect of court decisions as to its scope.

The scope of the legal meaning of "charitable" was laid down in *Commissioners for Special Purposes of Income Tax v Pemsel* [1891] AC 531, where Lord Macnaghten, after considering the preamble and the many cases following it, classified those objects into four principal divisions. He stated:

> " 'Charity' in its legal sense comprises four principal divisions: Trusts for the relief of poverty, trusts for the advancement of education, trusts for the advancement of religion, and trusts for other purposes beneficial to the community not falling under any of the preceding heads".

This explanation obviously leaves a great deal of scope for difference of opinion on whether particular objects are charitable or not. However, although the meaning of "charitable" has been elaborated as a result of innumerable court decisions, Lord Macnaghten's classification remains the basic test. See Appendix 3 for a more details. Some extensions in the meaning

17 The relief of aged, impotent and poor people; the maintenance of sick and maimed soldiers and mariners, schools of learning, free schools and scholars in universities; the repairs of bridges, ports, havens, causeways, churches, sea-banks and highways; the education and preferment of orphans; the relief, stock or maintenance for houses of correction; the marriage of poor maids; the supportation, aid and help of young tradesmen, handicraftsmen and persons decayed; the relief or redemption of prisoners or captives; and the aid or ease of any poor inhabitants concerning the payment of fifteens, setting out of soldiers and other taxes.

of "charitable" have been made by the Charitable Trusts Act 1957 but, as we are going to see, this Act is concerned primarily with the administration of charitable trusts. Also, the facts of some cases may bring them under more than one class of charity, so that they do not fit exactly into one category.

This is not the end of the matter. We must also make the point clearly that, to be "charitable", it is not sufficient merely for a trust to have a charitable object — it must also meet three further requirements that we now consider.

1. *The trust must have public purpose.* This means that the beneficiaries must not be numerically negligible, and that their distinction from the rest of the community must not rest on their relationship to a particular individual or firm. In other words, the trust must be for the public or a section of the public. The requirement of public purpose has been rigorously applied by the courts in the past, although its exact scope is not now entirely certain. For example, in *Oppenheim v Tobacco Securities Trust Co Ltd* [1951] AC 297; [1951] 1 All ER 31, a large business concern set up, in perpetuity, an education fund for the children of its employees and former employees, and those of related companies, under which the children of approximately 100,000 employees would have qualified. The House of Lords held that the scheme failed as a charitable trust because membership of it was not open to the public, but was dependent upon an employment-relationship with the businesses concerned. However, in *Dingle v Turner* [1972] AC 601, which confirmed that, by way of exception, a trust for the relief of poverty among employees of a company is a valid charitable trust, the House of Lords stated that the requirement of public purpose generally is not dependent on any one factor alone. It is a question of degree, which must be considered in all the circumstances of each and every case, and, in particular, with regard to the purpose of the trust. In the light of this latter case, it is almost certain that a scheme such as was before the Court in the *Oppenheim* case, would be more liberally regarded today.[18]

   As we have implied, trusts for the relief of poverty constitute an exception to this requirement of public purpose.[19]

18 Regarding the uncertainty that has been created primarily by *Dingle v Turner* (supra), Somers J said in *New Zealand Society of Accountants v C of IR* (1986) 8 NZTC 5,205; [1986] 1 NZLR 147 (the facts of which will not illuminate our discussion), at 5,206–5,207:

> "While it has been repeatedly held that a trust to be charitable must be of a public nature, that is to say for the benefit of the community or a section of it, as opposed to a gift for the benefit of particular individuals or a fluctuating body of private individuals, it is not possible, at least in the present state of the authorities, to state with any confidence how the line is drawn between the two or to say that it is drawn in the same way as between different types of charitable trust".

19 As was recognised by the Supreme Court of Canada, following *Dingle v Turner* (supra), in *Jones v TEaton Co Ltd* [1973] SCR 635.

2. *The trust must be*, at least to some extent, *of benefit to the public*. This similar requirement has always been more generously interpreted by the courts and, although it must be proved in relation to trusts falling within Lord Macnaghten's fourth category (trusts for other purposes beneficial to the community not falling under any of the preceding heads), it will be *presumed* in the case of trusts for the relief of poverty, trusts for the advancement of education, and trusts for the advancement of religion. However, the presumption is not irrebuttable, as is illustrated by *Cocks v Manners* (1871) LR 12 Eq 574, and *Gilmour v Coates* [1949] AC 426; [1949] 1 All ER 848 — both cases that involved bequests to closed ("contemplative" as opposed to "active") orders of nuns who did not preach the gospel to the public, perform any works of charity in the community or, indeed, engage in any activities outside the convent. The objects of the trusts were undoubtedly religious, but they were simply not of any benefit to the public. In *Gilmour v Coates*, it was contended that the example of the nuns' cloistered and devoted lives, and the effect of their prayers, were of some benefit to the public. The House of Lords held that neither of these contentions were susceptible of proof, and that the requirement now under discussion was not met.

3. *The trust must be capable of control by the court*. This means that, if it becomes necessary to do so (such as if the trustee dies), the nature of the trust must be such that the court is able to direct a due administration of it. There are not many cases on this requirement — the best known one probably being *Re Hummeltenberg* [1923] 1 Ch 237; [1923] All ER 49, which concerned a trust for "training and developing suitable persons, male and female, as [spiritualistic] mediums". Russell J, as well as holding that it was not proved that the trust was of benefit to the public, obviously considered that the court could not give directions on the training of persons for the purpose of communicating with the dead. After quoting a passage from Lord Eldon's judgment in *Morice v Bishop of Durham* (1805) 10 Ves 522, 539,[20] he said that the present case "would appear to be a trust the administration of which the Court would be quite unable to undertake or control".

The Crown has a duty to protect property devoted to charitable objects, and it is one of the duties of the Attorney-General (through the Crown Law Office) to represent and protect the interests of beneficiaries.

20 "As it is a maxim, that the execution of a trust shall be under the control of the court, it must be of such a nature that it can be under that control; so that the administration of it can be reviewed by the Court; or, if the trustee dies, the Court itself can execute the trust; a trust therefore, which, in case of mal-administration could be reformed; and a due administration directed; and then, unless the subject and the objects can be ascertained, upon principles, familiar in other cases, it must be decided, that the Court can neither reform mal-administration, nor direct a due administration."

It can be important to determine whether or not a trust is charitable, because charitable trusts enjoy certain privileges not accorded to private trusts. The principal privileges of charitable trusts are:

- Charitable trusts will not fail for uncertainty of purpose and/or uncertainty of beneficiaries, as we are going to see in the next chapter.
- Charitable trusts enjoy special taxation exemptions — the principal statutory provisions being cited below.
- Charitable trusts enjoy 2 exemptions, which we are also going to see in the next chapter, from the rule against perpetuities:
  - Where there is a disposition of a limited interest to a charity and the remainder is given to a second charity, the disposition of the remainder to the second charity (on a charitable trust) does not have to comply with the rule against perpetuities.
  - Provided that the interest of the charitable trust itself vests within the perpetuity period, charitable trusts of income do not have to comply with the rule. Such trusts can therefore be perpetual, which private trusts cannot. (You can now see why the issue of "charitable" was so important in *Oppenheim*'s case above.)

It is conceded that, from what has been said so far in this text, the reader will not yet be able to fully appreciate the above privileges. Nevertheless, in our brief discussion, it is best to introduce them at this point. The meaning of privileges will emerge later from the next chapter and Chapter 13 — *Illegal Trusts*.

11.1.5 Trusts inter vivos [classification (C) 1]

Trusts inter vivos are set up directly as such by settlors to operate during their lifetime. The most satisfactory way for a settlor to create a trust inter vivos is by deed, although a deed is not essential, as the reader will realise from the preceding discussion.

As with all trusts, no formal language is necessary for the creation of a trust inter vivos. Such a trust over personal property can even be created orally. However, trusts inter vivos of land have to be in writing.

As we are going to see under Subheading 12.2.2.1 — *Cases where the intended trustee is to be someone other than the settlor*, where the trustee of a trust of land is someone other than the settlor, a Transfer Instrument (in favour of the trustee) must be registered at Land Information NZ (LINZ). Where the settlor is the trustee, the modern statutory provisions [replacing those of the Statute of Frauds 1677 (United Kingdom)] provide that a declaration of trust of land must be *evidenced* in writing signed by the settlor.

Section 25 of the Property Law Act 2007 provides that a trust must be created in writing and signed by the settlor if it relates to land; and it is to take effect in the lifetime of the settlor. However, this does not apply to a short-term lease, the creation or operation of a resulting, implied, or constructive trust, the making or operation of a will; or the disposition of any interest in land by operation of law.

The Statute of Frauds 1677 (United Kingdom) required written evidence (of the transactions to which it applied), and was in force for a long period of time, during which it became an established principle in the courts that they would not allow the statute to be made an instrument of fraud. This still appears to apply in spite of the clear statutory requirements. Notwithstanding the lack of writing, the courts will, in appropriate cases, admit oral evidence that a conveyance was not to a person beneficially but was really on trust. *Pearce v Public Trustee* [1916] GLR 125, affords an example.[21]

11.1.6 Trusts arising under wills [classification (C) 2]

These are trusts that come into operation only on the death of the will-maker and then constitute part of the administration of the will-maker's estate pursuant to the will-maker's will. Such trusts are expressed in the will and form part of the will. As wills, other than those of military or seagoing persons, are required to be in writing, it follows that (apart from the "doctrine of secret trusts", which is beyond the scope of this text), such trusts, as part of the will, must necessarily be in writing.

This type of trust is common. It is often created by will-makers who have infant children and wish that there should not be an immediate distribution of their property should they die soon, but that property be held for distribution to their children on their attaining the age of majority or such later age as the will-maker may direct.

Law: Property (Relationships) Act 1976, ss 4, 11
Estate and Gift Duties Act 1968, s 73
Property Law Act 2007, s 25

21 This case concerned a separated husband and wife. The house property involved was inhabited by the plaintiff (the wife) with most of her children, and had been built up entirely at her cost. The husband had contributed nothing to the family. The plaintiff had transferred the property to a son, allegedly with his consent, and with the objective of keeping it away from the husband, upon the following terms:

> "After my death he was to hold it for his sisters and brothers, including himself. . .. The property was not given to him. He was to hold it as trustee for his sisters and brothers. It was mine during my life, and then to go to my children, to three sons and two daughters".

This statement was completely corroborated by the evidence of the plaintiff's solicitor, who had prepared the Memorandum of Transfer to the son. There was nothing in writing about the trust. The son died intestate, and the husband (as he was entitled, on the face of it, to do under the law as it stood in 1916, but would not be entitled to do now — see Chapter 9 — *Succession on Intestacy*) claimed an interest in the property under the rules of intestate succession.

Chapman J shortly held that the relevant provisions of the Statute of Frauds — the precursors to our present statutory provisions, had no application to a case like this, and that the son's estate was not entitled to the property beneficially but held it on an express trust for the plaintiff for life and thereafter for her children.

Chapter 12

Creation of an Express Trust and the Parties to a Trust

12.0 The parties to a trust

The settlor — Although certain special classes of persons, such as intellectually disabled persons, minors, and persons recognised by the court (under the provisions of the Protection of Personal and Property Rights Act 1988) as being incapable of managing their own affairs, have restricted capacity to create a trust, the general rule is that any person or body corporate legally capable of owning and dealing with property may create a trust. (Under the basic law of trusts [still prevailing], voluntary settlements[1] made by minors are voidable by them during their respective minorities, but become binding if not voided within a reasonable time after attaining the age of majority [18 years]. A minor can be a trustee, but the court will, upon application, appoint another person to act until the minor attains majority.)

The trustee — Similar comments as to settlors apply to trustees. Any adult, other than those in the special classes above, including a company,[2] can be a trustee. The reader should be aware, however, that a trustee, although a usual ingredient of a trust, is not an essential. Whereas a settlor and a beneficiary or beneficiaries are essentials, a trust will not fail merely for want of a trustee. If need be, the court will appoint a trustee.

Beneficiaries — Any person may be a beneficiary — even a person under a legal disability, such as a minor or a person with mental disabilities. The only general requirement is that the beneficiaries must be ascertainable with certainty. If the beneficiaries are not named by the trust instrument, they must, at least, from its terms, be ascertainable with certainty when the time arrives for distribution of the trust property.[3]

Law: Trusts Act 2019, ss 12–15

1 The situation is different if the trust is created as part of a contract entered into by the minor — see now the provisions of the Minors' Contracts Act 1969.

2 However, only a trustee company (see Chapter 7 — *Administrators*, footnote 4) can administer the estate of a deceased person.

3 *Re Laird* [1982] 2 NZLR 325, although not a particularly important case, is an illustration of this point.

12.1 The trust property

Any property may be the subject of a trust except property that is inalienable (not capable of being transferred away from the settlor). However, very little property is inalienable. Such property comprises mostly life interests and pensions of various kinds, for example, National Superannuation.

12.2 Creation of a trust

Knight v Knight (1840) 3 Beav 148, 49 ER 58, which concerned rather vague precatory words, established that there are three basic requirements for the creation of a valid express trust, that are usually referred to as the "three certainties". In addition, most trusts must be completely constituted.

12.2.1 The three certainties

Section 15 **Trusts Act 2019** provides that an express trust may be created by or under an enactment; or by a person (the settlor) who, clearly and with reasonable certainty (and subject to any formalities prescribed by any enactment) —

(i) indicates an intention to create a trust; and

(ii) identifies the beneficiaries (or classes of beneficiaries) or the permitted purpose of the trust; and

(iii) identifies the trust property.

These have commonly been referred to as the 3 certainties:

1. *Certainty of intention* — The first requirement is that the settlor must have clearly intended to create a trust. Where the trust is embodied in a professionally drafted deed or will, the intention will usually be made clear by the use of the words "upon trust" or a similar phrase, but, as we have seen, such words need not be used. It is always a question of whether, upon a true construction of all the words used, it was clearly the intention of the settlor to create a trust.

   Considerable difficulty is faced by the courts in deciding this question when the settlor has used precatory words, such as "in the hope that . . .", "in the belief that . . .", "in confidence that . . .". For example, a person may by will leave their property to their spouse "in the confident hope" that on their spouse's death they will in turn leave it to their children. Formerly, such expressions were regarded as creating a trust, but nowadays the courts are less inclined to recognise a trust unless this intention can be gathered from the tenor of the document as a whole.[4]

4 If such expressions are followed by a commonly inserted phrase such as "without however creating a binding trust in that regard", such phrase will, in all normal circumstances, negate the existence of a trust — *Re Singh (Deceased)* [1995] 2 NZLR 487.

If it appears that, although the will-maker used precatory words, they nevertheless intended such words to be imperative and intended to leave no element of discretion to the donee as to whether or not the expressed wish should be complied with, the court will uphold the existence of a trust.

On the other hand, a person may execute a deed that has the appearance of creating a trust by using such legal words as "upon trust", but, on a true construction of the document as a whole, it is clear that it was not their intention to create a trust at all. For example, they may merely intend to transfer their property to an agent for the purpose of paying creditors, while still retaining full control of the property. Such an arrangement is called an "illusory trust". Although it has the superficial appearance of a trust, it is not a trust at all.

2. *Certainty of subject-matter* — The property that is to be the subject-matter of the trust must be defined in clear and unambiguous terms. It must be certain. For example, this requirement was not met in *White v White* (1909) 28 NZLR 129, where the will-maker, after making prior gifts, made a gift of "a small portion of what is left" to Mary. It was held that this was too vague, and that Mary's gift failed for uncertainty of subject-matter.

3. *Certainty of object* — This requirement refers to the 2 related ingredients of purposes and beneficiaries. Under the "three certainties" doctrine, the objects of a trust must be clearly identifiable, and also the share or interest that each is to receive must be readily ascertainable.[5]

   A gift to a person with the direction that, on their death, it should be "kept in the family" would not result in an effective trust. The direction would fail as a trust on the ground of uncertainty of object.

We have said "Under the three certainties doctrine" in the "Certainity of object" paragraph because, in modern times, this third "certainty" is breaking down. In the many family trusts which are now being created (see Chapter 14 — *Introduction to Asset and Tax Planning*), it has become the practice to insert wide powers for the trustees to add or delete beneficiaries, and the validity of such provisions has been upheld in *Re Manisty's Settlement Trusts* [1973] 2 All ER 1203 and in *Re Hay's Settlement Trusts* [1981] 3 All ER 786. In *Re Manisty's Settlement*, the trustees were given power to add any beneficiaries except

5 In *Re Sparrow* [1984] 1 NZLR 750, the testatrix, a keen rugby fan, in a home-made will, left money to All Blacks Alex Wyllie and Sid Going, but the amounts that each was to receive, respectively, were not specified — the testatrix indicating that these would be decided later. The Court of Appeal rejected the contention that the dispositions were effective dispositions of the residue of her estate. Somers J, delivering the judgment of the Court, said "In the event the quantum of such benefit was never determined by her [the testatrix]. The gap cannot be filled by the Court". It was held that the gifts failed, and the case resolves itself into one of uncertainty of subject-matter.

certain specified persons and corporations,[6] and the Court held that, as long as it is possible to tell whether or not any given person falls within the specified class, it does not matter how wide the class is. The power was held not to infringe the certainty of objects rule. In *Re Hay's Settlement Trusts* (supra), where Sir Robert Megarry V-C said "dispositions ought if possible to be upheld, and the Court ought not to be astute to find grounds on which a power can be invalidated", the same reasoning was adopted, and an even wider power upheld. The effect of this development is that modern discretionary trusts can have beneficiaries that are far from certain.

A traditional exception to the requirement of certainty of object are trusts for charitable purposes. Under the 3 certainties doctrine, a trust would fail unless the beneficiaries were ascertainable with certainty (and the property concerned in an attempted testamentary trust would fall into residue)[7], except a trust for charitable purposes which, as we noted in the previous chapter, would be held good even though no particular charity was specified by the settlor. We are going to have to look somewhat further at the position regarding charitable trusts because, as we have said, trusts for charitable objects that have failed can be applied for other charitable purposes. Today, the relevant law is found principally in the Charitable Trusts Act 1957.

The relevant law was originally known as the cy-pres doctrine. Under this case-law, if a settlor or will-maker exhibited a general charitable intention, but the object of the trust was uncertain or unattainable, the trust would not fail because the court would apply the trust property to some other charitable object — approximating as closely as possible the original object selected by the settlor or will-maker. These cases must, however, be distinguished from cases of lapsed legacies, which were not saved (see Subsection 3.3.2 — *Lapse*). Thus, to take a typical example, in *Re Davis* [1902] 1 Ch 876, the testatrix (will-maker) left legacies to "the Home for the Homeless, 27 Red Lion Square, London". These were not lapsed legacies, as the "Home for the Homeless" had not been wound-up — it was non-existent; there was not at the date of the will, and never had been, any such charitable institution. Because a general

---

6 The relevant provision in *Re Manisty's Settlement* (supra) gave the trustees power:

> "by any Deed or Deeds revocable or irrevocable to declare that any person or persons corporation or corporations or charity or charities (other than a person or corporation who shall for the time being be a member of the Excepted Class or one of the Trustees) shall thenceforth and for such period as shall be specified in such Deed or Deeds (not extending beyond the Closing Date) be included in the class of Beneficiaries hereinbefore defined PROVIDED ALWAYS that any such Deed shall not take effect unless and until the same (or a memorandum stating the effect thereof) has been endorsed on this Settlement".

7 *Re Bagot* [1893] 3 Ch 348, *Re Leitch* [1997] 1 NZLR 38 at 41. "The property concerned will therefore fall into residue unless there is no true general residuary gift or unless there is some contrary indication in the will" — if there is no true general residuary gift the property concerned passes as on an intestacy — *Re Leitch* (supra).

charitable intention could be inferred, the legacies did not fail, and the court directed that they be paid to certain other charitable institutions mentioned in the will, that is, directed a cy-pres application.

The cy-pres doctrine has been largely replaced by Part 3 of the Charitable Trusts Act. Under s 32, where any property or income is held on trust for a charitable purpose, and:

- it is impossible, impracticable or inexpedient to carry out that purpose, or the amount available is inadequate to carry out that purpose, or that purpose has been effected already, or that purpose is illegal or useless or uncertain, or
- the property or income is more than is necessary for the purpose,

the property may be disposed of for some other charitable purpose, whether or not there is any general charitable intention.

The section indicates, as we saw in connection with *Re Davis*, that it does not operate to save gifts to specific charities that have gone out of existence before the death of the will-maker (or gifts that would fail in accordance with some specific rule of law)[8]. This is consistent with the cy-pres doctrine, but, in other respects, the statutory provisions are wider in that:

- they apply whether or not the settlor or will-maker has exhibited a general charitable intention, and
- the object approved by the court no longer has to approximate as closely as possible the original object — under the Act, the court has freedom to approve the application of the property to a new charitable purpose, without regard to the resemblance of that purpose to that specified by the settlor or will-maker. However, the court is not exercising this freedom but is, in fact, adhering to the original cy-pres doctrine. In *Re Twigger* [1989] 3 NZLR 329, where two of three organisations benefiting under a long-established charitable trust had become defunct, the Court, while acknowledging that it had this freedom, declined to approve the scheme submitted because the new substitute beneficiaries did not approximate as closely as possible the original organisations.[9]

---

8 See *Re Pettit* [1988] 2 NZLR 513, which illustrates how arcane is the law of charities.

9 Tipping J said at 341–342:

> "... a consistent line of authority spanning 80 years has developed whereby this Court on a Part III application, while not bound to adopt a cy-pres approach, will endeavour to see that the scheme propounded comes as close as possible in the changed circumstances to fulfilling the original charitable purpose.
>
> Part III does not make a cy-pres approach mandatory. However, this Court has held in the series of decisions, which I have traversed, that those promoting a scheme under Part III should seek to substitute beneficiaries or purposes resembling as closely as possible in the changed circumstances those which originally commended themselves to the person who established the trust. That is simply another way of saying ... that the wishes of the testator must be followed as far as possible by the scheme".

The Court also indicated that, although not mandatory, it is desirous of a trustee in the position of the trustee in the *Twigger* case, making full inquiries, and possibly advertising, in order to ascertain what organisations may fulfil this requirement.

(The remainder of Part 3 contains principally machinery provisions — they provide for the preparation by the trustees of a scheme for the disposition of the property, for its submission to the Attorney-General, and for its advertisement and approval by the court. The term "trustees" here includes executors and administrators. The court is also empowered to extend or vary the powers of trustees when the administration of the trust could be facilitated by so doing. For a successful application under Pt 3, see *Re Tennant* [1996] 2 NZLR 633.)

The Charitable Trusts Act also provides that when a trust provision includes, or could include, mixed charitable objects and objects that are non-charitable and invalid (and this includes uncertain), the provision shall not fail, but the property shall be applied exclusively for the charitable objects.[10]

12.2.2 The requirement that the trust be completely constituted

Section 15 Trusts Act provides that an express trust commences when a trustee holds property of the trust.

A trust arising under a valid will is completely constituted as from the point of time when the will comes into operation, that is, as from the death of the will-maker. The requirement arises, therefore, only in relation to trusts inter vivos.

Also, it is not necessary to fulfill the requirement *if consideration has been given for the trust*, in which event the agreement concerned is a contract and enforceable as such.

However, for a *voluntary* trust inter vivos to be binding and enforceable, the settlor must, *in addition* to satisfying the requirements of the "three certainties", completely constitute the trust — otherwise it is a mere imperfect (or incomplete) gift and is unenforceable.[11]

To ascertain whether or not this requirement has been met, we must distinguish between the following 2 types of cases, namely:

- cases where the intended trustee is to be someone other than the settlor, and
- cases where the settlor is to be the trustee.

10 For a modern case where the section is discussed, see *Re Beckbessinger* [1993] 2 NZLR 362.

11 Three fairly specialised exceptions to this exist, which are beyond the scope of this text.

12.2.2.1 Cases where the intended trustee is to be someone other than the settlor

In these cases, the settlor must have:

- effectively vested the legal title to the trust property in the trustee, or
- put trustees in a position where they can vest in themselves the legal title to the trust property without requiring any further assistance from the settlor. For example, this requirement would be met if the settlor handed to the trustees' solicitors the completed A&I form authorising the registration of a transfer by *edealing* to the trustee.

What is actually required to vest the legal title to the trust property in the trustee will, of course, *varies* with the type of property concerned. The legal title to chattels, for example, vests merely by words of transfer plus delivery (or deed of gift), but under land law, as we have already implied, the legal title to land vests only when a transfer instrument is registered at the Land Titles Office while, under company law, the legal title to company shares vests only when a share transfer is registered in the books of the company. The requirements of the law for the transfer of the particular type of property involved in the trust must be met.

12.2.2.2 Cases where the settlor is to be the trustee

These are cases in which the settlor intends, henceforth, to hold the property concerned (the legal title to which is already vested in them) as trustee for another person or persons (of whom the settlor may be one). The law here requires that the settlor make a "declaration of trust", that is, a declaration that the settlor henceforth holds the property concerned as trustee. This is the creation of a trust and, while under the basic law of trusts there are no formal requirements, *writing is required in the instances that we have specified in Subsection 11.1.5 — Trusts inter vivos.*

Although the settlor may be a trustee a sole trustee cannot be the sole beneficiary of a trust — Trusts Act s 14.

12.2.2.3 Classic quote

The classic statement of the requirement that the trust be completely constituted was made in *Milroy v Lord* (1862) 4 De GF & J 264.

The essential facts of the case, stated in modern terminology, were that the settlor, by a deed of settlement, purported to transfer company shares to Lord as trustee for the plaintiff. The dividends were handed to the plaintiff, *but no share transfer was ever prepared and registered with the company.*[12]

12 The Louisiana Bank. Lord held a power of attorney from the settlor, but the Court was of opinion that he could not exercise this without the assistance of the settlor.

[As we have seen, a deed is not an effective method of transferring the legal title to company shares.] Three years later, the settlor died, and the plaintiff claimed the shares as beneficiary.

It was held (reversing the decree appealed from) that:

- as the settlor intended to transfer the shares to Lord as trustee [refer to Subsection 12.2.2.1 — *Cases where the intended trustee is to be someone other than the settlor* mentioned above], the deed of settlement could not operate as a declaration of trust, and
- as the plaintiff had given no consideration, the purported disposition of the shares was an imperfect gift, and failed.

Turner LJ said at 274:

I take the law of this Court to be well settled, that, in order to render a voluntary settlement valid and effectual, the settlor must have done everything which, according to the nature of the property comprised in the settlement, was necessary to be done in order to transfer the property and render the settlement binding upon him. He may, of course, do this by actually transferring the property to the persons for whom he intends to provide, and the provision will then be effectual, and it will be equally effectual if he transfers the property to a trustee for the purposes of the settlement, or declares that he himself holds it in trust for those purposes; and if the property be personal, the trust may, as I apprehend, be declared either in writing or by parol; but, in order to render the settlement binding one or other of those modes must, as I understand the law of this Court, be resorted to, for there is no equity in this Court to perfect an imperfect gift. The cases, I think, go further to this extent, that if the settlement is intended to be effectuated by one of the modes to which I have referred, the Court will not give effect to it by applying another of those modes. If it is intended to take effect by transfer, the Court will not hold the intended transfer to operate as a declaration of trust, for then every imperfect instrument would be made effectual by being converted into a perfect trust.

Law: Charitable Trusts Act 1957, ss 31–37, 61B

Land Transfer Act 1952, s 41(1)

Companies Act 1993, ss 84, 89, 96(a)

Property Law Act 2007, s 25(2), (4)

Chapter 13

Illegal Trusts

13.0 Introduction

Even though all the ingredients of a trust are present, they will nevertheless not be regarded as valid if they amount to what is termed an "illegal trust". In the law of trusts, the word "illegal" is used in a sense very much wider than the common everyday meaning (criminal).[1]

There are now established in the law of trusts, a number of purposes which the courts have regarded as undesirable. A trust provision for any of these purposes is an "illegal trust" and void. The principal illegal trusts are:

- trusts of excessive duration
- trusts designed to defraud creditors
- trusts restricting the alienation of property
- trusts constituting a general restraint of marriage
- trusts encouraging the separation or divorce of husband and wife
- trusts encouraging the separation of parent and child or trusts interfering with parental duty, and
- trusts encouraging immorality, fraud, or dishonesty or otherwise against public policy.

These illegal trusts will now be discussed. Finally in this chapter, we will mention "purpose trusts".

13.1 Trusts of excessive duration

For centuries, English law has allowed people to determine how their property shall be disposed of after their death, but they must *dispose* of their property.

There are definite limits on how far into the future people can tie up their property by creating a succession of limited interests. Thus, those who wish to ensure that property that has been in the family for years shall continue to be so for generations to come, will find that they cannot legally enforce their wishes, because our law has only limited regard for "the dead hand of the will-maker". For instance, New Zealand law would clearly not permit a trust

1 See Chapter 3 — *Gifts under Wills*, footnote 4.

for X for life, and then to the children of X for life, and then to the grandchildren of X for life, and then to the great-grandchildren of X for life, and then to their children for life, with remainder to the Hutt Golf Club (Inc).

Under the law as it stood until 11 November 1964, there were 2 major restrictions on the duration of trusts — the "rule against perpetuities", and the "rule against accumulations". More trusts have been declared illegal for infringement of these restrictions than for infringement of any other illegal purpose. We shall first consider the rule against perpetuities, the more important rule — sometimes called the "rule against remoteness of vesting", which name better describes its operation.

13.1.1 The rule against perpetuities

Section 16 of the Trusts Act abolished the rule against perpetuities and provides that the maximum duration of a trust is 125 years. However the terms of a trust may specify or imply a shorter duration.

If the terms of a trust do not specify or imply a duration or a mechanism for or means of determining the date on which the trust property will be finally distributed, the trust continues until the date that is 125 years after the creation of the trust.

If the terms of a trust specify or imply a mechanism for or means of determining the date on which the trust property will be finally distributed, the trust continues until the earlier of —

(a) the date determined by that mechanism or means; and

(b) the date that is 125 years after the creation of the trust.

The following trusts may continue indefinitely:

(a) a charitable trust

(b) the trusts of a superannuation scheme to which s DC 7 of the Income Tax Act 2007 applies

(c) the trusts of an exempt employee share scheme (ESS) (within the meaning of s YA 1 of the Income Tax Act 2007)

(d) a trust that is created by or under, or is subject to, another enactment that allows the trust to continue indefinitely

(e) a trust that may continue indefinitely under common law or equity.

If property is held on a trust to which s 16(1) applies and is transferred as a part of a resettlement to be held on 1 or more other trusts without first being finally distributed, the maximum amount of time that may elapse between the property being settled on the first trust and being finally distributed is 125 years.

Section 18 of the Trusts Act provides that a trust may accumulate income to the extent that is consistent with its terms.

Law: Trusts Act, s 16

13.2 Trusts designed to defraud creditors

Speaking very generally, a trust designed to defraud creditors will be void as against the creditors. Although the general principle is clear, this branch of the law is complex, and it is summarised in the following propositions:

1. A person cannot, to any avail, settle property *on themself with* a gift over to someone else in the event of their bankruptcy — the gift over will not be upheld and the property will pass (under the provisions of the now Insolvency Act 2006) to an Official Assignee for the benefit of their creditors. Thus, in *Re Burroughs-Fowler* [1916] 2 Ch 251, the settlor settled property on himself for life "or until he shall . . . be declared bankrupt . . ." with a gift over to his wife for life, and remainder to his children. Ten years later, he was adjudicated bankrupt, and it was held that his life interest did not pass to his wife but vested in his trustee in bankruptcy for the benefit of his creditors.
2. Section 346 of the Property Law Act 2007 cited below, applies to dispositions of property made after 31 December 2007 by a debtor who was insolvent at the time, or became insolvent as a result, of making the disposition; or was engaged, or was about to engage, in a business or transaction for which the remaining assets of the debtor were, given the nature of the business or transaction, unreasonably small; or intended to incur, or believed, or reasonably should have believed, that the debtor would incur, debts beyond the debtor's ability to pay. The debtor must make the disposition with the intent to prejudice a creditor, or by way of gift, or without receiving reasonably equivalent value in exchange. Section 348 provides that the court may, if satisfied that the applicant for the order has been prejudiced by a disposition of property to which this subpart applies, either vest the property that is the subject of the disposition in the Official Assignee or the debtor or require a person who acquired or received property through the disposition to pay, in respect of that property, reasonable compensation to the person.

   Sections 344–350 of the Property Law Act 2007 include certain transfers of property to a trust. The provisions replaced s 60 of the Property Law Act 1952, which enabled the court to set aside alienations of property made with "intent to defraud creditors". However, s 60 remains relevant to creditors wishing to reverse prejudicial dispositions to trusts as it continues to apply to transactions made before 1 January 2008.

   Section 60 provides:

   60 Alienation with intent to defraud creditors

   (1) Save as provided by this section, every alienation of property with intent to defraud creditors shall be voidable at the instance of the person thereby prejudiced.

(2) This section does not affect the law of bankruptcy for the time being in force.

(3) This section does not extend to any estate or interest in property alienated to a purchaser in good faith not having, at the time of the alienation, notice of the intention to defraud creditors.

Previously, the section had been considered of limited effectiveness since it was difficult for a creditor to prove "intent to defraud" on the part of the debtor. However, the 2008 Supreme Court decision in *Regal Castings Ltd v Lightbody* [2009] 2 NZLR 433 at [53]–[56] has substantially increased its potential impact. Regal Castings Ltd was a supplier to a jewellery business (C Ltd) owned by L. L was personally responsible for a debt owed from C Ltd to Regal Castings Ltd. L subsequently transferred his home to a trust of which he, his wife and their solicitor were the trustees. Five years later, C Ltd went into liquidation, still owing Regal Castings Ltd $165,000. Regal Castings Ltd brought a claim under s 60.

The judgment of Blanchard and Wilson JJ emphasised the fact that L had made himself personally liable for the debts of C Ltd, but had subsequently divested himself of his only substantial asset without telling Regal Castings Ltd. The circumstances of the transfer (to a trust in a manner so that he continued to have enjoyment of the property, and for an unsecured debt repayable 7 years later), and the fact that at the time of the transfer, C Ltd was substantially indebted to Regal Castings Ltd, were also relevant.

The Court placed a new, broader interpretation on the meaning of "intent to defraud". Whereas, previously, an applicant had to show actual intent to defeat creditors' rights at the time of the disposition, Blanchard J said: "Whenever the circumstances are such that the debtor must have known that in alienating property, and thereby hindering, delaying or defeating creditors' recourse to that property, he or she was exposing them to a significantly enhanced risk of not recovering the amounts owing to them, then the debtor must be taken to have intended this consequence, even if it was not actually the debtor's wish to cause them loss".

The result was a declaration that the trustees held a one-half share of their interest in the property on trust for the Official Assignee, to be dealt with by the Assignee for the benefit of L's creditors. The decision is important, as it indicates a shift in approach in favour of creditors: whereas previously it was relatively easy for a debtor to avoid his liabilities by disposing of property, the decision in Regal Castings suggests that the courts may limit this in order to satisfy a creditor's claim.[2]

2 The combined effect of Part 6 of the Property Law Act 2007 and s 192 of the Insolvency Act 2006.

3. Provided that a person is not intending to defraud their own creditors, they can settle property *on someone* else with a gift over in the event of that other person's bankruptcy.[3]
4. If a person settles property on trust and then goes bankrupt, the trust may be open to attack by an Official Assignee under the provisions of the Insolvency Act. We will not examine this Act in detail, but will confine our attention to the main provisions concerning voluntary settlements:
   (a) Section 204 of the Insolvency Act provides that a gift by a bankrupt to another person may be cancelled on the Official Assignee's initiative if the bankrupt made the gift within 5 years immediately before adjudication and the bankrupt was unable to pay their due debts immediately after making the gift.
   (b) Section 205 of the Insolvency Act provides that a gift that is made within 2 years immediately before the bankrupt's adjudication is presumed, unless the contrary is proved, to be made at a time when the bankrupt is unable to pay their due debts.

As Elizabeth Toomey has stated,[4] practitioners should take note: "If your client is insolvent when he or she voluntarily transfers the family home into a trust, the property will be restored for the benefit of the creditors. A comprehensive knowledge of the client's financial circumstances is essential".

The author does not wish to digress into a lot of detail in the final two paragraphs of this section, but feels that the section should conclude by mentioning the development in recent years of international financial "havens". Of particular concern in this regard is the International Trusts Act 1984 [Cook Islands], which severely restricts the rights of creditors regarding assets in international trusts in the Cook Islands. Proposition 2 in the list given above deals with settlements or alienations (trusts) *in New Zealand*.

In 1992, the purchasers of some apartments in a condominium project at 515 South Orange Grove in Los Angeles, America, sued the developers for over $5 million (United States dollars) on account of the faulty construction of the apartments, and obtained judgment for such amount in 1994. Following the entry of judgment in the Californian Court, the purchasers sought to enforce their judgment, only to find that the developers had deliberately[5] divested themselves of most of their property in America and transferred it into international trusts in the Cook Islands. The best that can be said of the outcome of the litigation that followed, is that the New Zealand judges sitting in the Cook Islands Court of Appeal attempted to apply the Act moderately

3 *Brandon v Robinson* (1811) 18 Ves 429 (consistent with *Re Burroughs-Fowler* above), *Mackintosh v Pogose* [1895] 1 Ch 505.

4 E Toomey "Gifting the family home to a trust" (2009) NZLJ 131 at 133.

5 And with knowledge that the Californian judgment was imminent.

and in the interests of the purchasers, and that the relevant decision in *South Orange Grove Owners Association v Orange Grove Partners Cook Islands*, CA 31/96, 25 and 26 September 1996 is some measure of consolation.

Law: Property Law Act 2007, Part 6

Insolvency Act 2006, ss 204, 205

13.3 Trusts restricting the alienation of property

When an interest is given *absolutely*, any condition attached that provides that it is to cease on alienation is void. The beneficiary takes the gift absolutely and the condition is ignored.

However, this illegal purpose, like the following one, is largely a matter of words because, by skilful drafting, a will-maker or settlor can validly create limited interests or contingent interests to attain their objectives.

13.4 Trusts constituting a general restraint of marriage

The law has traditionally regarded marriage as a good and proper thing. Because of this, a trust that constitutes a *general* restraint on a first marriage is illegal. Hence, if will-makers provide that a certain house property is to go to B, a single person, but if B marries, the disposition is to determine and the property is then to go to C, the disposition to B is valid while the contingent gift over to C is void. B takes the property absolutely, and the condition about marriage is ignored.

However, will-makers can achieve their objective if they provide that the property is to go to B *until* B marries and then to C. A provision in restraint of marriage is distinguished from an interest limited until marriage. The distinction, based on the presumed motive of the will-maker, is that, in the first case, the will-maker is trying to prevent the beneficiary from marrying, whereas in the second case, the will-maker is not trying to restrain marriage but merely to provide for the beneficiary while unmarried.

A *partial* restraint of marriage is permitted, provided that the beneficiary is still left a reasonable choice of spouse. For example, a disposition to the will-maker's niece or nephew on condition that they do not marry a real estate agent or a taxi driver would be permitted.

13.5 Trusts encouraging separation or divorce of husband and wife

Very briefly, trusts coming into operation upon the future separation or divorce of the beneficiary are illegal and void.

13.6 Trusts encouraging separation of parent and child or trusts interfering with parental duty

These trusts are similar to trusts encouraging separation or divorce. An example is a provision terminating the interest of beneficiaries, not having custody of their children, should they gain custody of their infant child.

13.7 Trusts encouraging immorality, fraud, dishonesty, or otherwise against public policy

Generally speaking, any attempt to create a trust will be illegal and void if it requires the beneficiary, in order to obtain or retain the gift, to act in an illegal or immoral way or in any way contrary to established principles of public policy.

Most obviously, this includes trusts with criminal purposes, but it also includes some trusts for future ex-nuptial children and trusts deterring the beneficiary from taking a public office. The law on trusts for future ex-nuptial children (as they were then called) is rather archaic, but the main rule, that trusts for future ex-nuptial children are void,[6] is not affected by the Status of Children Act 1969 and is still with us. The provisions of the Act[7] are not relevant to this main rule.

13.8 Purpose trusts

The general rule is that a *non-charitable* (private) trust must have a *human beneficiary* or a beneficiary that constitutes a legal person (such as a company). Trusts merely for the carrying out of some purpose, that is, "purpose trusts", are not normally recognised and are normally void. For example, a trust "for the upkeep of my Jaguar car in its present good condition for the next 20 years" would not be recognised.

Although anomalous in the law of trusts, three types of purpose trusts are exceptions that are valid. The specialised law involved is not discussed here, but these exceptions are mentioned merely to acknowledge their existence. They are:

- trusts for animals
- trusts for the building and upkeep of tombs, and
- trusts for the saying of masses.

---

6 "Future" means conceived after the time of the coming into operation of the instrument creating the trust. In this context, remember that a will does not come into operation until the time of the death of the will-maker.

7 Mentioned in Subsection 8.1.3 — *Application for probate or Letters of Administration*, and elsewhere.

Chapter 14
Introduction to Asset and Tax Planning

14.0 Definition of the topic

In the last chapter, we have seen that the law will not allow settlors to attain some of their more dubious objectives. However, the law has not carried these ideas too far. It has also shown a degree of tolerance for people who wish to organise their assets to best advantage for themselves and their family, and it is now appropriate, before we conclude our examination of the law of trusts, to pause to glance at this aspect. We emphasise (as we will again later in this chapter) that, in the space available here, we are not going to deal comprehensively with this branch of the law[1] — we are going to merely introduce it.

For many years now, people have sought means whereby they can alienate property in such a way that they can retain the benefit of it while, at the same time, the property is not available to answer claims against them. In this regard, *at the moment*, settlors can get the best of both worlds by setting up a discretionary family trust[2] with themself as trustee (or one of them) and with themself as one of the discretionary beneficiaries, but this facility may be short-lived because of potential legislative changes. The protection sought may be from the claims of

1 Reading references for this purpose will be given.

2 There are various general reasons why people may want to put their assets in a trust, for example, they may not have confidence in their spouse or relatives who may succeed them — more specifically they may want:

(a) to provide continuity of ownership of assets for successive generations

(b) to protect property from property relationship claims. For example, an elderly father who is sharing his home with his daughter and his son-in-law may wish to protect the home from claims from the son-in-law in the event of the future break-up of the marriage

(c) to provide funds for education of children and grandchildren

(d) to provide continued care for disabled family members, for example, a "peace of mind" trust — especially for elderly parents who are concerned to provide for continued care of intellectually or physically handicapped children who may outlive their parents

(e) to effect a transfer of life style and other assets into a trust to protect those assets from exposure to creditor claims in the event of business failure

(f) to improve the likelihood of availability of subsidies for rest homes, and

(g) to guard against the possibility of the reintroduction of estate duty.

creditors, Inland Revenue (including the facility of income-splitting),[3] or Work and Income New Zealand (WINZ). Formerly, a major motive was the reduction or elimination of estate duty but, with the suspension of estate duty in 1993, this is not now such a strong motive but remains potentially so, should a future government decide to reintroduce it.

The protection from the claims of creditors has already been examined in Section 13.2 — *Trusts designed to defraud creditors*, and is subject to the reservations made in that section. We now summarise those reservations in a couple of sentences by saying that:

- The settlor must be solvent at the time of the setting up of the trust as the Property Law Act 2007 provides that every dispositions of property made after 31 December 2007 by a debtor who was insolvent at the time, or became insolvent as a result, of making the disposition may be rearranged by the court if satisfied that the applicant for the order has been prejudiced by the disposition of property by vesting the property that is the subject of the disposition in the Official Assignee or the debtor, and
- The trust must survive for at least 2 years prior to adjudication in bankruptcy, otherwise it is open to attack by an Official Assignee under the Insolvency Act 2006.

A more modern variation on the general theme in italics above is the interest that has been taken in recent years in rest home subsidies — people desire to alienate property (usually for the benefit of their children) so as to, when old, qualify for a rest home subsidy for which they would not otherwise be eligible.

It is the extent to which the law allows this general theme to be attained that constitutes the topic of Asset and Tax Planning. At the present time in New Zealand, there is nothing to prevent a person organising their property and affairs so as to attract the minimum amount of tax and so as to be generally to their best advantage and, in modern times, many people have shown an interest in this possibility.

As we have said, we will not examine this topic in detail in this text.[4]

3 Although trusts are taxed at the same rate as companies (33%), they are a very good means of income-splitting (the division of taxable income between several individuals, thus allowing lower tax rates).

By placing income-earning assets, such as commercial property, in trusts, the income from those assets can be diverted to beneficiaries. In many cases, the beneficiaries may be children who have no other income.

4 This is a large topic occupying a full branch of the law, but a brief and readable overview can be found in the revised 7th edition of Martin Hawes *Family Trusts: A New Zealand Guide* (Penguin Books, 2012). This book gives a particularly good summary of the advantages of family trusts.

We will outline the means of achieving asset and tax planning objectives, the relevance of the Income Tax Act 2007, the advantages and disadvantages of family trusts, and pursue the particular example of rest home subsidies in more detail. We will also make mention of the rather flimsy, and possibly temporary, state of the law on asset and tax planning. It is the author's intention to be conservative in this chapter as it is possible that some of the many family trusts which are now being set up may be attacked or rendered less effective in the future. Future changes to the law may render family trusts ineffective in achieving the intended purposes. For example, gift duty has now been repealed; however, a gifting regime may still be appropriate if a purpose of the Trust relates to the rest home subsidy. As a result, advice can be given about the current law, but with no future guarantees.

Law: Property Law Act 2007, Pt 6.
Insolvency Act 2006, s 192

14.1 The means of achieving asset and tax planning objectives

Asset and tax planning objectives can be achieved by 2 main means and these are, in order of importance, firstly, discretionary family trusts and, secondly, registered companies.

14.1.1 Discretionary family trusts

By a discretionary family trust, we mean a trust in which the trustees are given discretion (subject to the terms of the trust deed) as to how the assets are dealt with. These are sometimes called "sprinkler trusts". There is usually no requirement for the trustees to bestow a benefit onto any particular beneficiary in any particular proportion. It is all at the trustees' discretion and, theoretically, all that a beneficiary can hope for is a trustees' decision in the beneficiary's favour. We say "theoretically" because most discretionary family trusts give the settlor very considerable power over the trustees through rights to "hire and fire" (and, indeed, the settlor may be one of the trustees). Assets are transferred to the family trust, either in small amounts from time to time (under $27,000 per year), or else in large bulk amounts and discounted by means of a gifting program.

For example, if the settlor transferred to the family trust the settlor's home, worth $150,000, the result would be that the family trust (theoretically the trustee or trustees) now owns the home. To avoid having made a gift, the settlor takes a debt back from the trust (the settlor now owns the debt instead of the home), and forgives this debt by $27,000 per year. By this method, the settlor has, over a period of years, transferred the ownership of the home from the settlor to the trust free of tax, and the home is no longer the settlor's property available to answer claims against the settlor, although the settlor is probably still living in it in a secure manner and enjoying the benefits of it.

14.1.2 Registered companies

Although companies primarily satisfy the motive of protection from creditors, we should note that registered companies are still a very useful legal mechanism to dispose of business assets in a planned way while still retaining control over the business.

A registered company is formed that buys the original private owner's business and issues shares for its value. Only a small number (it may be only one) of the shares would need to be issued with voting rights. The original owner would retain these. All other shares may then be transferred to those persons whom the original owner wishes to benefit. Initially, the price would be paid by a debt for the corresponding amount of their value.

The debt can subsequently be repaid under a gifting program, or by crediting dividends declared by the company to its repayment.

If the shareholder beneficiaries are taxed at the lower rate,[5] there can be advantages in saving tax, while at the same time divesting the original owner of the business assets, although the tax aspect is complex and is beyond the scope of this text.

The original owner can retain control of the business and, if engaged in its management, be paid an income by way of salary (which, however, has to be adequate and on which tax is paid), or can retain management control as sole director and be paid director's fees at a lesser amount.

A registered company may also be used in conjunction with a trust. The trust could own all of the earning shares and the original owner retain control by owning all of the voting shares and retaining sole directorship. This can sometimes be a very versatile and useful solution. It separates the trust from management of the business asset. The transfer of the shares must be for real value, and be completed by legal transfer in the ordinary way.

14.1.3 The effect of the Property (Relationships) Act on companies

If a disposition is made to a "qualifying company", this may result in orders under the Act. A "qualifying company" is defined under s 44D of the Property (Relationships) Act 1976. (Note this definition is quite different to that under the Income Tax Act 2007.) Section 44D states that:

- a qualifying company is one in which the controlling interest is held by one of the spouses or relationship partners or their personal representative

5 See footnote 3 of this chapter.

- the controlling interest is constituted by equity securities (as defined under s 2 of the Securities Act 1978) in that company which carry the right to 50% or more of the votes at a general meeting of the company's shareholders
- those equity securities must be held by the spouse or partner or their personal representative:
  - — absolutely, or
  - — beneficially (whether directly or through a sub-trust), or
  - — by the spouse, partner or personal representative holding a controlling interest in another company which holds equity securities in the qualifying company.

Section 44F allows the court to make an order if any spouse or relationship partner has disposed of relationship property to a qualifying company and that disposition has the effect of defeating the claim or rights of one of the spouses or partners and the disposition is not one to which s 44 applies.

The court can, in that case, order the spouse or partner to pay money to the claimant or transfer other property to the claimant. The court can make such orders if it decides it is just to do so, having regard to the value of the relationship property disposed of to the qualifying company, the value of the relationship property available for division, the time at which the relationship property was disposed of, whether the company gave consideration and the amount of such consideration, and any other relevant matter.

Section 44F does not provide for the court to order the transfer of any asset owned by the company.

Law: Estate and Gift Duties Act 1968, s 62

14.2 The relevance of the Income Tax Act 2007

Having outlined the means of achieving asset and tax planning objectives, it is essential for us to note at this point that, in implementing these means, regard must be had to 2 important general sections of the Income Tax Act 2007.

The first,[6] in effect, allows the Commissioner of Inland Revenue to void any arrangement for tax purposes where the purpose or effect of the arrangement is the avoidance of tax. However, although the section is very general in

6

BG 1 – TAX AVOIDANCE

(1) A tax avoidance arrangement is void as against the Commissioner for income tax purposes.

(2) Under Part G (Avoidance and non-market transactions), the Commissioner may counteract a tax advantage that a person has obtained from or under a tax avoidance arrangement.

GA 1 – COMMISSIONER'S POWER TO ADJUST

(1) This section applies if an arrangement is void under section BG 1 (Tax avoidance).

nature, the similar section under the previous Act was not applied too severely by the Commissioner. Provided that the purpose of the arrangement is to bestow a genuine benefit on beneficiaries other than the settlor,[7] the Commissioner did not void it merely because an incidental effect is the avoidance of tax. The significance of the section, for our purposes, is that a person cannot set up trusts or companies just for the purpose of avoiding tax, and expect them to stand up against the Commissioner. We would strongly suggest that a person considering asset-planning arrangements to minimise tax should seek expert advice, as this is a highly specialised area.

Law: Income Tax Act 2007, ss BG 1, GA 1

14.3 Effect of Property (Relationships) Act on trusts

Any right or interest received by a spouse, civil union partner or de facto partner as part of a trust will be relationship property where the trust is settled from relationship property. Section 8 of the Property Relationships Act states that relationship property includes all property acquired by a spouse or de facto partner after the inception of the relationship subject to the exceptions set out in ss 9 and 10. Section 10(1)(a) describes as separate property:

(a) Property that a spouse or de facto partner acquires from a third person—

(i) by succession, or

(ii) by survivorship, or

(iii) by gift, or

(iv) because the spouse or de facto partner is a beneficiary under a trust settled by a third person.

consequently any equitable interest or other right in a trust (see definition of "property" in s 2)

- arising after the date of the relevant marriage or commencement of the de facto relationship, and
- held by a spouse or partner who settled that trust, and
- obtained out of relationship property

will be relationship property. Thus the equitable interest or other right can be the subject of orders made under Pt 7 of the Act. Because all relationship

(2) The Commissioner may adjust the taxable income of a person affected by the arrangement in a way the Commissioner thinks appropriate, in order to counteract a tax advantage obtained by the person from or under the arrangement.

(3) The Commissioner may—

(a) disallow some or all of a tax credit of a person affected by the arrangement; or

(b) allow another person to benefit from some or all of the tax credit.

...

7 It is a good idea to state such a purpose in writing at the inception of the arrangement.

property will be shared equally (subject to certain limited exceptions) there is no need to value it before an order can be made vesting it equally in the parties. An order under s 33(3)(m) varying the terms of the trust may then follow, such as appropriating equal shares in the trust fund in each spouse or partner.

In addition, ss 44B and 44C of the Property (Relationships) Act give the court new powers to make orders relating to trusts.

14.3.1 Information

The court can make an order for disclosure of information under s 44B to assist claimants to obtain information relating to the disposal of assets to a trust. Such an order:

- can only be made in relation to information dealing with the disposition of relationship property, and
- will only be made against the spouse or de facto partner of the claimant.

14.3.2 Orders relating to trusts

Section 44C of the Property (Relationships) Act provides that, if relationship property has been made subject to a trust by a spouse or de facto partner and that has the effect of defeating the claim or rights of the other spouse or partner and if no order under s 44 can be made, the court can order:

- the settlor-spouse or partner to pay money to the other spouse or partner
- the settlor-spouse or partner to transfer property to the other spouse or partner
- a trustee to pay to a spouse or partner any of the trust income either for a specified period or until the specified amount has been paid.

No order can be made against trustees if:

- payment of money or transfer of property by the settlor-spouse or partner would compensate the claimant, or
- a third party has in good faith altered their position in reliance upon the trustee's power to distribute income from the trust in such a way that it would be unjust to make the order.

The court can take into account relevant factors including:

- the value of the relationship property made subject to the trust
- the value of the relationship property available for division
- the time when the relationship property was made subject to the trust
- whether the trustees paid an appropriate amount for the property
- whether the parties or any of their children are, or have been, beneficiaries of the trust.

Section 44C only applies to the disposal of relationship property to trustees where that has the effect of defeating the rights of the other spouse or partner. If that person has an equitable interest or expectancy conferred by the trust, it may be difficult to determine whether that effect has occurred. The use of the expression "defeating" rights otherwise conferred by the Property (Relationships) Act may be interpreted as requiring a substantial reduction in the entitlement that the claimant would otherwise have had. To deal with the effects of s 44C, it may be decided to structure a trust to hold relationship property in a way that would allow a potential claimant to receive benefits equivalent to those available under the Property (Relationships) Act. The trustee might be required, should a property relationship dispute arise, to act in a manner that will lead to outcomes in accordance with those that would have resulted from the application of the Property (Relationships) Act.

It seems likely that a spouse or relationship partner could either:

- apply under s 25 for a vesting order together with an order under s 33(3)(m) to modify the trust to give further effect to the claimant's right or interest under the trust and conferred by the vesting order, and/or
- apply under s 44C for payment of a sum of money or the whole or part of the income of the trust.

14.4 Section 21 agreements and asset planning

Section 21 agreements may be used for the purpose of asset planning between married spouses, civil union partners and de facto partners so long as the agreement complies with the procedural requirements of s 21F. The parties can reach an agreement over which property is to be relationship property and which to be separate property. They can agree to define their shares of property.

14.5 Brief summary of the advantages and disadvantages of family trusts

The advantages of family trusts are that you may be able to achieve the asset and tax planning objectives mentioned at the beginning of this chapter. However, we have just seen that there is the potential disadvantage that you have to have regard to the provisions of the Income Tax Act 2007. This is not the only disadvantage. In addition there is the major disadvantage, from which there is no escape, that the settlors have legally alienated the property that they have settled on trust — they are no longer the owners of the property, and they no longer have *direct* control over it. They may sometimes be dependent upon the decisions of relatives, accountants, solicitors, etc. There will also be a degree of inconvenience — the more so if the trust owns income-earning assets and has to file tax returns and, of course, there is the relatively minor factor of cost. It costs several thousand dollars to set up a complete set of family trust arrangements (or more if several properties are involved). However, the settlor may well consider that these disadvantages are outweighed by the asset and tax planning objectives that the settlor hopes to achieve, and today many people do so consider.

A family trust is one of the most flexible and rapidly developing institutions of modern English law, but it is essential when setting one up to obtain competent professional assistance. Those who ignore this advice do so at their peril. It is like buying a car — there are many different types of vehicle available, and your choice will depend upon circumstances and upon which of many different purposes you seek to achieve. If established and monitored with care, trusts may serve all the various uses that they are intended to serve in family and commercial contexts.

14.6 The flimsy state of the law on asset and tax planning

Despite what we have just said, it remains to mention that, due to the flimsy state of the law on asset and tax planning, there is no complete guarantee that these objectives will be achieved. It is essential to realise that arrangements can only be made in light of the existing law at the time the asset plan is set up — there are no guarantees that future legislative changes will not render plans ineffective.

The legislature has taken a very benign attitude towards family trusts over the past few years, but this may not continue. In particular, we note:

1. The possibility that estate duty may be reintroduced (and we have alluded to in Chapter 8 — *Functions of a Personal Representative*, footnote 6).
2. The very flimsy basis upon which some present asset and tax planning opportunities rest.
3. The possibility of a concerted legislative attack on family trusts generally, should a future government have a change of heart.[8]
4. The possibility of lack of judicial support. This potential dry-rot can already be identified in some parts of the English-speaking world. The use of language appropriate to the law of trusts is not conclusive, and the courts are starting to look at the substance of the transaction. Two things are relevant here, namely, the arrangements by which the trust is set up, and the subsequent administration of the trust. Too little power exercised by the trustee, and too much control retained by the settlor, may result in the trust being held to be a sham. This viewpoint, in short, envisages that settlors must effectively divest themselves of the trust property — they

8 Hawes (see footnote 4 of this chapter) hopes that such a possible legislative attack would not be retrospective in effect.

cannot, thereafter, continue to deal with the trust property as if it were their own, and the trustee must thereafter perform with professional competence (and not as a mere agent of the settlor).[9]

5. The effects of the Property (Relationships) Act in allowing the court to override the trust.

14.7 Residential care subsidies

We have already said at the beginning of this chapter that we cannot, in the space available here, examine the topic of asset and tax planning in detail, but we have now introduced it. To attain our stated aims, it remains to examine one particular asset-planning objective in more detail, namely, that of eligibility for residential care subsidies. In recent years, people have taken considerable interest in the possibility of alienating assets so as to qualify for a residential care subsidy for which they would not otherwise be eligible, and this objective, as we have just seen, has been fostered by a lenient attitude on the part of WINZ. Although Inland Revenue has the ability to look very closely at family trust situations, this objective is usually achieved by means of a family trust, and the property is usually alienated for the benefit of the settlor's children.

14.7.1 Residential Care Subsidy

The Residential Care Subsidy (the Subsidy) is funded by the Ministry of Health (MOH). The Subsidy was initially provided for under Pt 4 of the Social Security Act 1964 and the Social Security (Long Term Residential Care) Regulations 2005, but as of November 2018, is now provided for by the Residential Care and Disability Support Services Act 2018 (the RC Act) and Residential Care and Disability Support Services Regulations 2018 (the Regulations).

The Subsidy is available to people aged 65 and over, who are eligible for funding, who have been positively assessed as needing long-term residential care (LTR care),who are receiving contracted care services and who are entitled to make an application for a means assessment. Section 11 of the RC Act states that LTR care means age-related LTR care in a hospital or rest home.

The Subsidy will only pay the maximum contribution that applies in each district for LTR care. That is, the maximum weekly amount (inclusive of GST)

9 For example, in *Rahman v Chase Bank (CJ) Trust Company Ltd* [1991] JLR 104, where the trustee had never taken control of the trust assets (and had never acted other than after seeking and receiving instructions from the settlor) the trust was held to be a sham and was interfered with by the Court. This extreme decision was a decision of the Royal Court of Jersey (British Isles). The Court disregarded the terminology used and held that the trustee was a mere agent of the settlor. For a discussion of the case, and other authorities, see Michael C St J Birt *"The Meaning of the Rahman Decision"* 1992 Offshore Tax Review [UK] Volume 3, Issue 1.

that a resident assessed as requiring LTR care is required to pay for contracted care services provided to them in the region in which their rest home or continuing care hospital is located.

A Means Assessment has 2 parts under the RC Act.

1. an asset assessment; and
2. an income assessment.

14.7.2 Asset assessment

If the applicant has assets which are over the applicable asset threshold, they will be required to pay for their care. If their assets are at, or below, the applicable asset threshold, they may be eligible for a Subsidy.

There are 2 asset thresholds:

Threshold A: is for a single person who is entering LTR care or where both partners are entering LTR care at the same time.

Threshold A, as at 1 July 2021, was $239,930.

Threshold B: is for a couple where one partner is entering LTR care, but the other partner continues to live in the community. The value of the family home and one car will be exempt (as long as the family home is the principal place of residence of the partner who is not in care, or a dependent child) but the threshold level is lower to reflect this. Threshold B, as at 1 July 2021, was $131,391.

The thresholds increase on the 1 July each year, in accordance with the Consumer Price Index.

MSD will not take a Relationship Property Agreement into consideration. The result is that if a spouse is in care, and notwithstanding the Relationship Property Agreement, the assets of the partner who is living in the community will be included in a Means Assessment for the partner who is living in care. A couple is considered by MSD as being a single economic unit.

A separation or divorce will bring the previous partner's obligation in regard to assistance with care costs to an end. However, it is common for MSD to request evidence that the separation or divorce is more than just a physical separation, particularly where a separation comes close after an assessment that a partner requires LTR care.

The question of whether the MSD had correctly interpreted the Regulations was asked and answered by the Court of Appeal in *G B v The Chief Executive of the Ministry of Social Development* [2013] NZCA 410; (2013) 2 NZCC ¶55-042 where it was found that the Chief Executive had correctly applied the test in that — the Act:

> "... explicitly require[d] the Chief Executive conducting a means assessment process to treat the assets of two spouses or partners as one for the purposes of assessing the value of assets that have been gifted".

Assets means those assets of the person and the person's spouse or partner (if any) that are capable of being realised by the person or the person's spouse or partner. (Residential Care and Disability Support Services Act, Sch 2, cl 4.)

14.7.3 Gifting

On 1 October 2011 gift duty was abolished. That means that on the face of it a person may gift as much as they wish, but if a person gifts assets, it will have consequences should they require LTR care and/or a Subsidy later in life.

The MSD's gifting regime has not been abolished and it is applied to every Subsidy application. This stems from the MSD's expectation that people will use the resources available to them (Section 3F Residential Care and Disability Support Services Act) until such time as they are at, or under, the thresholds above.

Gifting is allowed under the Subsidy regime but only within strict parameters. If a person gifts over those parameters, the excess gifts will be added back into the Financial Means Assessment, which is used to assess their eligibility.

Currently, gifts of $27,000 per year are allowed. This is not $27,000 per year, per person but $27,000 per year, per application, which includes both the applicant's assets and the assets of their spouse or partner. Each person is therefore able to gift $13,500 each for a total combined annual gift of $27,000.

In the 5 years directly preceding a Subsidy application, allowable gifting is reduced to $6,500 per application, per year.

There are anti-avoidance provisions in the Residential Care and Disability Services Act 2018 and a person's attempts to dispose of, or deprive themselves of assets, which might have otherwise been available to pay for their care costs, will be subject to rigorous scrutiny.

Section 39 applies where MSD is satisfied that a person who has applied for a means assessment or their spouse or partner, has directly or indirectly deprived himself or herself of any income or property. In conducting the person's means assessment, MSD may include the income or property as if the deprivation had not occurred. In this section, property does not include an exempt asset.

Clause 12 of the Regulations states that for the purposes of ss 39 and 40 of the Act, instances of deprivation of property or income include, but are not limited to, the following:

(a) gifts that are gifted in the 12-month period prior to the commencement of the gifting period, or in any 12-month period preceding that period, to the extent that the total value of the gifts in each such period exceeds $27,000

(b) a disposition of property at any time before the commencement of the gifting period for no consideration, or for a consideration less than the market value of the property at the time of disposition, may be treated as a gift for the purposes of paragraph (a)

(c) a disposition of property during the gifting period for no consideration, or for a consideration less than the market value of the property at the time of disposition

(d) a failure at any time to exercise any right or entitlement to demand a payment:

(e) a waiver of a right at any time to receive any entitlement or payment:

(f) an investment at any time in non-income-earning assets.

14.7.4 Income assessment

Once an applicant has met the relevant asset threshold, an income test will be undertaken to see what, if any, contribution they will need to make toward the cost of their LTR care. This assessment is not restricted to the applicant but may also include income their partner receives, gifting both partners have done, individually or as a couple, depending on their circumstances and whether they are considered to be a single economic unit.

Law: Section 39(2) Residential Care and Disability Support Services Act 2018.

Section 9 Residential Care and Disability Support Services Regulations 2018.

Section 10(2) Residential Care and Disability Support Services Regulations 2018.

Income includes:

- New Zealand Superannuation, Veteran's Pension or any other benefit
- 50% of private superannuation payments
- 50% of life insurance annuities
- overseas government pensions
- contributions from relatives
- earnings from interest and bank accounts
- investments, business or employment
- income or payments from a trust or estate.

Income does not include:

- any money a partner has earned through work
- income from assets when the income is under:
  - $1,027 a year for single people

- $2,054 a year for a couple when both have been assessed as needing care; and
- $3,081 a year for a couple where one partner has been assessed as needing care.

- a War Disablement Pension from New Zealand or any other Commonwealth country.

The applicant will need to provide the MSD with more information if they have ever:

- transferred assets to a trust; and/or
- been the settlor, trustee or beneficiary of a trust or estate.

Notional Income may be calculated in a situation where MSD believes that the applicant should have received income, but did not. The MSD's calculation of notional income was considered in *Broadbent v the Chief Executive of the Ministry of Social Development* [2017] NZHC 1499; (2017) 2 NZCC ¶55-053 and on appeal in *Chief Executive of the Ministry of Social Development v Broadbent* [2019] NZCA 201; (2019) 5 NZTR ¶29-002.

The case considered whether notional income could be calculated on a gifted asset for the purposes of an income assessment on an application for a Subsidy.

Mrs Broadbent had sold property to family trusts at market value. The MSD's contention was that she had deprived herself of income that could have been earned had the trusts not held non-income earning assets, which resulted in notional income being added to Mrs Broadbent's income assessment, putting her over the applicable threshold.

The High Court found in Mrs Broadbent's favour noting that an "... unconditional gift of an asset necessarily involves the relinquishment of all future income streams from that asset" (Katz J at [44]). Notional Income cannot be assessed on deprived assets.

The MSD appealed the High Court's decision and asked the Court of Appeal to determine whether the MSD could include any income capable of being derived from gifted assets valued below the permitted threshold in a person's means assessment. Ultimately the Court of Appeal dismissed the appeal and answered the question in the negative. However, the Court of Appeal also noted that the wrong question had been asked and identified the actual question as being whether notional income could be calculated on "... the deprived income (if any) of the debt back, that is, any interest free component".(*Chief Executive of the Ministry of Social Development v Broadbent* [2019] NZCA 201; (2019) 5 NZTR ¶29-002).

14.7.5 Preservation of rights

A debt back can provide security for a donor who has sold all his or her assets to a trust. This security can mean that the donor is able to effectively preserve a right to live in trust property or ensure that capital will be repaid to the donor if required. This can be particularly important where the donor does not have powers of appointment.

For this reason, the deed of trust should be reviewed before any major gift is made to ensure that the donor could not be disadvantaged by the gift. Where there is any question as to disadvantage, the prudent course of action is to recommend independent advice before the gift is made and for the reasons and basis for the gift to be recorded.

14.7.6 Solvency/Creditor protection

In a post-gift duty era, proof of solvency at the time a gift is made will be critical for some donors and the recipient donee(s). Historically, while it has only been possible to make small gifts each year, the question of donor solvency has rarely been an issue. However, now that bigger gifts can be made, care must be taken to assess and confirm solvency at the time of a gift. If, as a result of a gift, the donor is unable to pay debts as they fall due or if personal liabilities exceed personally owned assets, the gift may be able to be clawed back from the recipient of the gift, whether or not that recipient is a trustee.

For the purposes of the Insolvency Act, the Official Assignee can claw back gifts made in the two years prior to an adjudication of bankruptcy: Insolvency Act 2006, s 204. Gifts made between 2 and 5 years prior to bankruptcy can also be set aside if the bankrupt was insolvent at the time of the gift. The liability to prove solvency rests on the recipient of the gift: Insolvency Act 2006, s 205. There is a rebuttable presumption of insolvency in this case.

Given the claw back tests for solvency, it may be appropriate to make gifts as early as possible, sometimes on multiple occasions during the year as each gift recorded provides a "marker" in relation to claw back provisions.

To minimise risks when making substantial gifts the prudent donor should consider that person's financial position before and after the gift is made. Where the donor has no contingent debts or liabilities this will be a straightforward exercise.

However, it will be prudent for some donors to document their financial situation at the time of a gift so that a contemporaneous record of solvency can be provided if the donor's solvency is challenged in the future. Proof of solvency would present a substantial burden for the Official Assignee in the face of a claim under the Insolvency Act. The best evidence of solvency would be a solvency certificate provided by a qualified external adviser. Alternatively a declaration of solvency may also assist.

Any gifts that have the effect of defeating creditors can also be set aside at any time: Property Law Act 1952, Property Law Act 2007. While a solvency certificate or declaration of solvency may not be a total defence to a claim under either Property Law Act, it could be helpful.

However, more useful might be communications at the time of a transfer putting any person who might be disadvantaged on notice. If transfers could be shown to have been made by consent, together with some evidence as to solvency, it might then be possible to defend a claim that a disposition was made to defeat a creditor's interests.

14.7.7 Relationship property

The relationship property legislation is not being amended due to the abolition of gift duty. Accordingly, as was the case prior to the abolition of gift duty, if relationship property is disposed of into a trust, either through a gift of property or through the forgiveness of a relationship debt, it may be possible for the disposition or gift to be overturned on application under the Property (Relationships) Act or lead to additional remedies against the donor or the trust. Any significant gifts of relationship property should be recorded in a s 21 agreement if the gift is being made in fulfilment of relationship property rights. The possibility of claims under the Family Proceedings Act 1980 must also be taken into account. Again, where there is any question as to disadvantage, the prudent course of action is to recommend independent advice before the gift is made and for the reasons and basis for the gift to be recorded.

14.7.7.1 Clayton's case

This long-running litigation has considered trusts in the context of a relationship break up.

Mr and Mrs Clayton began a relationship in 1986, married in 1989, separated in 2006, and divorced in 2009. They had two children.

Shortly before they married, the Claytons signed a contracting out agreement. Under that agreement, Mrs Clayton was to receive a maximum of $10,000 for each year of marriage up to a maximum of $30,000. At the time, Mr Clayton owned a small timber supply business and a block of land near Rotorua. By the time they separated, Mr Clayton had built up a significant sawmilling and timber processing business.

The Claytons' assets were primarily held in a number of trusts, settled during and after their relationship. For the purposes of the court proceedings, the principle claims were against the Vaughan Road Property Trust (VRPT) and the Claymark Trust. These trusts were each established by Mr Clayton during the marriage. He was the sole settlor, principal family member and sole trustee of the VRPT. He was also the settlor and one of two trustees of the Claymark Trust.

After the Claytons' relationship ended, the contracting out agreement was set aside by the Family Court, deciding that giving effect to the agreement would cause serious injustice. Court proceedings then turned to the extent to which Mrs Clayton could claim the assets held in the trusts.

In relation to the VRPT, Mrs Clayton claimed that the trust was either a sham trust or an illusory trust, and therefore the assets of the trust still belonged to Mr Clayton and could be taken into account in the division of relationship property.

In the alternative, if the VRPT was valid, then Mrs Clayton claimed that the rights and powers held by Mr Clayton under the trust deed themselves amounted to property within the definition of the Property (Relationships) Act.

Mrs Clayton also argued that the Claymark Trust was set up during the marriage and that she had an expectation of benefit under the trust, and that the Claymark Trust was therefore a nuptial trust in terms of s 182 of the Family Proceedings Act.

On 23 March 2016, the Supreme Court delivered its judgments on Mr and Mrs Clayton's appeals against the Court of Appeal judgment handed down 12 months previously in *Clayton v Clayton* [2015] NZCA 30. Before the judgments were delivered, the Claytons settled all matters in issue between them; but, because of the importance of the issues, the Supreme Court still delivered its judgments. The judgments comprised three separate decisions. Two were on Mrs Clayton's appeal — both as to the status of the Claymark Trust, the application or otherwise of s 182 of the Family Proceedings Act and s 44C of the Property (Relationships) Act (*Clayton v Clayton* [2015] NZSC 30).

One was on Mr Clayton's cross-appeal — both as to the status of the VRPT and his power of appointment under the deed of trust (*Clayton v Clayton* [2016] NZSC 29).

The Court held that:

- The Claymark Trust was not a nuptial trust and so Mrs Clayton could not rely on s 182 of the Family Proceedings Act to seek a variation of it in her favour.
- There had been no transfer nor disposition of relationship property into the Claymark Trust and so Mrs Clayton could not claim a compensatory adjustment under s 44 of the Property (Relationships) Act.
- The VRPT was neither a sham nor an illusory trust; but Mr Clayton had effective control over VRPT and its assets by virtue of his power to add and or remove beneficiaries; that the power was unconstrained and/or affected by fiduciary obligations or responsibilities and was therefore in the nature of a personal (as opposed to fiduciary) power compromising

relationship property, the value of which could be determined by reference to the net assets of VRPT.

The *Clayton* decision will result in family trusts being more vulnerable to attack as courts try to ensure that assets accumulated by partners during long relationships are shared equitably whether they are held in trusts or not.

Where the parties were married or in a civil union, the chances of bringing a successful claim under s 182 against a traditional succession planning trust which was settled during the relationship has also increased. However, s 182 of the Family Proceedings Act does not apply to de facto relationships.

In May 2016, following the *Clayton* decision, the Law Commission announced that it would be undertaking a Property (Relationships) Act review. That review will also look at de facto relationships, protection of children, prenuptial agreements, and division of property after death. The Law Commission expects to report its findings by November 2018.

14.7.8 Other considerations

When assessing whether to gift or not it will often be useful to consider why the trust was settled. For example, if the primary motivation was to ensure inter-generational asset protection, the fact that a large gift might mean that a residential care subsidy will never be available may be largely ameliorated by the subsequent asset protection afforded.

14.7.9 How to gift

Following the abolition of gift duty there is no requirement to file gift statements and associated deeds. This means that it is necessary to reconsider how gifts are recorded and what documents are required. Trustees will still be required to keep a record of all forgiveness of debt and distributions to beneficiaries over the life of the trust: Tax Administration Act 1994, s 22B.

Although there is no legal requirement that gifts (other than real property) are recorded in writing, in the absence of any formal record of a gift, proving that a gift has been made may be difficult.

Where a gift cannot be proven, it may be treated as an advance or as having failed such that the "gift" is still the donor's property and is available to creditors.

Requirements to ensure the legal certainty of gifts, such as deeds of gift for trusts, will still be required. See the special report on the abolition of gift duty at taxpolicy.govt.nz.

Chapter 15

Revocation and Avoidance of Trusts

15.0 Revocation and avoidance of trusts

It should be remembered that a will can create a written trust and that, as a will does not come into operation until the death of the will-maker, a trust arising under it is not completely constituted until that time. During the lifetime of the will-maker, a will is regarded only as a provisional statement of the will-maker's intention, and so the will-maker can revoke its contents at any time.

Apart from factors that obviously taint any legal transaction, such as fraud, mistake, or undue influence, which can be grounds for the avoidance (cancellation) of a trust under a will or a trust inter vivos, a trust, once it has been completely constituted,[1] cannot usually be revoked. As Jessel MR said in *Dutton v Thompson* (1883) 23 Ch D 278; 52 LJ Ch 661; 49 LT 109; 31 WR 596, "It is not the province of a Court of Justice to decide on what terms or conditions a man of competent understanding may choose to dispose of his property. If he thoroughly understands what he is about, it is not the duty of a Court of Justice to set aside a settlement which he chooses to execute on the ground that it contains clauses which are not proper".[2]

Ignorance, however, can be a ground for the avoidance of a voluntary settlement. In *Dutton v Thompson* (supra), the settlor was cajoled by his uncle, who was a trustee in the estate in question, into executing a deed restricting his rights to immediate payment from the estate, which deed the uncle believed would be for the settlor's benefit. Although the settlor *was* a person sui juris (of full capacity), the Court of Appeal accepted the view that he was nevertheless a person of weak intellect, and that he did not fully comprehend the effect that the deed would have on his rights in the estate. The uncle should have taken steps to ensure that he did fully comprehend and, as these steps had not been taken, the deed was set aside.

Apart from the tainting factors, to which we have already alluded, the general position is that a trust inter vivos can be revoked or avoided only if:

- the settlor has inserted an express power of revocation
- the court considers that the purpose for which the trust was created has totally failed (the most common occurrence of this being marriage settlements where the intended marriage has not taken place), or

---

1 See Subsection 12.2.2 — *The requirement that the trust be completely constituted.*

2 He went on to say "No doubt if the settlement were shewn to contain provisions so absurd and improvident that no reasonable person would have consented to them, or if provisions were omitted that no reasonable person would have allowed to be omitted, that is an argument that he did not understand the settlement. But in no other way would it be a reason for setting it aside".

- the court chooses to vary, or even revoke, the trust under the discretion given to it by s 64A of the Trustee Act 1956 (dealt with in Subsection 16.5.2 — *Adherence to the terms of the trust*).

In our brief outline, a long discussion of the tainting factors is not appropriate, but a further word needs to be said about *undue influence*, because the position is not the same for wills, and trusts inter vivos, respectively. In Section 1.4 — *The free expression of the will-maker's intentions*, we noted with regard to wills, that a special relationship between the parties is all the more reason for one person wishing to leave a gift to another. The existence of a special relationship will not render voidable a gift by will, as long as the will-maker was still free to exercise their own judgment. The burden of proof is usually on the person alleging undue influence. However, in the case of trusts inter vivos, the position under the *general law* prevails, that is, when the beneficiary stands in a fiduciary position[3] in relation to the settlor, undue influence will be *presumed* (and the gift avoided) *unless* the beneficiary proves[4] that the settlor:

- fully understood the transaction
- was provided with independent advice,[5] and
- exercised the settlor's own free judgment.

The following examples provide some illustration:[6]

In *Huguenin v Baseley* (1807) 14 Ves 273; 33 ER 526; [1803–13] All ER Rep 1, a recently-widowed woman who was under the influence of a clergyman (who

3 A position of dominance and influence.

4 The burden of proof is now on the beneficiary.

5 Preferably legal advice. The topic of independent legal advice is not one that has neatly formulated rules.

For example, "There is no general rule of law to the effect that a solicitor should never act for both parties in a transaction where their interests may conflict. Rather is the position that he may act provided that he has obtained the informed consent of both to his acting". — Lord Jauncey in *Clark Boyce v Mouat* (1993) 2 NZ ConvC 191,706; [1993] 3 NZLR 641 in NZ ConvC at 191,712; NZLR at 646. In *Haira v Burbery Mortgage Finance & Savings Ltd (In Receivership): Koya v Haira* (1995) NZ ConvC (digest) 192,249; [1995] 3 NZLR 396, where a solicitor acted for both mortgagee and mortgagor, the Court of Appeal found that there was a clear conflict of interest, and the solicitor was in breach of his fiduciary duty in not recommending to the mortgagor that she get independent legal advice. The solicitor was further in breach of his fiduciary duty in carrying through the transaction without the informed consent of both to his acting.

In each case, the lawyer must exercise their professional judgment dependent on their assessment of such factors as the age, experience, competence and character of the client, the history and nature of any business involved, and the personal relationships involved. The topic is examined in more detail in Auckland District Law Society Seminar *General Practice Pot Pourri*, May 1995 (Presenters Ann Miller, Kerry Knight and John Sheppard) at 1–8, which contain quite an extensive bibliography. The Lawyers and Conveyancers Act (Lawyers: Conduct and Client Care) Rules 2008 Rule 6.1 provides that a lawyer may not act for more than one client on a matter in any circumstances where there is more than negligible risk that the lawyer may be unable to discharge the obligations owed to one or more of the clients.

6 See also *Day v Mead* [1987] 2 NZLR 443.

was managing her affairs), who by more than one deed, alienated considerable wealth — some of which went to the clergyman and his family. Lord Eldon LC said "if the [deeds were] executed under the effect of that which has always been considered in this court as undue influence, if . . . they are not the pure, well understood, acts of her mind, this court will undo them". He held that, quite apart from the question of independent advice, it was not proved that the woman understood the deeds. The deed conveying to the clergyman and his family the interests in the "Hampton Gay" estates, the subject of the proceedings, was set aside.

In *Re Craig (deceased)* [1971] Ch 95, an old widower, over the last five years of his life (when he was aged 84-89), gave three quarters of his wealth to his secretary-companion, Mrs Middleton. After the old man's death, the gifts were challenged by the residuary beneficiaries in his estate. The Court held that the gifts could not be accounted for on the ground of ordinary motives, that Mrs Middleton stood in a fiduciary position in relation to the old man and, although it was not proved that she had exerted undue influence over him, *she* had failed to discharge the onus of proving that the settlor had fully understood the transaction, had been provided with independent advice and exercised their own free judgment. The gifts were set aside.

The House of Lords in *National Westminster Bank plc v Morgan*[7] (reversing the decision of the English Court of Appeal) held that the weaker party must be disadvantaged (had an unfair advantage taken of him) to enable a transaction to be set aside on the ground of undue influence. Lord Scarman quoted the following passage[8] with approval:

> "Where a person who is in a position to dominate the will of another enters into a contract with him, and the transaction appears on the face of it, or on the evidence, to be unconscionable, the burden of proving that such contract was not induced by undue influence shall lie upon the person in the position to dominate the will of the other".

A fiduciary position automatically arises in the case of solicitor and client, doctor and patient, parent and child, guardian and ward, and religious advisor and pupil, but it is not confined to these set categories and, in modern times, the number of cases in which it is being held to arise is expanding.

With regard to cases outside the above set categories, Lord Scarman, in *Morgan*'s case (supra) at 831, had this to say:

> ". . . the relationships which may develop a dominating influence of one over another are infinitely various. There is no substitute in this branch of the law for a 'meticulous examination of the facts'.
>
> . . .

7 [1985] AC 686; [1985] 1 All ER 821.

8 From *Poosathurai v Kannappa Chettiar* (1919) LR 47 Ind App 1.

There is no precisely defined law setting limits to the equitable jurisdiction of a court to relieve against undue influence. This is a world of doctrine, not of neat and tidy rules. The courts of equity have developed a body of learning enabling relief to be granted where the law has to treat the transaction as unimpeachable unless it can be held to have been procured by undue influence. It is the unimpeachability at law of a disadvantageous transaction which is the starting point from which the court advances to consider whether the transaction is the product merely of one's own folly or of the undue influence exercised by another. A court in the exercise of this equitable jurisdiction is a court of conscience. Definition is a poor instrument when used to determine whether a transaction is or is not unconscionable: this is a question which depends on the particular facts of the case".

Chapter 16

Trustees

16.0 Appointment of trustees

As the reader will now appreciate, the original trustees are usually appointed by the settlor (except in the case of implied or constructive trusts, when the trustee will be the person deemed to be such by the court). When a person has clearly intended to create a trust but has not appointed a trustee, the trust will not be permitted to fail for want of a trustee, and the court will appoint a suitable person or, perhaps, the Public Trust. Similarly, if the trustee appointed by the settlor dies or declines to act before the trust takes effect, the court will make an appointment. No person appointed as trustee is compelled to accept the appointment, and they may disclaim the office, provided that they have not already expressly accepted or manifested acceptance by their conduct in dealing with the trust property.

Law: Trusts Act 2019, s 98

16.1 Retirement of trustees

Just as trustees cannot be compelled to accept their appointments, similarly, they cannot usually be compelled to continue in office and are entitled to retire. In some cases, the trust instrument itself makes provision for the voluntary retirement of the trustees.

Even when the terms of the trust do not make provision for retirement, a trustee may retire under various statutory provisions contained in the Trusts Act 2019,[1]

Section 101 provides that a trustee who expresses in writing a wish to retire may be discharged in writing:

(a) by a person with the power to remove trustees; or

(b) if there is no person authorised under paragraph (a) or that person is unable or unwilling to act, by the remaining trustees; or

(c) if there is no person authorised under paragraph (a) or (b) or that person is unable or unwilling to act, and the trustee's retirement will reduce the number of trustees below the minimum number of trustees required by the terms of the trust, by the retiring trustee and a replacement trustee (selected by the retiring trustee) together; or

1 These provisions are cited at the end of this Section.

(d) if there is no person authorised under paragraph (a) or (b) or that person is unable or to act, and the minimum number of trustees required by the terms of the trust will remain, by the retiring trustee alone.

Law: Trusts Act 2019, s 101

16.2 Removal of trustees

An incompetent or dishonest trustee is worse than no trustee at all, and the law makes provision for the removal of trustees from office in certain cases. The trust instrument may contain provisions governing the removal of trustees, but if there are no such provisions, or if those contained in the instrument are inappropriate in the circumstances, the statutory powers in the Trusts Act may be resorted to. Specific provision is made in the Trusts Act for trustee removal, trustee retirement, trustee replacement and when a trustee has died. In all cases, the first "port of call" is the person nominated in the trust deed. If no one is nominated in the trust deed, or the nominated person is unable or unwilling to act, the remaining trustees have the power of appointment and removal (s 92).

If there is no nominated person or remaining trustee who is able or willing to act, then the power to remove and replace a trustee may be exercised by:

- a property manager of a trustee appointed under the Protection of Personal and Property Rights Act 1988 (PPPR Act)
- the attorney of a trustee who has lost capacity, appointed under an Enduring Power of Attorney; or the liquidator of a corporate trustee
- a retiring trustee may appoint a replacement
- the executor or administrator of a trustee who has died may appoint a replacement; and
- if it is difficult or impractical to replace a trustee otherwise, the High Court may appoint a trustee.

16.2.1 How a trustee is removed

A trustee may be removed by the service of notice upon them (s 106). The notice itself will be immediately effective to remove a trustee if they are subject to a property order under ss 31–33 of the PPPR Act. In other cases, the document takes effect 20 working days after the trustee receives the notice, if they have not made an application for the decision to remove them to be reviewed (s 107).

If the trustee cannot be located, then a statutory declaration must be signed recording the decision and the efforts to locate and contact the trustee. The statutory declaration will amount to a document of removal (s 108).

A trustee may apply to the court for an order preventing their removal (s 109). The application must be made within 20 working days of the date the trustee receives the notice of the decision to remove them.

The court may also make an order for removal if it is difficult or impracticable to do so without the assistance of the court (s 112).

Apart from the statutory provisions, the court has always exercised an inherent jurisdiction when it considers that removal of a trustee is clearly necessary in the interests of the beneficiaries and the preservation of the trust property, but this jurisdiction will not be exercised lightly. In *Osborne v Wilson* HC Auckland, CIV-2005-404-1252, 27 June 2005, there was a successful application by Osborne for the removal of trustees. Osborne and Wilson had formed a family trust with Wilson's long-time friend and solicitor, T, as third trustee; when Osborne and Wilson's relationship broke down, so too did management of the trust, with Osborne alleging that T was partisan and biased. It was held that actual misconduct is not required for the removal of a trustee. The decision to remove was based on the course that would best serve the beneficiaries, taking into account all the relevant circumstances. The Court had no confidence that the trustees could work together to properly manage the trust property for benefit of beneficiaries as a whole, so the application was granted.

In *McCartney v Cox* [2012] NZHC 1369, following a marriage breakdown, a trust settled by the parties was unable to be administered when one of the partners refused to participate in the administration of the trust. The trustees applied, amongst other things, for an order removing both partners as trustees and appointing an additional independent trustee (the deed of trust requiring a minimum of 2 trustees).

The legislative jurisdiction for considering the request was pursuant to the Trustee Act, s 51, which as well as allowing the court to appoint a new trustee also allowed the appointment of a trustee in substitution for a trustee who, amongst other things, has "misconducted himself in the administration of the trust". In agreeing to the requested removal and appointment, the High Court considered the applicable principles set out in *Miller v Cameron* [[1936] HCA 13; (1936) 54 CLR 572], where Dixon J outlined the matters to take into account in exercise of the discretion pursuant to s 51 of the Trustee Act:

> "The jurisdiction to remove a trustee is exercised with a view to the interests of the beneficiaries, to the security of the trust property and to an efficient and satisfactory execution of the trust and a faithful and sound exercise of the powers conferred upon the trustee. In deciding to remove a trustee the court forms a judgment based upon considerations, possibly large in number and varied in character, which combine to show that the welfare of the beneficiaries is opposed to his continued

> occupation of the office. Such a judgment must be largely discretionary. A trustee is not to be removed unless circumstances exist which afford grounds upon which the jurisdiction may be exercised".

In the case in hand, the Court found that the absence of one trustee and his refusal to engage with the trust or respond to proceedings equated to misconduct in the administration of the trust in terms of s 51(2)(a) and, in accordance with the principles outlined in *Miller v Cameron*, the removal and replacement sought should be ordered.[2]

Law: Trusts Act 2019

16.3 New trustees

When original trustees have died, retired, or been removed from office, it will be desirable to have new trustees appointed to ensure the continuance of the trust. The trust instrument may contain provisions giving a power of appointment of new trustees either to the existing trustees or to some specified persons, and, if such a power of appointment exists, it should be used. The power may give a completely free choice to the donees of the power, or it may place restrictions on who they may appoint.

If the trust instrument contains no power of appointment, or if the powers given are inappropriate in the circumstances, statutory power to appoint new trustees is given by the Trusts Act. Appointments and replacements must be made in writing (s 92). If the appointment or replacement is taking place under the power in the trust deed, then any limitations specified in the empowering clause must be complied with (s 92(4)).

A person with the power to appoint or remove may apply to the court for directions on exercise of power (s 93). The exercise of a power to appoint or remove a trustee must be exercised honestly and in good faith and for a proper purpose (s 94). A beneficiary may apply to the court for review of an exercise of the power to appoint and remove a trustee (s 95).

Law: Trusts Act 2019, ss 92–95

16.4 Vesting of trust property in new trustees

Whenever a new trustee is appointed, the trust property must be transferred into the new trustee's name, or, if the new trustee is not the sole trustee, the trust property must be transferred into their name jointly with the continuing trustees. Previously, if a trustee lost capacity, it was usually possible to replace

2 Good reasons why a trustee should be removed must be put before the court. It should be noted that *mere friction* between a trustee and a beneficiary or beneficiaries is not, *in itself*, a reason why the trustee should be removed, and may even be a reason why they should be retained — for example, where a trustee adheres to the terms of the trust against the wishes of a particular beneficiary or beneficiaries.

them using the broad power in s 43 of the Trustee Act 1956. If the trust included land, it was then necessary to apply to the court for a vesting order. This was to meet the requirements of the Land Transfer Act 2017 for the registration of land.

Under the Trusts Act, the execution of a document of appointment, removal, or discharge divests the trust property from the former trustees and vests it in the new trustees without any conveyance, transfer, or assignment (s 116). In other words, the trustee replacement documents suffice as "vesting by statute" under s 90 of the Land Transfer Act.

A court order appointing or removing a trustee amounts to a vesting order for the purposes of s 89 of the Land Transfer Act. If a court order is made, the statutory declaration is not necessary.

Trustees may complete the formal requirements necessary for vesting and divesting on behalf of a former trustee who loses capacity (s 118). The Trusts Act includes a specific limitation of liability for any person who registers, notifies or records the transfer of property in accordance with these provisions, and a requirement for the new trustees to give the departing trustee a copy of documents demonstrating that they have been divested of the trust property. This must take place as soon as possible after the registration is complete (s 120).

(Note: In this section, we are talking about "trustees". A person who started off as executor under a will, may later become trustee under the will. The office of trustee does not devolve as the office of executor devolves. The discussion of the devolution of executorship in Section 6.5 — *The devolution of executorship*, therefore, does not apply to trustees. It applies only to executors.)

Law: Life Insurance Act 1908, s 43

Land Transfer Act 1952, s 41(1)

Trusts Act 2019

16.5 Duties of trustees

The Trusts Act specifies the core trustee duties that were already part of the law. It then incorporates a new concept by classifying the duties as either "mandatory" (ss 23–27) or "default" (ss 29–38). In exercising any duty, a trustee must have regard to the contents and objects of the trust (as well as the s 4 principles). Mandatory duties must be performed by the trustee and may not be modified or excluded by the terms of the trust. Any purported exclusion of a mandatory duty will have no effect.

Arguably, the exclusion of mandatory duties may also be evidence that there was no intention to create a trust in the first place (an argument accepted in *JSC Mezhdunarodniy Promyshlenniy Bank v Pugachev* [2017] EWHC 2426 (Ch)) and thereby undermine the asset protection strategy if the trust is ever challenged.

Default duties may be modified or excluded by the terms of the trust, subject to certain limits as set out in s 5 and Sch 2. Many default duties are commonly excluded by trust deeds. This practice will continue to be acceptable (provided that the exclusions fit within the permitted limits).

However, the Act imposes a statutory duty on any person advising on or preparing the terms of a trust to take reasonable steps to ensure that the settlor understands the meaning and effect of any modification or exclusion of any default duty.

16.5.1 Trustee duties

The Trusts Act clearly sets out the legal duties of a trustee.

Some trustee duties, known as "mandatory duties", are compulsory and apply to all trusts. Under these duties, all trustees must:

- know the terms of the trust — this means what is set out in the trust deed or other trust documents, or matters that are implied in those documents
- act in accordance with the terms of the trust
- act honestly and in good faith
- act for the benefit of beneficiaries, or to further a permitted purpose. Most trusts are set up for the benefit of beneficiaries. There are a limited number of situations where trusts can be set up for a purpose; these will be usually be charitable trusts
- exercise powers for a proper purpose.

Other trustee duties, known as "default duties" also apply, but are not compulsory and can be modified or excluded by the trust. These duties apply unless the trust specifies that they do not apply, or that they are modified, or it is otherwise implied that this is the case. Under these duties, trustees must:

- exercise the care and skill that is reasonable in the circumstances. This will depend on the knowledge and experience of the trustee and whether the person is acting as a trustee as part of their business or profession, such as a trustee who is a lawyer or an accountant
- use appropriate powers to invest trust property with the care and skill expected of a business person dealing with someone else's property. This will also depend on the knowledge and experience of the trustee and whether they're acting in a professional capacity
- not exercise a power directly or indirectly for the trustee's own benefit. This duty will be limited by implication where the trustee is also a beneficiary

- actively and regularly consider whether they should be exercising their powers as a trustee
- not bind or commit trustees to a future exercise or non-exercise of a discretion
- avoid a conflict between the interests of the trustee and the beneficiaries
- act impartially in relation to the beneficiaries, and not be unfairly partial to one beneficiary or group. This does not require all beneficiaries to be treated equally
- not make a profit from acting as a trustee
- not to take any reward for acting as a trustee, although they may be reimbursed for their legitimate expenses
- if there is more than one trustee, to act in agreement with each other.

Section 130 gives the court statutory authority to extend or vary a trustif —

(a) the court considers that the variation or extension is necessary or desirable for the proper management or administration of the trust property; and

(b) the variation or extension does not alter a beneficiary's interest under the trust; and

(c) the variation or extension does not involve a power to distribute trust property to a beneficiary.

An application for an order may be made by a trustee or a beneficiary of the trust.

The court will almost always grant authority for a variation proposed by the trustees if consent to such variation has been obtained from all beneficiaries affected, all being sui juris.[3]

This gives the court power to authorise virtually any transaction that is expedient in the management or administration of the trust, or would be in the best interests of the persons beneficially interested under the trust.[4]

Under the previous legislation this provision was thought to enable only the authorisation of administrative acts for which the trustee may lack the necessary power. It was held in *Re Smith (deceased)* [1975] 1 NZLR 495 that it did not permit the court to alter the trust itself. In that case, Cooke J (as he then was) declined to approve the sale of a farm under this provision, on the ground that the will-maker clearly intended the farm to be settled on trust,

3 Baragwanath J said in *Re Philips New Zealand Ltd* [1997] 1 NZLR 93 at 101 "If all beneficiaries are sui juris and consent to an amendment proposed by the trustees it is difficult to visualise a successful challenge to it".

4 "... but it is inexpedient or difficult or impracticable to effect the same without the assistance of the court, or the same cannot be effected by reason of the absence of any power for that purpose vested in the trustee by the trust instrument (if any) or by law" — s 64(1).

and that to permit the trustees to sell it would "savour of a rewriting of the substantive trusts more than of a step in the management or administration of the estate". However, in *Re Greenwood* [1988] 1 NZLR 197, Tipping J in a dictum[5] expressed the view that s 64(1) [the provision in question], *in addition* to enabling the authorisation of transactions that are expedient in the management or administration of the trust, enables the court to authorise any of the specified wide range of transactions that can be shown to be in the best interests of the beneficiaries.[6]

The Tax (Income Tax Rate and Other Amendments) Act 2020 has also been enacted, which provides the Inland Revenue Department with new information gathering powers for trusts. Trustees of certain income generating trusts will now be required to disclose financial, distribution, settlement, and identity information.

Law: Trusts Act 2019

Trustee Companies Act 1967, ss 18, 19

16.6 Powers of trustees

Trustees do not have unlimited power to deal with the trust property as they would with their own. However, to carry out their various duties, trustees must obviously have certain powers to act in relation to the trust property.

16.6.1 Sources of a trustee's powers

Trustees can derive their powers from any of the following sources:

- *A legal duty* — Trustees automatically have power to carry out any duty that the law imposes upon them.
- *The trust instrument itself* — This frequently confers express powers. A trustee also has implied power to do those things that are necessarily incidental to the express powers.
- *Statute, principally the Trusts Act* — Many powers are given to a trustee by statute, and these apply to all trusts except when a contrary intention is

5 An application under s 64A, not s 64(1), was before the court.

6 Tipping J said at 208:

> "The power to approve a sale granted by s 64 is not however limited only to a case of expediency in the management or administration of any property vested in a trustee. The power arises additionally where, in the opinion of the Court, such a sale would be in the best interests of the persons beneficially interested under the trust".

He said again at 209:

> "In my view this Court has power, subject to the terms of s 64, to authorise a sale, or indeed any of the other transactions referred to in s 64(1), if the transaction is expedient in the management or administration of the trusts, or would be in the best interests of the persons beneficially interested, but one or more of the various impediments referred to in the section stand in the way of the trustees".

expressed in the trust instrument. These powers are summarised in the following subsection.

- *The court* — A trustee may apply to the court for directions on matters of administration. Trustees who are in doubt as to the extent of their powers should always obtain the court's directions.
- *The consent of the beneficiaries* — If all the beneficiaries are of full legal capacity, trustees may act in any manner authorised by all, even though it may not be within the scope of the powers given to them by the trust instrument or by statute.

16.6.2 Statutory powers of a trustee

The trust instrument may invest a trustee with any powers that the settlor considered necessary for the proper administration of the trust. In the absence of any such express powers, or when they prove inadequate, trustees will find that various statutes have invested them with most of the powers that they are likely to need to carry out their duties. For certain purposes, however, trustees must exercise their statutory powers only with the consent or under the direction of the court (and, as we are going to see, the exercise of all of them is subject to possible review by the court).

Section 56 gives trustees all the powers necessary to manage the trust property including the powers of an absolute owner. Sections 58–79 set out specific powers including the matters to consider when deciding to invest (s 59). Section 29 provides that when administering a trust (other than when exercising a discretion to distribute trust property), a trustee must exercise the care and skill that is reasonable in the circumstances, having regard, in particular —

(a) to any special knowledge or experience that the trustee has or that the trustee holds out as having; and

(b) if the person acts as a trustee in the course of a business or profession, to any special knowledge or experience that it is reasonable to expect of a person acting in the course of that kind of business or profession.

Section 30 provides that when exercising any power to invest trust property, a trustee must exercise the care and skill that a prudent person of business would exercise in managing the affairs of others, having regard, in particular —

(a) to any special knowledge or experience that the trustee has or that the trustee holds out as having; and

(b) if the person acts as a trustee in the course of a business or profession, to any special knowledge or experience that it is reasonable to expect of a person acting in the course of that kind of business or profession.

Law: Trusts Act 2019, ss 56–74

16.7 Rights of trustees

The powers of trustees, discussed above, refers to things that they are entitled to do to administer the trust properly. In addition, trustees are recognised as having certain rights that relate to their own personal position as regards the trust. We have already noted that trustees may not make profit out of their position, but it is equally true that they are not expected to incur a personal loss in carrying out their duties.

The Act makes it clear that trust deeds must not limit a trustee's liability or provide an indemnity for dishonesty, wilful misconduct or gross negligence. Any terms in a trust deed that purport to limit the liability of the trustee or to indemnify them in breach of these provisions is invalid. This means that trustees can no longer rely on broad indemnity clauses that purport to protect them against gross negligence. They may still be protected in relation to ordinary negligence, if this is covered by an appropriately drafted limitation of liability and indemnity clause.

A trustee's rights may be summarised as follows:

- *Reimbursement and indemnity* — Under the Trusts Act, a trustee is entitled to be indemnified against expenses properly incurred in the execution of the trust. They may reimburse themselves from trust money for all proper trust expenses paid out of their own money, and they have the right to be indemnified for any liabilities they have properly incurred in the course of their duties.
- *Set-off* — Trustees have the right to cancel an amount due by them to the trust against an amount due by the trust to them and, thus, pay only the balance to the trust.
- *Contribution* — Trustees are jointly and severally liable for breach of trust. (This means that a beneficiary can sue all, or any one or more, of the trustees.) When any loss has been incurred and has been made good by one trustee, that trustee has the right to call on the co-trustees for contribution, so that the loss is spread equally among all trustees.

  However, there are some exceptional circumstances in which the court may refuse to make an order for contribution. These are:

  — When the trustee has committed a fraudulent breach resulting in a loss, and the other trustees have played no part in the fraud and cannot fairly be held responsible for it.

  — When the trustee is also a beneficiary. In this event, their share of the trust property normally goes in satisfaction of damages.[7]

7 When a trustee-beneficiary has committed the breach of trust, the court will order that their beneficial interest in the trust property be applied towards making good the breach — *Fox v Buckley* (1876) 3 Ch D 508 (CA).

Trustees can normally seek contribution only in respect of the amount by which the loss exceeds their share of the trust property.

— When the trustee is a solicitor and, because of the confidence of the other trustees in the solicitor-trustee's professional knowledge and skill, they were enabled to commit the breach without the other trustees having knowledge of it.

- *Right of indemnity by impounding beneficiary's interest* — Under the general law of trusts, when a beneficiary has consented to a breach of trust by a trustee, the beneficiary is not permitted to complain about any loss that results and cannot bring an action for damages against the trustee. However, when the breach has been committed at the instigation or request or with the written consent of a beneficiary,[8] the law now goes further by providing (in the Trustee Act) that the court may, if it thinks fit, indemnify the trustee by impounding any part of the beneficiary's interest in the trust property. The property impounded is then available to answer claims for damages.

The above rights, as we have said, relate to trustees' own personal position as regards the trust but, in addition, no trustee is in a position where they are forced to expose themselves to liability. They always have the underlying right to seek the guidance and protection of the court. Hence, a trustee who is uncertain as to whether or not a proposed action is correct, can apply to the court for directions. However, if difficult questions of law are involved, they should institute an action.

Law: Trusts Act 2019

16.8 Liability of trustees

That the duties of trustees are numerous has been noted. Their primary duty is to carry out the terms of the trust, but they must also adhere to the general duties imposed by the law. Corresponding to their duties is their liability for any loss resulting from their breach. This liability extends not only to active breaches, for example, when trustees overpay a particular beneficiary, but also to passive breaches when trustees refuse or simply neglect to carry out their duties.

There is no direct relationship between the *liability* and the *power* of a trustee. That a trustee had the power to do some act, is not in itself a defence to an action for breach of trust. Trustees must observe their general duties. However, the amount of the trustees' liability is limited to the loss incurred as a result of the breach of trust. This will be the amount of damages awarded. It follows from this that, if no loss results either to the trust estate or to any beneficiaries, there is no liability. The two main exceptions are:

8 The beneficiary having knowledge that the proposed action is a breach of trust.

- when trustees have made a personal profit through the trust property, they will be held liable to account to the beneficiaries for such profit, and
- when trustees have advanced excessively large amounts on a mortgage that would be a proper investment for a smaller sum, they are liable only for the excess above the smaller sum.

It has been mentioned previously that the office of trustee is an onerous one. Any deviation from the terms of the trust, or from the duties incidental to its proper administration, will impose liabilities on the trustees, if a loss of either capital or income is the result. Trustees are not permitted to plead as a defence that the loss would have occurred even if they had not been guilty of the breach. Provided that the loss actually incurred flows directly from the breach, they will be liable. Under s 59 of the Trusts Act, the general quality of the trustees' investment strategy can be taken into account and the court can offset losses against gains. Hence, if a trustee made nine good and prudent investments, and one somewhat imprudent investment that was held to be a breach of trust, and if all returned substantial dividends to the trust except the tenth, which was sold at a loss of $100, the court may well now offset the $100 against the substantial dividends returned by the other 9 investments. Breaches of trust, and the consequent liability that may occur, vary infinitely, but the most common examples are improper investment, or failure to invest at all, and failure to realise or sell property when directed to do so.

The liability for breach of trust that we have spoken of in this section is a *civil* liability (it is a liability to make good the loss). However, it is also possible for trustees to incur criminal liability. Trustees who, *with intent to defraud* and in violation of their trust convert anything of which they are trustee to any use not authorised by the trust, commit a criminal breach of trust and may, with the leave of the Attorney-General, be prosecuted (and imprisoned for a term of up to 7 years).

Law: Crimes Act 1961, s 230

Trusts Act 2019, ss 158, 59

16.9 Remedies of beneficiaries

This topic follows on directly from, and is related to, the duties and liabilities of trustees. Naturally, there is no point in a trustee being held liable, unless the liability gives rise to some remedy on the part of the beneficiaries. From what has been said previously, the reader will be aware that the main remedy of the beneficiaries is to sue the trustee for damages.

Following trust property — The usual remedy of damages is a personal action against the trustee. (Trustees who are being so sued can attempt to protect themselves by taking action to follow and recover trust property if this is possible. They can also, with the leave of the court, join to the proceedings any person from whom they may be able to recover the property.) However, the beneficiaries may have a right of action to recover trust property that has been wrongly converted or disposed of by the trustee. This is called following the trust property, and this right of action is not prevented by the fact that the beneficiaries could have sued the trustee for damages.

The general rule is that, while trust property can be followed and recovered from the holder if it can be identified in their hands, *it cannot be recovered from a bona fide purchaser* who has acquired the legal title to the property without notice of the trust.

Trust monies can also be followed and recovered when they have been misappropriated by the trustee, but only if the actual money can be identified and the present holder had notice of the trust. When trustees have mixed trust monies with their own, the beneficiaries are entitled to a charge against the mixed fund thereby created and to be reimbursed out of such fund.

Additional remedies of beneficiaries — In addition to the usual remedy of suing the trustee personally, and the right to follow trust property in certain cases, the beneficiaries may also have the following rights:

- to apply to the court for an injunction to restrain a breach of trust contemplated by a trustee
- to apply to the court for an order that the trustee carry out some specific lawful act, or for the appointment of a receiver when the trust property is in jeopardy
- to bring an action for accounts, whereby a trustee is required to substantiate their actions
- to apply to the court to review what a trustee has done under the authority of the Trustee Act, or to give directions relating to such matter (or even to appoint a new trustee[9])
- to apply to the court for an order that the trustee or trustees carry out the terms of the trust, and
- to terminate the trust, if all possible beneficiaries are of full legal capacity and all act jointly.

Law: Administration Act 1969, ss 49, 50
Trusts Act 2019

16.10 Relief of trustees

Statutory relief — The point that the office of trustee is an onerous one has already been made. Under the basic law of trusts, trustees who have acted

9 We noted in Section 16.2 — *Removal of trustees* that the court will not over-readily appoint a new trustee.

with the best of intentions and with the welfare of the beneficiaries in mind will nevertheless be liable for breach of trust if they deviate in any way from their duties and a loss results.

To mitigate the harshness of this principle, s 131 of the Trusts Act makes provision for the relief of a trustee in certain circumstances. (Under the Act, "trustee" includes personal representatives.) The section gives a general discretion to the court to relieve a trustee from personal liability, either wholly or partly, if the court considers that the trustee "has acted honestly and reasonably, and ought fairly to be excused".

In order to obtain relief, trustees must satisfy all three requirements. It is not sufficient that they merely acted honestly — they must also have acted reasonably, as an honest fool will not be relieved by the court. They must, in addition, satisfy the court that, in the circumstances, they ought fairly to be excused, and the fulfilment of this requirement does not automatically follow the fact that they have acted honestly and reasonably. For example, in *National Trustees Company of Australasia Ltd v General Finance Company of Australasia Ltd* [1905] AC 373 (PC), the essential issues of which were set out in Subsection 16.5.5 — *Diligence and prudence*, the National Trustees Company (the trustee) was held to have acted honestly and reasonably, but it failed to make out a sufficient case[10] that, in the circumstances, it ought fairly to be excused for the breach of trust. In reaching this conclusion (and in affirming the decisions of the courts below under which the National Trustees Company was held liable in damages to the extent of two-thirds of the fund), the Privy Council was influenced by the following factors:

- When the error was discovered, the National Trustees Company did not attempt to put matters right.
- If the Council relieved the National Trustees Company from liability, the result would be that the loss fell on the respondent, which was an innocent party.

Special limitation periods — A personal representative can distribute an estate without fear of incurring personal liability under the Law Reform (Testamentary Promises) Act 1949 or the Family Protection Act, if the personal representative has held the estate property for 6 months from the date of grant of probate or Letters of Administration and, during that period, has received no notice of any claims, or pending claims, under either of these above two Acts. Such claimants can still follow the estate property, but the personal representative is protected from liability.

A further time limit arises as a consequence of the Property (Relationships) Act 1976. Section 71 provides that the administrators or trustees of the estate of a deceased spouse or de facto partner must not distribute any part of the estate until six months from the grant of administration or before the

10 Under the precursor of s 73 of the Trustee Act.

surviving spouse elects whether to apply for a division of the relationship property under that Act or take under the will or intestacy, whichever happens first. If proceedings have been commenced, distribution may not take place until the proceedings are finally concluded, including any possible appeal. The court has the discretion to extend the time available to a spouse to make the choice above, even if the time has already expired.

General limitation of actions — Trustees (or personal representatives) are also protected by the Limitation Act 1950, which prevents an action for breach of trust being taken after the lapse of six years from the breach of trust.[11]

However, where the right of action has been *concealed by the fraud* of the trustees, the limitation period does not begin to run until the beneficiaries have discovered the right of action or could, with reasonable diligence, have discovered it. Moreover, the limitation period does not apply to prevent beneficiaries from bringing an action after 6 years against trustees who have been guilty *of a fraudulent* breach of trust, or who have converted trust property to their own use.

Concurrence, consent, acquiescence, or release by beneficiaries — Trustees will be exonerated from liability for breach of trust in so far as it affects beneficiaries who have consented to the breach or have subsequently released the trustee from liability. A release may even be informal in nature if the trustees give valuable consideration for it and if the intention is clear. For any of the matters mentioned above to be effective, however, the beneficiaries must be of full legal capacity and in full possession of all relevant information about the breach and their rights in respect of it.

Concurrence usually requires active agreement on the part of the beneficiaries, and to this extent is the same as consent, but, in some cases, mere passive acquiescence, if continued for a long time, will suffice to release the trustees. This will depend upon whether the court considers that, in the circumstances, the failure of the beneficiaries to take active steps about the breach indicates their willingness to concur in the breach and to release the trustees from liability.

Law: Limitation Act 1950, ss 21, 28
Family Protection Act 1955, s 2(5)(b)
Trusts Act 2019, s 131
Administration Act 1969, s 47
Property (Relationships) Act 1976, s 62

11 The six years do not begin to run against beneficiaries entitled to a *future* interest under a trust until their interest falls into possession.

Chapter 17
Administration of Insolvent Estates

17.0 Introduction

We have already alluded to the fact that, fortunately, the usual estate (with which this text is primarily concerned) is solvent, that is, there is still something available to be distributed to beneficiaries after the payment of expenses and debts. The word "insolvent" simply means expenses and debts exceeding assets, and this final chapter is intended to give the legal executive some guidance when confronted with such an estate. It follows from our definition that, in such estates, there is nothing available for distribution to beneficiaries — there is not even enough to pay all of the debts. The main questions arising are in what order, and to what extent, are the debts to be paid.

17.1 What the legal executive essentially needs to know

The Insolvency Act 2006 came into force on 3 December 2007. Part 6, which involves an application to the court, makes provision for insolvent estates to be administered in a manner analogous to bankruptcy, and gains for them the benefit of bankruptcy provisions. However, legal executives can avoid the application to the court, because the most useful provision, for their purposes, is s 31 of the Administration Act 1969, which enables small or uncontentious insolvent estates to be administered without such an application. The section provides that where the estate of any deceased person is insufficient to pay their debts, funeral and testamentary expenses in full, it shall be lawful for the executor or administrator to distribute that estate in accordance with the priorities that would be applicable if it were being administered under Pt 6 of the Insolvency Act, without the executor or administrator being under any obligation to apply under that Part.

It, therefore, remains to consider the priorities that would be applicable if the estate were being administered under Pt 6 of the Insolvency Act. The assets should be applied in the following order of priority (within each group, creditors rank on an equal footing):

- (Secured creditors rank first by virtue of their respective securities — they are outside the ambit of Pt 6 altogether.)
- Section 389 provides that, if the estate includes any of the deceased's household furniture and effects that would have passed to the deceased's surviving spouse if the estate had not been insolvent, the spouse may

select and retain as their own property so much of the furniture and effects as the administrator determines. The spouse must make the selection within the time that the administrator allows. The spouse's selection does not affect any rights under a valid charge or hire-purchase agreement in respect of the goods selected. And, if the goods are subject to a charge or hire-purchase agreement, it does not give the spouse any rights to any other part of the deceased's property.

- All proper costs, charges, debts, and expenses attending the due administration of the estate (that is, administration expenses).
- Reasonable funeral expenses of the deceased.
- The duty of the administrator is to realise the assets and pay creditors regardless of the deceased's will and then apply the surplus, if any, as directed by the court. If the surplus is ascertained to exist, the administrator should not realise further assets, but should apply to the court: *In re Loveridge (dec'd), Silk v Public Trustee* [1937] NZLR 534; *In re F Hall and Sons Ltd* [1939] NZLR 408.

Section 390 of the Insolvency Act provides that the administrator may make an allowance out of the estate to the surviving spouse or to any of the relatives or dependants of the deceased or the surviving spouse for the support of any of them. However, the appointee must first obtain the consent of the creditors.

Law: Administration Act 1969, s 31
Insolvency Act 2006, Pt 6

17.2 Notes on the administration of insolvent estates under Part 6 of the Insolvency Act 2006

As we have said, Pt 6 of the Act makes provision for the estates of deceased insolvent debtors to be administered in a manner analogous to bankruptcy, and gain for such estates the benefit of bankruptcy provisions.

Much of bankruptcy law is imported into the administration of these estates. We cannot, in this text, cover bankruptcy law, which is a separate branch of the law, but a one-paragraph nutshell view follows. When a person (who must necessarily be insolvent) is adjudicated bankrupt, their property is placed under the control of a government official called an Official Assignee. An Official Assignee has the power to gather in property owned by the bankrupt, not only as at the date of adjudication, but also as at previous dates,[1] and they may, in some cases, set aside gifts made by the bankrupt as much as five years prior to the date of adjudication.[2]

1 These retrospective powers of an Official Assignee are the subject of a complete branch of the law of bankruptcy.

2 Even longer if they are able to apply the Property Law Act 2007, which deals with property alienated by the bankrupt *with intent to defraud creditors*.

Having enlarged the bankrupt's estate as much as possible, the Official Assignee then distributes the proceeds among creditors, in accordance with a set order of priorities, on what the legislature considers to be a fair basis. There are few bankruptcies in which there are sufficient assets to go beyond the priority of general unsecured creditors, and these creditors normally receive only a small dividend. The Insolvency Act provides for alternatives to bankruptcy and a simplified process for a person who declares themselves bankrupt with minimal assets. This process can only be used once.

The following brief notes on the full procedure are for reference, and are intended for use in conjunction with bankruptcy texts.

17.2.1 Who can apply?

When an executor or administrator, or a person who is applying to the court to be appointed an executor or administrator of a deceased person, has ascertained that the money in the estate, together with the assets that can conveniently be converted into money, are not, or are not likely to be, sufficient to meet the claims on the estate, they may apply to the court to have the estate administered under Pt 6. When they apply to the court, or within the prescribed time thereafter, they must also file in the court an account showing the assets, debts, and liabilities of the deceased so far as they are known to them, which account they may from time to time amend.

A creditor of the deceased's estate, if the creditor's debt has reached the threshold for a creditor's application for adjudication or a beneficiary may also apply to the court for an order under Pt 6.

A creditor or beneficiary may apply for an order if—

- the administrator has not applied under this Part, and after being requested in writing to apply, fails to apply within 15 working days after receiving the request, or
- after four months from the date of the debtor's death, no administrator has been appointed and no application has been filed in the court under s 380.

The court must not make the order before two months have expired after the date when the administration was granted, but this restriction does not apply if the administrator has consented; or the applicant proves that the deceased committed an act of bankruptcy within three months before their death; or the administrator has favoured or is about to favour any creditor; or, in the court's opinion, the administrator is not properly administering the estate.

The court may allow an application filed before four months after the date of the debtor's death have expired if the court is satisfied that the deceased committed an act of bankruptcy within three months before their death or the estate that should have been available for the deceased's creditors is reducing.

17.2.2 Powers of court on hearing application

In the case of an application by a creditor, the Court of Appeal held, in effect, in *Moulder v Fischer* [1979] 2 NZLR 662, that an application to administer under Pt XVII of the previous Act should not (in the absence of cause being shown) be withheld once the simple conditions in the Act are made out. In that case, a divorced wife of the deceased, to whom he owed money, applied a considerable time after the granting of probate to have his estate so administered, in circumstances which were not blameworthy on her part and which were assumed did not prejudice the respondent. Somers J, delivering the judgment of the Court, said at 665:

> "The way in which the Court is to approach the exercise of the discretion to make or refuse an administration order is indicated by [the Act]. In the first place if the Court is satisfied that there is a reasonable probability that the estate will be sufficient for payment of debts and as well creditors will not be prejudiced by the usual administration the application will be dismissed. Unless both those matters are made out the Court may make the order 'or (upon cause being shown) may dismiss the application'.
>
> Where the creditor proves his debt and establishes that there are insufficient assets to pay creditors in full it is for those resisting the making of an order to establish grounds why it should not be made. It is essentially the same approach as is the case on a bankruptcy petition when the creditor has satisfied the Court of the truth of his allegations — see s 26(1) and (2) of the Act. The creditor has no absolute right to an order. But where the appropriate circumstances are made out, if an order is to be refused it is for the debtor to establish some ground. . .
>
> In the present case the debt was proved and it is clear that there were and are not assets sufficient for its payment".

The Court reversed the decision of the [then Supreme Court] and made an order under Pt XVII.

17.2.3 Who may be ordered to administer?

The person ordered to administer is referred to in the Act as "the appointee". The appointee can be:

- with their consent, the executors or administrators of the estate, OR if the court is of the opinion that the estate is likely to be better administered by some person other than the person who is or may become the executor or administrator
- an Official Assignee, or
- the Public Trust, or
- with the court's consent, some other person.

17.2.4 Power of Public Trust and Maori Trustee in regard to insolvent estates

The appointee has, in relation to the estate, the same authority, powers, and functions as the Assignee has in relation to the property of a bankrupt.

Where estates that they are administering, respectively, or would be entitled to administer, are apparently insolvent, they may file a certificate in the court to the effect that they elect to administer, respectively, under Pt 6. Such a certificate has the effect of an application *and an order* under Pt 6. All the powers conferred on the Public Trust or the Maori Trustee under Pt 6 are in addition to the powers conferred on them by any other Act or law.

17.2.5 The effect of an order under Part 6

At last, what is the manner of administration outlined in this chapter. In short, the order deems the appointee to be an Official Assignee, and renders the deceased a bankrupt. More specifically, it is as follows:

1. The executor or administrator (if there is one) must immediately deliver to the appointee an account of their dealings and administration of the estate, and must at the same time furnish such particulars of the affairs of the deceased as may be required by the appointee.
2. Subject to the modifications made by Pt 6, the whole of the estate, at the date of the presentation of the application upon which the order is made, vests in the appointee as the court by that order or any subsequent order directs, and the appointee must proceed to realise, administer, and distribute the estate in accordance with the law and practice for the time being in force with respect to the realisation, administration, and distribution of the property of a bankrupt debtor.
3. With respect to every estate ordered to be administered under Pt 6 (and every estate as to which such an application is pending), the court has the same powers and functions as belong to the court in its bankruptcy jurisdiction and are necessary for the purposes of Pt 6.
4. The appointee has the same authorities, powers, and functions, as an Official Assignee has under the law for the time being in force relating to bankruptcy, with respect to the property of a person adjudged a bankrupt.
5. Notice to the executor or administrator of a deceased debtor of the presentation by a creditor of an application under Pt 6 is, in the event of an order being made thereon, deemed to be equivalent to notice of an act of bankruptcy, and after that notice no payment or disposition of property made by the executor or administrator, except pursuant to the order, shall operate as a discharge to them.

6. Everything in the deceased's lifetime that would, if the deceased had become bankrupt at the time of their death, have been voidable as against an Official Assignee or the creditors of the deceased, shall be liable to be set aside by the appointee as if the deceased had been alive.

7. However, proceedings to set aside any gift or voluntary settlement, or to recover the value of voluntary improvements made by the deceased to another person's property, can be taken only with the leave of the court. Also, such voluntary transactions can be set aside only in so far as is necessary to enable the debts to be paid.

8. Unless it was completed more than three months before the date of the order to administer under Pt 6, an execution against the deceased's estate is voidable as against the appointee.

9. Before the deceased's estate is distributed as in 10. below, the deceased's spouse, if the estate includes any of the deceased's necessary household furniture and effects that would have passed to the spouse if the estate had not been insolvent, is entitled to take out and receive as their own property such necessary household furniture and effects to which they would have been so entitled.[3]

   If the estate had not been insolvent, the deceased's necessary household furniture and effects would have passed to the spouse if they had been left to them by will, or if the deceased left no will effectively disposing of them.

10. The deceased's estate is distributed in accordance with the following priorities:
    (a) payment of all proper costs, charges, debts, and expenses of the due administration of the estate, whether incurred before or after the order is made
    (b) payment of the deceased's reasonable funeral expenses
    (c) payment of the following expenses of the deceased incurred during the three months immediately before the deceased's death:
        (i) medical expenses
        (ii) reasonable expenses for hospital care (as defined in s 4(1) of the Health and Disability Services (Safety) Act 2001) provided for the deceased, so far as those expenses are lawfully recoverable
    (d) payment of other claims and interest in accordance with s 274
    (e) all other claims, which rank equally and abate in proportion if there is insufficient to pay them in full.

3 See footnote 1 of this chapter.

17.2.6 Appointee's right of indemnity

Nothing in the Insolvency Act invalidates any payment made, or any act or thing done, in good faith by the administrator before the administrator had notice of an intention to apply for an order that the estate be administered under Pt 6.

If the appointee has *properly* incurred debts for which the appointee is personally responsible, the appointee has a right of indemnity against the estate assets — *Hope v Public Trustee* [1943] NZLR 398. In that case, the Public Trustee had elected to administer an estate under the provisions of Pt IV of the Administration Act — the equivalent provisions in 1943 of Pt 6 of the Insolvency Act. However, it is emphasised that, for the appointee to have this right of indemnity, the debts must be *properly* incurred.[4]

Law: Insolvency Act 2006, Pt 6
Administration Act 1969, s 77

4 In *Re Brooks (deceased), Official Assignee v Brooks* [1942] NZLR 523, an executrix, subsequently relieved of office by the Official Assignee under the provisions of Pt IV of the Administration Act 1908, had, for the purpose of providing a home for herself and for her own benefit, unprofitably carried on the deceased's hotel business for nine months after his death. It was held, among other things:

- The business could properly have been carried on only temporarily for the purpose of prudent realisation. "This carrying on of the business was not justified and was a breach of trust against the interests of the creditors to whom the executrix owed a duty." In principle, the business debts should be made good by the executrix, who had no right of indemnity.
- An order under Pt IV [now Pt XVII] relates back to the date of death and, as the provisions of bankruptcy law are applicable as from this time, an executrix or executor in the insolvent estate has no right to prefer some creditors over others. Preferences can be recovered for the benefit of the estate.

APPENDIX 1

Example of AFFIDAVIT FOR OBTAINING GRANT OF PROBATE

In the High Court of New Zealand
Wellington Registry

No: 2022-4310 CIV.

In the estate of
PETER JOHN BROWN
of Wellington in
New Zealand, Retired (deceased)

AFFIDAVIT FOR OBTAINING GRANT OF PROBATE

NAME OF FIRM Slough & Golightly

P O BOX 435 and DX NUMBERS 742

Telephone 04 568657 and Fax numbers 04 345789

Name of person handling the matter: Vera Slough

In the High Court of New Zealand
Wellington Registry

No: 2022-4310 CIV

In the estate of
PETER JOHN
BROWN of Wellington
in New Zealand, Retired
(deceased)

I, BRIAN BROWN of Wellington, Painter, swear:

1. THE deceased (whom I knew) died at Wellington, New Zealand on or about the 5th day of January 2022.
2. I attended the deceased's funeral.
3. When the deceased died, he resided at Wellington, New Zealand.
4. I believe the document dated the 5th day of May 2003 and marked "A" now produced and shown to me is the deceased's last will.

Initials: ________ Initials: ________ Initials: ________ Initials: ________

5. I am the sole executor named in the will.
6. I will faithfully execute the will of which probate is granted in accordance with the law. If the Court requires me to, I will file in the Court and verify by affidavit—
   (a) An accurate inventory of the deceased's estate; and
   (b) An account of the deceased's estate that—
      (i) Is accurate; and
      (ii) States the dates and details of all receipts and disbursements; and
      (iii) States which of the receipts and disbursements were, on capital account and which on revenue account.

SWORN at Wellington)
this day of)
2022 before me:) SIGNATURE OF EXECUTOR

A Solicitor of the High Court of New Zealand
Name of Solicitor:

Initials: __________ Initials: __________ Initials: __________ Initials: __________

Example of APPLICATION WITHOUT NOTICE FOR OBTAINING PROBATE

In the High Court of New Zealand
Wellington Registry

No: 2022-4310 CIV.

In the estate of
PETER JOHN
BROWN of Wellington
in New Zealand, Retired
(deceased)

APPLICATION WITHOUT NOTICE FOR OBTAINING PROBATE

NAME OF FIRM Slough & Golightly
P O BOX 435 and DX NUMBERS 742
Telephone 04 568657 and Fax numbers 04 345789
Name of person handling the matter: Vera Slough

In the High Court of New Zealand

Wellington Registry

No: 2022-4310 CIV

In the estate of

PETER JOHN

BROWN of Wellington

in New Zealand, Retired

(deceased)

TO: The Registrar of the High Court at Wellington

THIS DOCUMENT NOTIFIES YOU THAT:

1. The applicant, BRIAN BROWN of Wellington, Painter, will apply for an order that probate of the will of the above-named deceased be granted to him.
2. The grounds on which this order is sought is that the applicant is the sole executor named in the will.
3. The application is made in reliance on Section 5 of the Administration Act 1969, and Rule 27.4 and the rules following of the High Court Rules.

I certify that this application complies with the rules.

Dated this 20th day of January 2022

....

VERA SLOUGH

Solicitor for the Applicant

This application is filed by: Vera Slough

Of Slough & Golightly

5 Main Street

Wellington

P O BOX 435 and DX NUMBERS 742

Telephone 04 568657 and Fax numbers 04 345789

Comment

Rule 27.4 of the High Court Rules 2016 states that a lawyer may give the certificate above even though he or she—

(a) is one of the witnesses to the will that the application is about; or

(b) is named as an executor in the will; or

(c) is an executor of the will according to its tenor.

Example of PROBATE

In the High Court of New Zealand

Wellington Registry

No: 2022-4310 CIV.

In the estate of
PETER JOHN
BROWN of Wellington
in New Zealand, Retired
(deceased)

PROBATE IN COMMON FORM

NAME OF FIRM Slough & Golightly

P O BOX 435 and DX NUMBERS 742

Telephone 04 568657 and Fax numbers 04 345789

Name of person handling the matter: Vera Slough

In the High Court of New Zealand

Wellington Registry

No: 2022-4310 CIV

In the estate of

PETER JOHN

BROWN of Wellington

in New Zealand, Retired

(deceased)

1. The deceased, PETER JOHN BROWN, died at Wellington on or about the 5th day of January 2022, leaving a will. A copy is attached.

2. The will was proved before Registrar Brown at Wellington in chambers acting under Rule 27.14 of the High Court Rules and probate of the will was granted this day.

3. This probate document appoints BRIAN BROWN of Wellington, painter, the sole executor named in the will as administrator of the deceased's estate.

Dated: the 15th day of February 2022

Registrar

Sealed: 15th day of February 2022

Example of Trust Inter Vivos (Private Deed of Trust)

THIS DEED made this...................day of............................ 2022 BETWEEN JOSEPH BLOGGS of Wellington, Clerk, (hereinafter called "the settlor") of the one part AND WILLIAM SMITH of Wellington, Accountant, (hereinafter called "the trustee") of the other part WHEREAS it has been agreed by the settlor and the trustee that:

(a) The trustee should execute such declaration of trust as is hereinafter contained; and

(b) The settlor should pay to the trustee the sum of fifty thousand dollars ($50,000) to be held by him upon the trusts so to be declared, which sum the settlor has contemporaneously herewith paid to the trustee.

NOW THIS DEED WITNESSES THAT in pursuance of the premises the settlor HEREBY DIRECTS and the trustee DECLARES that the trustee shall stand possessed of the said sum of fifty thousand dollars ($50,000) (hereinafter called "the trust fund") upon the following trusts, namely:

1. UPON TRUST to invest the trust fund in such manner and in such securities as the trustee may in his absolute and uncontrolled discretion deem fit and to pay the income derived therefrom to JANE BLOGGS so long as she remains the wife or unmarried widow of the settlor.
2. UPON TRUST from and after the death or sooner remarriage of the said Jane Bloggs to hold the trust fund for such of them RICHARD BLOGGS, JAMES BLOGGS, TRACEY BLOGGS and NANCY BLOGGS (being the children of the settlor) as attain the age of twenty (20) years and if more than one in equal shares.

IN WITNESS WHEREOF these presents have been executed the day and year first hereinbefore written.

SIGNED by the abovenamed JOSEPH BLOGGS

as settlor in the presence of

SIGNED by the abovenamed WILLIAM SMITH

as trustee in the presence of

Example of Testamentary Trust (Created by Will)

THIS IS THE LAST WILL of me ALBERT JONES of Wellington in New Zealand, Builder.

1. I REVOKE all wills and testamentary dispositions at any time heretofore executed by me AND I APPOINT THE PUBLIC TRUST of New Zealand (hereinafter referred to as "my trustee") to be the executor and trustee of this my will.

2. I GIVE AND DEVISE the dwellinghouse and land owned by me at the date of this my will situate at and known as 17 Ohiro Bay Road, Wellington, unto my trustee upon the following trusts, namely:

   (a) UPON TRUST as from my death to permit my wife JANE JONES to have the free use income occupation and enjoyment thereof during her lifetime subject to her paying all rates taxes interest insurance premiums and other outgoings usually payable out of income from time to time payable in connection therewith and to her keeping the same in good order repair and condition to the satisfaction of my trustee except in respect of any injury or deterioration occasioned by fire lightning earthquake tempest or other inevitable accident.

   (b) UPON TRUST from and after the death of the survivor of my said wife and me (hereinafter referred to as "the period of distribution") to hold my dwellinghouse and land for such of them my children MOIRA JONES, NORMAN JONES and ELIZABETH JONES as survive the period of distribution and if more than one in equal shares.

3. I GIVE DEVISE AND BEQUEATH the whole of my estate both real and personal of whatsoever nature and wheresoever situate not hereinbefore otherwise disposed of unto my trustee UPON TRUST to pay thereout my just debts funeral and testamentary expenses and to stand possessed of the residue for my said wife Jane Jones but should she predecease me then for such of them my said children as survive me and if more than one in equal shares.

AS WITNESS my hand this .... day of .... two thousand and seventeen (2017).

SIGNED by the abovenamed ALBERT JONES

as his last will in our presence and attested by

us in his presence

Example of Discretionary Trust

(Clause regarding maintenance, education, advancement or benefit of will-maker's children)

I GIVE DEVISE AND BEQUEATH the whole of my estate both real and personal of whatsoever nature and wheresoever situate unto my trustee UPON TRUST to pay thereout my just debts funeral and testamentary expenses and to stand possessed of the residue for my husband RICHARD GIBSON but should he predecease me then and in that event only I DIRECT my trustee to stand possessed of such residue (hereinafter referred to as "my residuary estate") upon the following trusts, namely:

1. UPON TRUST as from my death to apply so much of the income arising therefrom as my trustee thinks fit and in so far as such income is insufficient for the purpose such part or parts of the capital thereof as my trustee thinks fit for or towards the maintenance education advancement or benefit of such of my children MOIRA GIBSON, NORMAN GIBSON and ELIZABETH GIBSON as there are from time to time living or of any one or more of them to the exclusion of the others or other of them in such shares and proportions and in such manner as my trustee thinks fit until the arrival of the first point of time (hereinafter referred to as "the period of distribution") when I shall have died and all of them my said children shall respectively either have attained the age of twenty-four (24) years or died under that age AND I DIRECT that until the period of distribution so much of the income arising from my residuary estate as is not applied in any year by my trustee as aforesaid shall be invested by my trustee so as to accumulate at compound interest to the intent that such accumulations shall be added to and form part of the capital of my residuary estate and follow the destination thereof but my trustee may at any time or times prior to the period of distribution resort to the accumulations of any preceding year or years and apply the same for or towards the maintenance education advancement or benefit of my said children as aforesaid.
2. UPON TRUST from and after the period of distribution to hold my residuary estate or so much as then remains for such of them my said children as are living at my death and if more than one in equal shares.

N.B. Clause 1. governing the payment of income (and possibly capital) during the trust period is an example of a *sprinkler trust*. Such payments are left entirely at the discretion of the trustee, and all that a beneficiary can hope for is a decision, on the part of the trustee, to give him part of the income.

APPENDIX 2

Modern Cases on Constructive Trusts

These cases remain relevant in situations where people share interests in property but are not in a relationship as defined in the Property (Relationships) Act 1976 (See Subsection 1.5.3 — *Meaning of de facto relationships*), such as friends or flatmates who have contributed to the acquisition of property.

Hussey v Palmer [1972] 1 WLR 1286. In this case, the plaintiff, an elderly widow, moved in with her daughter and son-in-law. However, the house was not big enough, and so the plaintiff, by way of an inexplicit loan, which is understandable in this context of family arrangements, advanced £607 to the son-in-law with which he had an additional room built on to the house. The arrangement did not work out in the long term, and the plaintiff left the house — her requests (to the son-in-law) for the £607 meeting with no response.

In the English Court of Appeal, the plaintiff claimed that the son-in-law held the house on trust for her to the extent of £607 and, in a *not unanimous* decision, she was successful. Although, under the principles of Equity, a loan to the purchaser does not give rise to a trust, Denning MR held that the son-in-law held the house (to the extent concerned) on a *constructive* trust, and said at 1289:

> "Although the plaintiff alleged that there was a resulting trust, I should have thought that the trust in this case, if there was one, was more in the nature of a constructive trust: but this is more a matter of words than anything else. The two run together. By whatever name it is described, it is a trust imposed by law whenever justice and good conscience require it. It is a liberal process, founded upon large principles of equity, to be applied in cases where the legal owner cannot conscientiously keep the property for himself alone, but ought to allow another to have the property or the benefit of it or a share in it. The trust may arise at the outset when the property is acquired, or later on, as the circumstances may require. It is an equitable remedy by which the court can enable an aggrieved party to obtain restitution".

Phillimore LJ agreed, but held that the son-in-law held the house on a *resulting* trust.

It now appears that the categories of "resulting trust" and "constructive trust" are not separate and distinct and that, in these joint enterprise property cases, there is overlap between the two.

In *Stratulatos v Stratulatos* [1988] 2 NZLR 424, the plaintiff believed that the property occupied by herself and her husband (when alive), but owned by the defendant, her mother-in-law, would be transferred to her husband as a gift on the death of the defendant. The defendant knew of this belief, and acquiesced in the couple effecting major renovations to the property, and regarded the property as "theirs". On the early death of the husband (and remarriage of the plaintiff), a dispute as to the property arose, the plaintiff claiming (inter alia) that the defendant "held the property under an implied or constructive trust in favour of the plaintiff and her [former] husband". McGechan J found that the defendant held the property on a constructive trust for the plaintiff (who was also next of kin in her late husband's estate) to the extent of the value of the improvements, that is, as to a one-quarter share. His Honour considered, but declined to commit himself on, *Hussey v Palmer* (supra), but clearly favoured the imposition of a constructive trust upon a wide basis. He cited a passage in *Hayward v Giordani* (see Subsection 11.1.2.2 — *Ownership of the family home when a de facto couple have split up* in the text) mentioning the expectations of the reasonable person, the "unjust enrichment concept used by the Supreme Court of Canada", unconscionability, and Lord Denning's "justice and good conscience"; but did not specify the exact base on which the constructive trust rested. He said at 436:

> "There has been a steady development in the doctrine of the constructive trust over recent years to cater for situations where one party has expended money or effort on the property of another, in the absence not only of any formal contract but of any actual intention as to a right to the property resulting. ... I have little doubt that the tide is running strongly in favour of the simple and overt imposition of a constructive trust when such is necessary to do justice, rather than fashioning 'phantoms of common intention' in order to resolve the property relationship . . . ".

In *Elders Pastoral Ltd v Bank of New Zealand* (1989) 2 NZBLC 103,667; [1989] 2 NZLR 180, Elders, a firm of stock agents, persuaded the Bank of New Zealand to advance money to a farmer named Gunn under an instrument by way of security (in favour of the bank) registered over Gunn's stock. Gunn was also indebted to Elders. Elders, acting as agent for Gunn, then sold some of the stock and applied nearly all of the proceeds of sale in satisfaction of the debt owing to itself. The bank claimed that it was entitled to the proceeds of sale, thereby giving rise to the proceedings. The Court of Appeal held that:

1. Elders had actual knowledge of the existence of the instrument by way of security.
2. On a construction of both the provisions of the instrument and the implied provisions in the Chattels Transfer Act 1924, Gunn had the right to sell the stock but was bound to pay the proceeds of sale to, or see that they were paid to, the bank.

3. Elders had constructive knowledge of the above provisions by virtue of s 4 of the Chattels Transfer Act (everyone is deemed to know of the contents of registered instruments).

4. Elders, who was the agent of Gunn, held the proceeds of sale on a constructive trust for the bank, in that it would be unconscionable for it to retain them as against the bank. In reaching this conclusion, Cooke P also spoke of the expectations of reasonable persons. Somers J said in NZBLC at 103,679; NZLR at 193:

> "The constructive trust, to which the passage in Goff and Jones refers, has not been left uninfluenced. It has come to be used as a device for imposing a liability to account on persons who cannot in good conscience retain a benefit in breach of their legal or equitable obligations. Its evolution or extension as a remedy may not yet have come to an end".

(The decision in favour of the Bank of New Zealand was later affirmed by the Privy Council, but on other grounds — their Lordships did not consider it necessary to consider the matter of a constructive trust — see (1990) 3 NZBLC 101,893; [1991] 1 NZLR 385.)

Powell v Thompson (1990) 1 NZ ConvC 190,663; [1991] 1 NZLR 597. A brief statement is given of the essential issues of this case — factual complications are omitted. Mrs Powell, an accountant's assistant handling Mr Thompson's financial affairs, over an eight-year period, embezzled nearly $300,000 of his money. The fraud was eventually discovered by Mr Thompson who, showing considerable tolerance, did not initially report it, but acquiesced in Mrs Powell's plans to get out of the difficulties herself. Part of these plans involved the transfer of Mrs Powell's home to Mr Thompson. However, Mrs Powell was not, in fact, the outright owner of the home — she was a tenant in common as to a one-third share, the other two-thirds share being owned equally by her two daughters, one of whom was also occupying the home. The former fact was known to Mr Thompson, who accepted a transfer of the property signed by Mrs Powell in her own right, and on behalf of the daughters under powers of attorney which she held. The daughters knew nothing of this and, indeed, the powers of attorney, although valid and unrevoked, were outdated, and had been forgotten by them. Mr Thompson's only concern, quite understandably it is submitted, was that the transaction was legally enforceable — Mrs Powell's daughters were her problem. Finally, the daughters discovered all that had transpired, and the balloon was up — they placed a caveat on the title and claimed that Mr Thompson held the property, which he had received, on a constructive trust for them as to a two-thirds share; and Mr Thompson reported the matter to Mrs Powell's employer and to the police.

Thomas J held that:

1. Mr Thompson had actual knowledge that the daughters were part-owners of the property.
2. Mr Thompson had actual knowledge that the daughters had not authorised Mrs Powell to sign the transfer under the powers of attorney, which transfer defeated the daughters' interests.
3. If he (Thomas J) was wrong in holding 2. above, Mr Thompson had constructive knowledge that the daughters had not authorised Mrs Powell to sign the transfer under the powers of attorney, in that a reasonable person in Mr Thompson's shoes would have been put on inquiry. (In other words, he ought to have checked the position out.)
4. Because of findings 1., 2., and 3. above, the property received by Mr Thompson was impressed with a constructive trust in favour of the daughters as to a two-thirds share, in that it would be unconscionable to allow Mr Thompson to retain this advantage. Thomas J said in NZ ConvC at 190,669; NZLR at 605:

> "A constructive trust is one of the most productive concepts by which equity reverses the unconscionable. It is also one of the most flexible, defying close definition. As McMullin J said in *Pasi v Kamana* [1986] 1 NZLR 603, at p 607:
>
> > 'There is . . . little purpose in endeavouring to lay down the metes and bounds of the constructive trust any more than there is in pursuing the parameters of the unconscionable bargain . . .'
>
> I agree, and perceive in this flexibility a real advantage. The judiciary is better able to shape a malleable principle so as to accommodate the changing needs and mores of society in order to achieve justice in a particular case than it is when the principle bears the imprint of rigidity (see Dickson J in *Pettkus v Becker* (1980) 117 DLR (3d) 257, at pp 273–274.)
>
> So while no claim may be certain, yet none is hopeless! But this is to be unduly cynical. The inequitable circumstances and unconscionable conduct which will attract the attention of equity must, in the nature of things, be boundless. No single formulation will suffice to embrace all the factual situations calling for an equitable response which will arise in the course of human affairs. But while the circumstances and behaviour may be incapable of precise definition, they are capable of identification. Equity is then at hand with a principle which will enable the courts to rectify the injustices which would otherwise occur. For it to do so effectively, equitable concepts such as the constructive trust must be as flexible as the subject matter with which they must cope".

And in NZ ConvC at 190,669; NZLR at 606:

> "However, whether the juristic basis has been expressed in terms of unconscionability, constructive or equitable fraud, unjust enrichment, imputed intention, denial of reasonable expectations, or proprietary or promissory estoppel, the outcome is the same; the courts will declare the defendant to be a constructive trustee of the property in question whenever, in all the circumstances of the particular case, it is perceived that it would be unjust or unfair not to do so. Almost invariably the element which underlies the finding is the unmerited enrichment of the defendant at the expense of the plaintiff.
>
> Thus, in this case I consider that, in all the circumstances, it would be manifestly unjust to permit the defendant to retain the moneys which represent the proceeds of the sale of the plaintiffs' two-thirds share of their property sold without their knowledge or consent. I do not propose to justify this decision by reference to the many authorities which the subject of constructive trusts has generated. It is widely acknowledged that the authorities are in disarray, and any attempt to analyse or reconcile them is not only unnecessary but is likely to add to the present confusion. In line with what I have said above, I prefer to decide the case on the basis of the principles of equity which underlie the varying decisions — and which accord with reason and common sense. My approach is, perhaps, not too dissimilar from that of Sir Robert Megarry V-C in *Re Montagu's Settlement Trusts* [1987] 1 Ch 264, at p 278, where he states:
>
> > 'There is today something of a tendency in equity to put less emphasis on detailed rules that have emerged from the cases and more weight on the underlying principles that engendered those rules, treating the rules less as rules requiring complete compliance, and more as guidelines to assist the court in applying the principles'."

In *DFC New Zealand Ltd v Goddard* [1992] 2 NZLR 445, Goddard, a trustee under an express trust, invested for a term of one year over $2,000,000 with DFC giving instructions that, at the expiration of the term, the funds were to be paid into a named account at the National Bank. At the expiration of the term, DFC did not pay the funds to the National Bank. DFC, after an ineffectual attempt to contact Goddard, in effect "rolled them over" — it held them (but on call) for a further term of one year under a negotiable certificate of deposit. A few days elapsed. Normally, no great difficulties would have arisen from this, but severe difficulties for Goddard did arise in that, on the very day that he took action to enforce his instructions, DFC went into statutory management and the funds became frozen. It thus became critical for Goddard to establish that DFC held the funds, not merely on the normal contractual basis prevailing between banker and customer, but on trust. In this latter event, the beneficiaries were ultimately entitled to the funds (thereby gaining priority over other creditors), in the former, the statutory manager was entitled to them. Goddard alleged that DFC, in purporting to make the reinvestment, so intermeddled in the affairs of the trust as to constitute itself a constructive trustee; and Gallen J upheld him. The judge held that DFC, as well as breaching the terms on which the funds had been deposited, with knowledge that the funds were trust funds made a decision as to investment that was the responsibility of the trustee, and intermeddled with the performance of the trust itself. Upon reinvestment, he held that DFC became a constructive trustee of the funds for the beneficiaries, because it made itself a trustee de son tort (see Chapter 6 — *Executors*, footnote 8).

However, this was reversed on appeal with the Court of Appeal holding that, by retaining the money on call as it had done, DFC did not become a constructive trustee of the funds. The normal relationship of debtor and creditor prevailed. The funds belonged to DFC (not to the trustee), and we are talking only about book entries within DFC. DFC had not "reinvested" the funds — it is indisputable that the normal relationship between banker and customer is one of debtor and creditor and DFC, in failing to pay the funds into the named account at the National Bank, had simply failed to pay a debt and had committed a breach of contract. It did not thereby constitute itself a trustee. Cooke P said at 448:

> "DFC did not intermeddle with trust matters by failing to pay a debt and purporting to accept a liability to pay a substituted debt".

In *Lankshear v ANZ Banking Group (New Zealand) Ltd* (1992) 4 NZBLC 102,770; [1993] 1 NZLR 481, the plaintiff, in furtherance of a property-development partnership that she had formed with Broadley, handed over to Broadley a cheque for a substantial sum for the purpose of the development of a Whangaparoa property. Broadley paid the cheque into the ANZ Bank, knowing that the bank was proposing to use the money in repayment of his pre-partnership overdraft. The Court held that, in doing this, Broadley was in breach of his fiduciary obligations as a partner, and in breach of the partnership agreement. Later, Broadley went bankrupt. Although bankers are not under a general duty to inquire into the circumstances of deposit or payment of a cheque, the plaintiff was successful in establishing that the bank held the money on a constructive trust for her. In reaching such a conclusion, Wallace J[1] made it clear that the knowledge of the bank becomes of crucial importance. As a result of several communications (with Broadley), the bank

1 Who said in NZBLC at 102,772; NZLR at 483:

> "This proceeding adds yet another to the burgeoning list of cases concerning the circumstances in which a bank or other third party may become a constructive trustee. In this area of the law some of the previously decided cases are difficult to reconcile and there is also debate concerning the underlying principles. Though I have endeavoured to give full consideration to the many authorities and published articles it is desirable first to consider the facts. In the end they are always of crucial importance and, once

manager had actual knowledge that the cheque was handed over by the plaintiff solely for the purpose of the development of the Whangaparoa property, and he knew or ought to have known that the bank could not properly apply the money in repayment of Broadley's overdraft for pre-partnership indebtedness. On this latter point, the judge confirmed that constructive knowledge will suffice — any inquiry from the bank manager would have conclusively resolved the matter, but he did not want to face up to it. On the contrary, "on the most favourable interpretation from [the bank manager's] point of view [he] simply closed his mind to the knowledge he acquired concerning the existence of the partnership and the intended use of the funds". In terms of legal principle, the bank acquired the money with knowledge of a trust, and then, to its own advantage, knowingly applied it in a manner inconsistent with the trust, thereby constituting itself a constructive trustee. It was also "unjust or unconscionable for the [bank] to retain at the plaintiff's expense the funds used to repay Broadley's overdraft".

However, if the bank has not obtained an advantage for itself out of the dealing (knowing receipt), it must have acted dishonestly or recklessly before a constructive trust will be imposed. In *Nimmo v Westpac Banking Corporation* [1993] 3 NZLR 218, where the proceeds of Nimmo's superannuation moneys were negligently paid by the bank (without advantage to the bank — knowing assistance) to Eaton, who then embezzled them, the Court declined to impose a constructive trust because the bank had been neither dishonest or reckless.[2]

Where the bank has not obtained an advantage for itself, constructive (as opposed to actual) knowledge of the claimant's interest is not in itself sufficient.

Attorney-General for Hong Kong v Reid [1994] 1 NZLR 1 concerns the matter of bribes. Reid, a New Zealand national employed by the Hong Kong Government as a crown prosecutor, accepted bribes for obstructing the prosecution of certain criminals, and with the bribe moneys bought three properties in Tauranga, New Zealand. The long-established decision of *Lister & Co v Stubbs* (1890) 45 Ch D 1 (CA) had settled that an employee who accepts bribes does not hold them on a constructive trust for the employer, because the employer was never entitled to them in the first place, but that the employer could merely claim them as a debt owing (the employer had no

established, may make it unnecessary to consider large tracts of uncertain or developing law".

And in NZBLC at 102,777; NZLR at 489:

"As I have indicated in the earlier discussion of the pleadings, the plaintiff's counsel finally advanced the claim on several alternative (but overlapping) grounds. That is understandable because this area of the law is difficult and still in the process of development".

2 The reasoning in *Nimmo*'s case was adopted in *Cigna Life Insurance New Zealand Ltd v Westpac Securities Ltd* [1996] 1 NZLR 80, and in *Equiticorp Industries Group (In Statutory Management) v The Crown (Judgment no 47)* 1996 7 NZCLC 261,143; [1998] 2 NZLR 481. A summary of the case can be seen in [1996] 3 NZLR 587.

initial proprietary interest). However the Privy Council, after looking at earlier authorities, overruled *Lister & Co v Stubbs*, and held that a false fiduciary (employee) who accepts bribes, holds the bribes or their proceeds on a constructive trust for the person to whom the false fiduciary owed the duty (employer). Reid, therefore, held the three properties as a constructive trustee for the Hong Kong Government, which was entitled to have caveats against them extended.

In *Dickie v Torbay Pharmacy (1986) Ltd* (1995) 5 NZBLC 103,918; [1995] 3 NZLR 429, a group of doctors practicing together as Hauraki Medical Centre, Takapuna, Auckland, entrusted B, an accountant/developer, to arrange the purchase of a block of land over the road that the doctors and B hoped to use for the further expansion of their respective businesses. For practical reasons, with which we need not concern ourselves, B arranged the purchase in the name of a nominee or agent J but, when the arrangements were complete, sought to make J a principal in the venture. This was contrary to the wishes of the doctors, who sought to exclude J, and now wished to claim sole ownership of the land. The Court held initially that J held the land on a constructive trust for the doctors and B. Furthermore, the law as to fiduciary relationships is one of the rapidly developing branches of Equity. Because B stood in a position of confidence and trust in the venture, he owed a fiduciary duty to the doctors,[3]

3 Hammond J said in NZBLC at 103,926–103,927; NZLR at 439–440:

> "The first issue I need to dispose of here is, *was* B a fiduciary as between himself and the doctors? As to that, it is now established that a fiduciary relationship can, on the facts of the particular matter, exist in a co-ventureship. See *United Dominions Corporation Ltd v Brian Pty Ltd* (1985) 157 CLR 1. And in *Marr v Arabco Traders Ltd* (1987) 1 NZBLC 102,732 at 102,745, Tompkins J said:
>
> > 'The essential issue will be whether the relationship, however it may be described or characterised, imports between the participants a duty to act in perfect fairness, in good faith and honestly to each other. That will depend on the nature of the dealings and the extent to which those dealings, by their very nature, require the participants so to act. If the course of dealing indicates an intention to carry out a common purpose by a joint association in a way that involves mutual confidence in each other, fiduciary duties may well result. This of course is clearly the case where there is a partnership and where there is a joint venture agreement other than a partnership. It can also be the case where the parties are negotiating to achieve either of those relationships or where they have formed an association of the kind I have described, which although it may not amount to a partnership or a joint venture, is akin to one or the other'".

Hammond J went on to say in NZBLC at 103,927; NZLR at 440:

> "In my view, B was in a fiduciary relationship with the doctors. Further, he breached that fiduciary relationship by making an unauthorised agreement with J that J would have a share in the development; and he turned his back on his co-venturers — to whom he owed a duty of loyalty — when a crisis arose and it became plain that his co-venturers would not agree to his proposals. He threw in his lot with J. That has to be a very serious breach of fiduciary duty. In everyday language, it involved 'jumping ship' and acting very directly against his co-venturers".

and as he had breached this fiduciary duty in a serious way by unauthorisedly including J as a principal in the purchase, the Court terminated the co-venturer relationship and forfeited his interest. The Court excluded B from the purchase subject to refunding to him the expenses that he had incurred.

Vernon v Public Trust [2016] NZCA 388; [2015] NZHC 1928

A son had, through undue influence, appropriated almost all of his father's assets for his own benefit and that of his wife. Justice Kós in the High Court found that all the funds misapplied by the son in breach of his fiduciary obligations were held by him on constructive trust, and ordered the son to account to his father's estate for half of those assets for the benefit of his nephew. The decision was upheld on appeal to the Court of Appeal.

Judd v Hawkes Bay Trustee Company Limited [2016] NZCA 397

In *Judd v Hawkes Bay Trustee Company Limited*, the Court of Appeal held that Mr Hodgkinson's family trust could not stand in the way of his wife's claim to a share of the trust property which was used as their home during their relationship. The Court imposed a constructive trust (in favour of a wife) on an express trust (which did not benefit her). Imposition of a constructive trust has emerged as a way of ensuring that an express trust is not used as a means of defeating a claim by someone who has a reasonable expectation of receiving a benefit from property used by partners in a relationship, should that relationship break down.

Mr Hodgkinson and Ms Judd were married for six and a half years. Over that period, they lived in a substantial residential property located in Havelock North, which was owned by the Richard Hodgkinson Trust ("the Trust"). Following their separation, Ms Judd claimed that the Trust held a share in the property on trust for her, reflecting her contributions to it.

The High Court agreed ([2014] NZHC 3298), valuing Ms Judd's contributions at $10,000 per year and totalling $65,000 in all. Although Ms Judd's contributions were indirect, they were found to have prevented the house from going to "rack and ruin" which, when proof of enhanced value is not always required, was sufficient to establish that her efforts benefited the Trust.

Ms Judd's claim was upheld on appeal. Following Lankow v Rose, the Court agreed that Ms Judd's contributions to the property gave her a reasonable expectation of a share in it. This would not be surprising had the property been owned by Mr Hodgkinson in his own right, but neither the fact that the property was owned by a trust, nor that she knew this at the outset, prevented Ms Judd's claim from succeeding. The Court noted that "Ms Judd's understanding of the situation that pertained to the Trust did not mean she expected she was to contribute in the way she did but, if the marriage broke up, receive nothing" (at [36]). It was not sufficient that she knew she was not a beneficiary of the trust.

The Court was influenced by the fact that Mr Hodgkinson treated the property as his own and was given "carte blanche" by his co-trustee to do as he wished with the assets of the Trust. The co-trustee knew of Ms Judd's contributions but nevertheless was content to allow the Trust — and Mr Hodgkinson as beneficiary — to take the full benefit of them. In this light the Court found that it would be unconscionable not to recognise the benefits freely accepted by the Trust.

Upholding the quantum of the award made by the High Court the Court of Appeal noted at [33]:

"One means of cross-checking the approach is to note that the judgment sum amounts to an award of some $200 a week for the course of the marriage. If we assume that Ms Judd would have otherwise made rental payments of, say, $200 per week that means she has received overall a payment of $400 a week. We do not consider it is unreasonable or unrealistic to say that her contribution equated to about $400 a week."

Crucially, Mr Hodgkinson and Ms Judd did not enter into a relationship property agreement. If a trust's primary purpose is to protect assets from becoming relationship property at least to the extent of improvement or maintenance provided by the other partner, it is vital to have relationship property agreement in place. Indeed, the Court of Appeal acknowledged that Mr Hodgkinson could have entered into a relationship property agreement with Ms Judd but noted that "absent such an adjustment of her expectations, where the contributions are to the matrimonial home and the trustees have encouraged or permitted these contributions, it would be wrong to treat a contributor like Ms Judd as a volunteer" (at [47]). A relationship property agreement which negatived any claim by her would have stood as a clear statement by Ms Judd that she was foregoing any claim despite her contributions and would have been upheld unless the Court considered that the circumstances between the parties had changed since the agreement was made so as to render the agreement "unfair or unreasonable".

Further, a co-trustee cannot simply abdicate responsibility and allow the other to operate a trust for his own benefit. This behaviour is what led to Mr Hodgkinson's downfall. He and his co-trustee could have taken advice on the issue at the time of the marriage, but did not. Trustees need to be alert to the possibility of a constructive trust claim and take proactive steps to preserve trust assets. The lack of engagement by the co-trustee in this case meant that the Court was able to see the case as more closely that of one spouse holding property to which the other had contributed, rather that property which was clearly held in a separate trust estate and outside the hands of the other spouse.

Ridge and Ridge v Parore and Lloyd [2014] NZHC 318 (28 February 2014)

Following the separation of Sally Ridge and Adam Parore, the division of property between them was made difficult as the majority of the assets were held in two family trusts. Both Sally Ridge and Adam Parore and their four children were beneficiaries of each trust. Sally and Adam were also trustees of each trust.

The parties' assets were restructured so that the family home was owned by Sally Ridge's trust and the business assets held by Adam Parore's trust. This structure was set up in early 2007 to protect their family home from any trading liabilities of the couple. The evidence showed that it was the intention of the parties that Adam's trust would fund the parties' lifestyle and allow the income and assets of both trusts to be shared equally between the parties.

It is not clear whether Sally Ridge received independent legal advice in relation to the restructure, but it is clear that she was kept well informed, as she attended meetings with, and received email correspondence from, the lawyer instructed to put the restructure in place. Sally was, however, not particularly interested in the details of the restructure and relied on Adam to ensure the arrangements were appropriate.

In mid-2008, Adam's trust purchased a company called Small Business Accounting (SBA). SBA was successful and allowed Adam's trust to fund the parties' living expenses.

Sally Ridge and Adam Parore separated in 2010. Sally claimed that the parties had a common intention that SBA would be held equally for the benefit of the parties and therefore Adam's trust was holding half of the shares in SBA on a common intention constructive trust for her trust.

While few, if any, cases of a common intention constructive trust have been recognised in New Zealand, the Australian and English authorities are clear that such trusts are founded on "proof of a subjective common intention, clearly and unequivocally established by words or conduct".

One problem that Sally faced was that in each of her pleadings before the Court, the parties to the alleged common intention kept changing. At one point, Sally claimed Adam's trust was holding the shares for the parties personally; at a later point, it was that Adam's trust was holding the shares for the benefit of the two trusts.

The Court found that Sally's claim was contradicted by the evidence:

- The 2007 restructure was completed to clearly separate the family home and business assets. There was never a suggestion that the trustees of Adam's trust would hold assets for the beneficiaries of Sally's trust, and

- The concept of equal sharing was achieved by the trustees of each trust exercising their discretions to benefit Sally and Adam as equal beneficiaries of each trust, not by sharing ownership of the assets between the two trusts.

As Sally could not show a clear and unequivocal intention that half of the shares in SBA were held by Adam's trust for her own trust, the Court declined to find in her favour.

APPENDIX 3

Cases that clarify what is charitable

The meaning of "charitable" has been further explained by the following cases:

1. *Trusts for the relief of poverty.*

The preamble to the Statute of Elizabeth speaks of "the relief of aged, impotent, and poor people". In *Re Glyn's Will Trusts* [1950] 2 All ER 1150, it was held that these words must be read disjunctively, so that a trust may be charitable if the beneficiaries fall within any of these descriptions. "Impotent" means physically infirm, for example, blind. In *Re Lewis* [1954] 3 All ER 257, a gift of £100 each to "ten blind girls Tottenham residents if possible" was held to have a charitable object even though the blind girls would not necessarily be poor in the financial sense. It is not necessary that the beneficiaries be destitute. As Lord Evershed MR said in *Re Coulthurst's Will Trusts* [1951] Ch 661, poverty "is a word of wide and somewhat indefinite import; it may not unfairly be paraphrased for present purposes as meaning persons who have to 'go short' in the ordinary acceptation of that term, due regard being had to their status in life and so forth".

2. *Trusts for the advancement of education.*

Trusts for the dissemination of any form of morally acceptable knowledge will be held to have a charitable object. Thus trusts for the establishment or support of schools and universities clearly qualify, as do trusts for the establishment or support of professorships, lectureships and scholarships. Also, trusts for research can qualify if the necessary conditions are met. However, in *Re Shaw* [1957] 1 All ER 745, where George Bernard Shaw in his will set up a trust to develop a new English alphabet, the Court did not regard the conditions as met because there was no element of dissemination of knowledge. As we are going to see when we deal with Lord Macnaghten's fourth category, trusts for political purposes do not have a charitable object. The significance of this last point for the present heading, is that it appears that a trust which is being operated for political purposes will not have a charitable object, even though it purports to be a trust for the advancement of education. In *Bonar Law Memorial Trust v Inland Revenue Commissioners* (1933) 49 TLR 220, there was a widely framed educational trust under which the trustees could, but did not have to, apply the income for education in Conservative Party principles. The Court held on the evidence that "one could not doubt that this place was being used as an education centre for the Conservative Party", and that the Bonar Law Memorial Trust was not charitable.

3. *Trusts for the advancement of religion.*

Any trust that is essentially for, or ancillary to, the worship of God (or a gift to an organisation that exists for this purpose, such as the Salvation Army) has a charitable object. It appears that the interpretation of "God" can be very general. In *Centrepoint Community Growth Trust v C of IR* (1984) 6 NZTC 62,010; [1985] 1 NZLR 673 (HC), the Court found that the members of the trust, under the leadership of Mr HT Potter, believed in a supernatural being, thing, or principle. They had an affinity to the world's revealed religions, and such objectives were expressed in the trust's provisions, even though these were far from easy to understand. The trust was held to be (inter alia) for the advancement of religion. The courts do not distinguish between different branches of religion, and nor do they attempt to concern themselves with the truth or otherwise of any particular religious beliefs. Thus in *Re Strickland's Will Trusts* [1936] 3 All ER 1027, a trust for the upkeep of the "K.H. Baptist Chapel and school", and in *Thornton v Howe* (1862) 31 Beav 14, a trust to publish the writings of a woman who claimed to have conceived the new Messiah, were held to have charitable objects. Again in *Centrepoint Community Growth Trust v C of IR* (supra), the Court declined to assess the truth or otherwise of the beliefs and writings of Mr HT Potter (and held the trust *also* to be charitable on the basis of the advancement of education, and on the basis of other purposes beneficial to the community).

As stated, trusts for purposes ancillary to the worship of God, qualify. Thus in *Re Eighmie* [1935] Ch 524, a legacy for the purpose of keeping Chiswick Church and the decorations thereof and the burial ground and monument therein to the testatrix's late husband and herself in good and sufficient repair, was held to have a charitable object, while *Re Pardoe* [1906] 2 Ch 184 left no doubt that so does a trust to keep in repair the churchyard around a church. In *Re King* [1923] 1 Ch 243, even a bequest for the erection of a stained-glass window in a church to the memory of the testatrix and certain of her relatives, was held to have a charitable object. In *Re Davies* [1915] 1 Ch 543, a trust for the vicar of Cilcennin for £50 to be invested and the income paid to him as an increase in his stipend, was held to have a charitable object.

4. *Trusts for other purposes beneficial to the community not falling under any of the preceding heads.*

The objects under this heading are many and varied.

However, it is not sufficient merely for an object to be beneficial to the community, it must *also* be within the spirit and intendment of the preamble to the Statute of Elizabeth. In *Re Strakosch* [1949] 2 All ER 6, there were trusts to "strengthen the bonds of unity between the Union of South Africa and [England]" and to appease "racial feeling between the Dutch and English speaking sections of the South African community". The English Court of Appeal held that, apart from the fact that these objects could possibly be regarded as political, they were not within the spirit and intendment of the preamble to the Statute of Elizabeth. The objects were undoubtedly beneficial to the communities of England and South Africa, but they were not charitable. Lord Greene MR said at 7:

> "In order to come within Lord Macnaghten's fourth class the gift must be not only for the benefit of the community but beneficial in a way which the law regards as charitable. In order to satisfy the latter it must be within the 'spirit and intendment' of the preamble of the Statute of Elizabeth. . .. We take it that one must find something charitable in the same sense as the recited purposes are charitable".

The same point was made in *New Zealand Society of Accountants v C of IR; New Zealand Law Society v C of IR (No 2)* (1986) 8 NZTC 5,205; [1986] 1 NZLR 147 (CA), where the accountants' and solicitors' fidelity guarantee funds, respectively, were held not to be within the spirit and intendment of the preamble to the Statute of Elizabeth.

Some of the many objectives that have been held to be charitable under this heading are to build a bridge over the river Don in Scotland — *Forbes v Forbes* (1854) 18 Beav 552, and the promotion of maternal welfare in New Zealand not only by the education of doctors and patients but by the taking of practical steps in co-operation with the Health Department — *McGregor v Commissioner of Stamp Duties* [1942] NZLR 164. (Indeed, many medical objectives have been held to be charitable under this heading.) In *Re Bruce* [1918] NZLR 16, the will-maker left the whole of his residuary estate "for the purpose of afforestation as well as to the making of domains and national parks in New Zealand". The Court of Appeal held that the words "in New Zealand" applied to afforestation as well as to the making of domains and national parks, and that they were all charitable objects.

As we have seen, political purposes are not charitable objects. In *Bowman v Secular Society Ltd* [1917] AC 406, which concerned a bequest to a company that was impliedly anti-Christian, the House of Lords stated this. Political purposes include promoting a change in the law, or promoting retention of the present law.

The promotion of sport, without more, is not a charitable object. Thus, in *Re Nottage* [1895] 2 Ch 649, a trust to provide annually a cup for the most successful yacht of the season, and in *Re Clifford* (1911) 106 LT 14, a gift to a society to improve angling in certain parts of a river, were held not to be charitable. But in *Re Marriette* (1915) 2 Ch 284, a gift to provide fives courts and squash racket courts at a school (sport allied to education), and in *Re Gray* [1925] Ch 362; [1925] All ER 250, a trust for the promotion of sport recreating and increasing the efficiency of the armed forces (sport allied to Lord Macnaghten's fourth category), were held to be charitable. This area of the law has been largely taken over by s 61A of the Charitable Trusts Act 1957, which provides:

> 61A Trusts for recreational and similar purposes
>
> (1) Subject to the provisions of this section, it shall for all purposes be and be deemed always to have been charitable to provide, or assist in the provision of, facilities for recreation or other leisure-time occupation, if the facilities are provided in the interests of social welfare:
>
> Provided that nothing in this section shall be taken to derogate from the principle that a trust or institution to be charitable must be for the public benefit.
>
> (2) The requirement of subsection (1) of this section that the facilities are provided in the interests of social welfare shall not be treated as satisfied unless—
>
> (a) The facilities are provided with the purpose of improving the conditions of life for the persons for whom the facilities are primarily intended; and
>
> (b) Either—
>
> (i) Those persons have need of such facilities as aforesaid by reason of their youth, age, infirmity, disablement, poverty, race, occupation, or social or economic circumstances; or
>
> (ii) The facilities are to be available to the members of the public at large or to the male or female members of the public at large.

The section goes on to indicate that, in terms of the section, it applies to the provision and maintenance of grounds and buildings, the provision of facilities at public halls, community centres, and women's institutes, and extends to organised activity for these ends. It is submitted that now, while a trust for the promotion of sport simpliciter may not be charitable, a settlor or will-maker, so minded, can achieve his objective by framing his trust in a manner which clearly complies with s 61A.

Trusts Act 2019

The Trusts Act recognises trusts for charitable purposes or "any other purpose for a trust that is permitted at law" as a separate category of trusts, which it designates as "permitted purpose" trusts. The Act distinguishes such trusts from trusts established for fixed or discretionary beneficiaries.

Most permitted purpose trusts are charitable trusts, established for purposes falling within the 4 heads of charity that are recognised by New Zealand law.

Charitable trusts and other permitted purpose trusts are generally registered under the Charities Act 2005, for tax concession purposes, and their trustees will often be incorporated as a board under the Charitable Trusts Act 1957.There are, however, other permitted purpose trusts that are not established for charitable purposes, or are not limited to charitable purposes (eg certain community trusts).

The focus of charitable and other permitted purpose trusts is their purposes, not "beneficiaries". They do not have "beneficiaries" as defined and referred to in the Trusts Act — even if the trustees may be required under the terms of the trust to pursue the trust's purposes for the benefit of a specified group or class of persons and/or a specified area or region.

Many trusts for charitable or other purposes are governed by a corporate entity, such as an incorporated board of trustees or a company. The Trusts Act also does not affect the continued application of other legislation to charitable and other permitted purpose trusts, including (where applicable) the Charities Act 2005, the Charitable Trusts Act 1957 or any other enactment by or under which a permitted purpose trust has been created.

The Greenpeace saga

In *Molloy v C of IR* [1981] 1 NZLR 688, the Court of Appeal had adopted the view that "a trust for the attainment of political objects has always been held invalid". This was considered further in *Re Greenpeace of New Zealand Inc* [2014] NZSC 105.

The Charities Commission declined Greenpeace registration as a charity on the basis that two of its objects were not charitable. The objects found to be not charitable were the promotion of disarmament and peace and the promotion of "legislation, policies, rules, regulations and plans which further [Greenpeace's other objects] and support their enforcement or implementation through political or judicial processes as necessary".

The Commission found that the political purposes of Greenpeace were not merely ancillary to its charitable purposes (as would be permitted by s 5 of the Act, in adoption of a similar common law latitude) but were independent purposes. In addition, the Commission concluded that the direct action which it found to be "central" to the activities carried on by Greenpeace could entail illegal activity, which also could not be said to be in the public interest and charitable.

Greenpeace was unsuccessful on appeal to the High Court.[1] Heath J considered that he was bound by *Molloy* to find that the two objects of promoting peace and disarmament and advocacy through political and other forums meant that Greenpeace was not "established and maintained exclusively for charitable purposes".

1 *Re Greenpeace of New Zealand Inc* (2011) 25 NZTC 20-045; [2011] NZHC 77.

Greenpeace then appealed to the Court of Appeal.[2] It indicated that it had resolved to recommend to a general meeting that the two objects which had caused the difficulty be changed. The promotion of "disarmament" would be restricted to the promotion of "nuclear disarmament and the elimination of all weapons of mass destruction" (on the basis that these purposes accorded with New Zealand's international obligations and domestic law and were not controversial) and the advocacy object would be changed to make it clear that it was truly "ancillary" to Greenpeace's charitable objects.

The Court of Appeal set aside the decision of the Commission declining to register Greenpeace as a charity. It affirmed the exclusion of "political" purpose, but it held that the foreshadowed amendments to the Greenpeace objects avoided the political purpose exclusion: first, it was not controversial in New Zealand that promoting nuclear disarmament and eliminating weapons of mass destruction are for public benefit; and secondly, the political advocacy object was now expressed to be limited to that which was "ancillary" only to other charitable purpose. The Court of Appeal considered however that the advocacy actually carried out by Greenpeace could well be beyond a level merely "ancillary" to its charitable purposes. If that proved to be the case, Greenpeace would not be maintained exclusively for charitable purposes. The Court of Appeal referred the application for registration for reconsideration by the chief executive of the Department of Internal Affairs and the Charities Board, Greenpeace then appealed to the Supreme Court which stated:

> "Just as promotion of the abolition of slavery has been regarded as charitable, today advocacy for such ends as human rights or protection of the environment and promotion of amenities that make communities pleasant may have come to be regarded as charitable purposes in themselves, depending on the nature of the advocacy, even if not ancillary to more tangible charity. That result was looked to as one that might well come about in relation to protection of the environment by Somers J in Molloy. In the present case the Board has accepted that Greenpeace's object to 'promote the protection and preservation of nature and the environment' is charitable. Protection of the environment may require broad-based support and effort, including through the participatory processes set up by legislation, to enable the public interest to be assessed. In the same way, the promotion of human rights (a purpose of the New Zealand Bill of Rights Act 1990, as its long title indicates) may depend on similar broad-based support so that advocacy, including through participation in political and legal processes, may well be charitable".

2 *Re Greenpeace of New Zealand Inc* [2012] NZCA 533; [2013] 1 NZLR 339.

The Supreme Court did not adjudicate on whether or not Greenpeace Inc qualified for charitable status, the Court instead referred the decision back to the Department of Internal Affairs (Charities Services).

Charities Services subsequently applied a restrictive interpretation of the Supreme Court decision which resulted in a number of challenges to Charities Services' interpretation and both Family First New Zealand and Better Public Media Trust brought cases before the New Zealand Court of Appeal.

On 10 August 2020 the High Court granted Greenpeace New Zealand Inc's judicial review application against the Charities Registration Board's decision disallowing it to become a registered charity. Mallon J ruled that Greenpeace was entitled to be registered as a charity because it met its requirements under the Charities Act 2006 (*Greenpeace of New Zealand Inc v Charities Registration Board* [2020] NZHC 1999).

Mallon J's decision states (at [101]) that the Board erred in finding that campaigning for the protection of the environment was not a charitable purpose. In so concluding, her Honour noted (at [85]–[86] and [97]) that protecting the environment will often come at the cost of competing interests, but advocating for its protection, in opposition to competing interests, is no less in the public benefit because of that. She found that the Supreme Court cannot have meant that the nature of the advocacy will be disqualifying if an organisation advocates for environmental protection of a kind for which there will be opposition and the public benefit comes from raising awareness of the environmental issues at stake and thereby assisting to ensure that the public's interest in protecting the environment is part of the decision-making process. Without advocacy from environmental groups, the environmental impacts may not be appreciated or understood, or they may be overlooked and underweighted.

Her Honour found (at [128]) that any other purposes are ancillary to Greenpeace's purposes of protecting the environment and advancing education (now re-confirmed as charitable).

With respect to Greenpeace's non-violent direct action activities, Her Honour noted (at [139]) that civil disobedience may sometimes be of public benefit and therefore not necessarily inconsistent with registered charitable status.

However, Her Honour cautioned that if Greenpeace engaged in unlawful non-violent direct action activities in a "more sustained or serious way", Greenpeace's registered charitable status may be put at risk (at [144]).

Case Table

Paragraph

Paragraph

Legislation Finding List

HIGH COURT AMENDMENT (WILLS ACT 2007) RULES 2007

HIGH COURT RULES

INCOME TAX ACT 2007

INSOLVENCY ACT 2006

LAND TRANSFER ACT 1952

LAW REFORM (TESTAMENTARY PROMISES) ACT 1949

LIFE INSURANCE ACT 1908

LIMITATION ACT 1950

PROPERTY LAW ACT 2007

PROPERTY (RELATIONSHIPS) ACT 1976

PUBLIC TRUST ACT 2001

RESIDENTIAL CARE AND DISABILITY SUPPORT SERVICES ACT 2018

Index

Made in United States
Orlando, FL
04 November 2026

90200184R00154